Tranquil Ireland

I will arise and go now, for always night and day
I hear lake water lapping with low sounds by the shore;
While I stand on the roadway, or on the pavements grey
I hear it in the deep heart's core.

William Butler Yeats

The Shell Guide to the River Shannon

Published by: ERA-Maptec Limited,
36 Dame Street,
Dublin 2, Ireland.
Tel: 353-1-679 9227
Fax: 353-1-679 9798

Managing Editors: Ruth Delany, Paul Kidney, Walter Borner.

Designer: Sharon O'Reilly.

Printed by: PRINTSTONE.

Corrections: Any changes, additions or deletions should be sent to
ERA-Maptec Ltd., for possible inclusion in subsequent editions.

Cover Photo: Walter Borner.

ISBN: 1-873489-90-0

Contents

Foreword

Adam Wolfitt-National Geographic

John Weaving with Brocky and Twiggy

The preparation of this fourth edition of the Shell Guide to the Shannon has coincided with the establishment of Waterways Ireland, one of the six North/South Implementation Bodies under the Good Friday Agreement. Waterways Ireland assumed immediate responsibility on 2 December 1999 for the Shannon Erne Waterway and on 1 April 2000 all of the island's currently navigable waterways will be transferred from Dúchas - Waterways and from the Rivers Agency in Northern Ireland. The headquarters of Waterways Ireland will be in Enniskillen, Co Fermanagh and there will be three regional offices: the Northern Region based in Carrick-on-Shannon, Co Leitrim, the Eastern Region based in Dublin and the Southern Region based in Scarriff, Co Clare. All these changes are subject to the full implacation of the Good Friday Agreement and none of these offices has been established to date; (the interim telephone number for Waterways Ireland is 01-6472557).

This fourth edition of the Shell Guide to the Shannon brings the third edition up to date and contains some changes in the illustrations. Walter Borner has once again supplied these new illustrations and has also edited the German translation.

In the Foreword to the first edition of this guide reference was made to the fact that John Weaving was to have been my co-editor. Sadly he died before its completion but during his last months in hospital he worked on various aspects of the guide, calling on his dwindling strength to complete the task. For many years he had been a familiar figure at the helm of the *Peter Farrell* as he plied up and down the river accompanied by his faithful dogs, Brocky and Twiggy. He became "at one" with the great river and now has become a permanent part of its legend. I hope that this guide will continue to be a fitting memorial to him. I know that I speak for his many friends when I say that it was a great privilege to have known him.

Finally, I would like to thank Dúchas-Waterways, the Northern Ireland Tourist Board and Irish Shell Ltd. for their continued interest and support.

May 2000 **Ruth Delany**

This Shannon Guide is dedicated to

John Weaving

who died on 24 May 1987

Ní h-aitheantas go h-aointíos

To know beauty one must live with it.

The spacious Shannon

Ruth Delany

Edmund Spenser in an oft quoted canto from The Faerie Queene refers to: "The spacious Shannon spreading like a sea". It is an apt description because this great river, the longest in Ireland or Britain, does indeed spread itself across the country like a great sea in places.

Walter Borner

Weaving memorial at Terryglass

The catchment area is over 15,000 sq km, representing one fifth of the area of Ireland. The source of the river is ascribed to the Shannon Pot on the slopes of Cuilcagh Mountain in Co Cavan. The Pot is 152 m above sea level and in the first 14 km to Lough Allen, the infant river, joined by the Owenmore and the Owennayle, drops 104 m. It leaves Lough Allen to commence its slow progress across Ireland's central plain, falling only 12 m in the 185 km between Battlebridge, and Killaloe at the south end of Lough Derg. From here it drops 30 m in the last few miles to Limerick.

From its source to Loop Head, where it meets the Atlantic Ocean, it is 344 km in length and it is joined by a number of river and lake systems which provide 258 km of cruising waterway: a total of 2,035 sq km. Some of the lakes are large inland seas which have to be treated with caution; Lough Allen is 11 km long, Lough Ree 29km and Lough Derg is 39 km. The Boyle and Carnadoe Waters and the Inner Lakes of Lough Ree are part of the Shannon Navigation and provide a series of small inter-connected lakes which are wildlife paradises.

Inevitably, a river of this size has made a significant contribution to the history and lives of the Irish people, from prehistoric times down to the present century. In the 1920s the Shannon hydro-electric scheme represented the emerging nation's first steps on the road to establishing a sound economy, and today the river is an important amenity for tourists and Irish people alike. You can trace this historical background in the articles which follow. There is also much to be seen in the landscape, birds, wild flowers and wildlife of the Shannon. It is only possible here to provide a short introduction to these topics and to recommend some good text books. Those with special interests will find many other books. The fishermen will find no shortage of good fishing grounds, and some indications of the type of fish and how and where to catch them is given, with more detailed locations referred to in the appendix.There is also a brief insight into the great wealth of poetry and legend of the river and this can be readily supplemented by the people you will meet along the way who are always happy to oblige with local lore. The Gazetteer section lists the places to visit and things to do and see for those travelling by water, but the guide also enables those travelling by road to search out interesting features.

Perhaps the most appealing characteristic of the Shannon is its unique quality of peace and tranquillity and this you will have no difficulty in finding for yourself.

Fishing on the weir at Clarendon Lock

Walter Borner

Der mächtige Shannon

'Der mächtige Shannon, weit wie ein Meer', so bezeichnete der englische Dichter Edmund Spencer in einem häufig zitierten Canto seines Vers-Epos 'Faerie Queene' zutreffend diesen grossen Fluss, der sich tatsächlich vielerorts wie ein weites Meer über die Landschaft ausbreitet. Als längster Fluss Irlands und Grossbritanniens hat er ein mehr als 15'000 Quadratkilometer, also fast ein Fünftel der Gesamtfläche Irlands, umfassendes Einzugsgebiet. Sein Ursprung liegt im Shannon Pot an den Hängen der Cuilcagh Berge in der Grafschaft Cavan. Auf den ersten vierzehn Kilometern zum Lough Allen überwindet der junge Quellfluss mit seinen beiden Zuflüssen Owenmore und Owenayle ein Gefälle von 104 Metern und beginnt dann, aus Lough Allen herauskommend, seinen gemächlichen Lauf durch die mittelirische Ebene mit einem Gefälle von nur noch zwölf Metern auf dem 186 Kilometer langen Abschnitt zwischen Battlebridge und Killaloe am Südende von Lough Derg. Von dort hat er auf dem letzten Stück nach Limerick ein Gefälle von dreissig Metern.

Von seiner Quelle bis nach Loop Head, wo er in den Atlantik mündet, hat der Shannon eine Länge von 344 Kilometern. Er hat eine grössere Anzahl von Zuflüssen und verbindet mehrere Seengebiete, die zusammen einen schiffbaren Wasserweg von 258 Kilometern und ein Gesamtgebiet von 2'035 Quadratkilometern ausmachen. Zwei der Seen, die er durchfliesst, sind grosse Binnenmeere und müssen mit Vorsicht befahren werden: Lough Ree ist 30 km und Lough Derg 39 km lang. Die Seenketten von Boyle und Carnadoe und die Inner Lakes von Lough Ree sind Teil der Schifffahrtsstrecke und stellen eine Reihe kleiner, miteinander verbundener Seen dar, die ein Tier- und Pflanzenparadies sind.

Natürlich ist ein Fluss dieser Ausmasse seit prähistorischen Zeiten von eminenter Bedeutung für Leben und Geschichte der Iren. Dies bis in unser Jahrhundert, als das Kraftwerk von Ardnacrusha zum Symbol für die ersten Schritte der jungen Nation auf dem Weg zu einer gesunden Volkswirtschaft wurde. Auch heute ist der Shannon äusserst wichtig als Erholungsgebiet für Iren wie für Ausländer. Für die Freunde von Landschaft und Natur, Vögeln, Wildblumen und Wildtieren gibt es viel zu sehen. Es ist in diesem Rahmen nicht möglich, mehr als eine knappe Einführung zu bieten und daher einschlägige Literatur zu empfehlen. Leute mit speziellen Interessen können aus einer Vielfalt von Fachbüchern auswählen. Angler erhalten hier eine grosse Zahl von Angaben über Fangplätze sowie über Fischarten. Der grosse, mit dem Fluss verknüpfte Reichtum an Dichtung und Legenden wird in einer kurzen Einführung vorgestellt, zudem erzählen sicher die Iren, die Sie unterwegs treffen, ausführlicher aus der örtlichen Überlieferung. Im Verzeichnis der Ortsnamen findet man eine Liste der Sehenswürdigkeiten, die besichtigt werden können. Für die Mehrheit der Besucher jedoch ist es die einzigartige, friedvolle Ruhe des Shannongebiets, die am meisten bezaubert.

Kilglass Cut

Walter Borner

The legend of the Shannon's origin

> ***The noble name of Sinann seek ye from me,***
> ***Its bare recital would not be pleasant,***
> ***Not alike now are its action and noise***
> ***As when Sinann herself was free and alive.***
> **Translated from the Irish of**
> **Cuan O' Lothchain**

Jan de Fouw

Sinann was the daughter of the learned Lodan, who was the son of Lear, the great sea-king of the Tuatha De Danann colony of Erinn, from whose son and successor, Manannan, the Isle of Man derives its name and ancient celebrity. In those very early times there was a certain mystical fountain which was called Connla's Well (situated, so far as we can gather, in Lower Ormond). As to who this Connla was, from whom the well had its name, we are not told; but the well itself appears to have been regarded as another Helicon by the ancient Irish poets. Over this well there grew, according to the legend, nine beautiful hazel-trees, which annually send forth their blossoms and fruits simultaneously. The nuts were of the richest crimson colour, and teemed with the knowledge of all that was refined in literature, poetry and art. No sooner, however, were the beautiful nuts produced on the trees, than they always dropped into the well, raising by their fall a succession of shining red bubbles. Now during this time the water was always full of salmon; and no sooner did the bubbles appear than these salmon darted to the surface and ate the nuts, after which they made their way to the river. The eating of the nuts produced brilliant crimson spots on the bellies of these salmon; and to catch and eat these salmon became an object of more than mere gastronomic interest among those who were distinguished in the arts and in literature without being at the pains and the delay of long study: for the fish was supposed to have become filled with the knowledge which was contained in the nuts, which, it was believed, would be transferred in full to those who had the good fortune to catch and eat them.

It was forbidden to women to come within the precincts of Connla's wonderful well; but the beautiful Lady Sinann, who possessed above every maiden of her time all the accomplishments of her sex, longed to have also those more solid and masculine acquirements which were accessible at Connla's well to the other sex only. To possess herself of these she went secretly to the mystical fountain; but as soon as she approached its brink, the water rose up violently, burst forth over its banks, and rushed towards the great river now called the Shannon, overwhelming the Lady Sinann in their course, whose dead body was carried down by the torrent, and at last cast up on the land at the confluence of two streams. After this the well became dry for ever; and the stream which issued from it was that originally known by the name of the Lady Sinann or Shannon; but having fallen into the great succession of lakes which runs nearly through the centre of Ireland, the course of lakes subsequently appropriated the name to itself, which it still retains, whilst the original stream is now unknown. The original Sinann is, however, believed to have fallen into the present Shannon, near the head of Lough Derg, not far from Portumna.

From On the Manners and Customs of the Ancient Irish by Eugene O'Curry.

The Shannon Pot on the slopes of Cuilcagh

Walter Borner

Prehistory and the Middle Ages

Peter Harbison

The Shannon has played a significant role in the history of Ireland down the ages and was an important line of communication from prehistoric times to the Middle Ages, when travel by road was very difficult. It also provided access into the heart of the country for the Viking invaders.

One of the delights of travelling on the Shannon today is being able to turn one's back on roads, and to enjoy the extensive views of the gently undulating countryside from a boat. But the more distant views were not always visible, for in earlier times Ireland was much more wooded than it is today, the country having been denuded of many of its trees in the sixteenth and seventeenth centuries. To travel along the Shannon in prehistoric times would have meant being often flanked by trees, or at least scrub and hazel which was difficult to penetrate. Thousands of years ago, the Shannon would, therefore, have provided the easiest method of travelling north or south in the centre of Ireland, and one which avoided the necessity of traversing watery bog or hacking through the hazel. Sadly, we know virtually nothing about early boats on the Shannon, though they were probably dug-outs of the kind which have occasionally come to light when the levels of midland lakes were lowered in recent times. These same midland lakes are now producing finds which show that the centre of Ireland was already occupied by man as early as the eighth millennium BC, and rivers—particularly the Shannon—must have been especially helpful in providing Stone Age settlers with access to various parts of the Irish midlands, as well as giving them fish for their proteins.

Prehistoric Times

Few prehistoric settlements have come to light on Shannon's shores, but when the river and its tributaries (particularly the Suck) were being drained in the middle of the last century, many bronze implements and weapons were dredged up from their beds. While this might conjure up a picture of early population groups fighting one another for control of the waterways, in fact these Bronze Age (second and first millennium BC) objects are perhaps better interpreted as being among the many items deposited in Europe's moors and inland waters as ritual offerings to appease some river or other god or goddess.

The lands surrounding the lower Shannon in counties Clare, Limerick and Tipperary are particularly rich in Late Bronze Age gold ornaments, including the famous gorgets, and they bear testimony to a richness in prehistoric craftsmanship in the area around 700 BC. It has even been suggested that foreign craftsmen may have settled in the region to work the considerable amounts of gold which seem to have been available at the time from some source now sadly unknown to us.

Vorgeschichte und Mittelalter

Bis etwa zum 16. Jahrhundert war Irland dicht bewachsen mit grossen Laubwäldern, Gebüsch und Haselsträuchern. Der Shannon war der einfachste Reiseweg von Norden nach Süden, ohne sich den Weg durch Wälder und Moorgebiete bahnen zu müssen. Dazu wurde wahrscheinlich eine Art Einbaum verwendet, wie sie in einigen Seen gefunden wurden. Aber auch andere Entdeckungen beweisen, dass bereits 8'000 Jahre vor Christus Menschen hier lebten.

Obschon es entlang des Flusses wenig Anzeichen prähistorischer Siedlungen gibt, wurden bei Baggerarbeiten am Shannon und seiner Nebenflüsse Geräte und Waffen aus Bronze gefunden, die beweisen, dass die Gegend um 2'000 bis 1'000 vor Christus bewohnt war. Der Unterlauf ist besonders reich an Funden von Goldschmuck aus der späten Bronzezeit, die Zeugnis geben von einer Hochblüte frühzeitlicher, möglicherweise von Ausländern beeinflusster Kunstfertigkeit und reichen Goldvorkommen, die uns leider nicht mehr bekannt sind. Die gefundenen Gegenstände waren vermutlich einem Flussgott dargebrachte Ritualopfer.

Vom 5. Jahrhundert an begann das Goldene Zeitalter des Shannon, als hier die frühchristlichen Klostersiedlungen gegründet wurden. Ein Beispiel ist diejenige des heiligen Ciaran in Clonmacnois. Dieses grösste Schmuckstück des Shannon-Gebiets liegt an der Stelle, wo sich die Hauptstrassen Irlands, nämlich die Ost-West-Strasse entlang des Eiscir Riada und die Nord-Süd-Strasse entlang des Shannon, kreuzten. Es gibt Hinweise dafür, dass hier bereits vor der Klostergründung ein wichtiger Ort an der Handelsstrasse existierte. Vom 7. bis zum 19. Jahrhundert war Clonmacnois einer der beliebtesten Wallfahrtsorte Irlands, ein Aspekt des Wirkungsbereichs des Klosters, der neben seiner hohen monastischen und künstlerischen Bedeutung gerne vergessen wird. Holy Island oder Inishcealtra im Lough Derg mit seinen vielen Sehenswürdigkeiten ist wie auch Hare Island im Lough Ree, wo St. Ciaran vor der Gründung

Office of Public Works

Clonmacnois: an aerial veiw of the settlement area

A conjectural reconstruction of Clonmacnois in monastic times

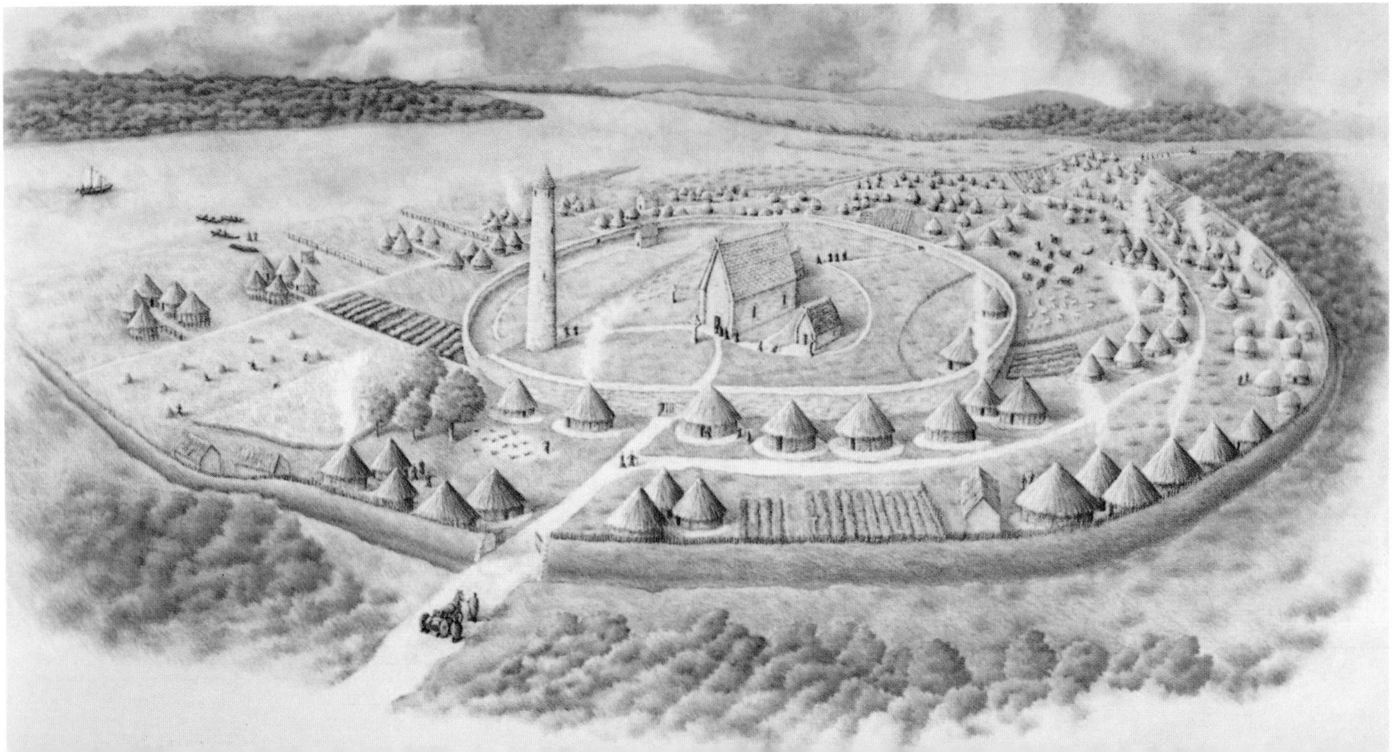

Office of Public Works

The Monastic Period

But it is with the dawning of the historic period from the fifth century AD onwards that the Shannon really begins to glisten in another Golden Age—that of the early Christian monasteries which have made Ireland famous. Prime among these was Clonmacnois, the Shannon's greatest gem. This venerable site, which attracts the visitor back again and again like a magnet, started its long recorded history when St Ciarán founded his monastery there around AD 545—only to die some months later, like his Lord and Master, at the age of 33. His choice of location was scarcely accidental for, unlike today, Clonmacnois was at the very crossroads of Ireland, where the Shannon—the country's main north-south traffic artery—was crossed by 'the great road' along the Eiscir Riada, Ireland's most important east-west thoroughfare in early historic times, though we can no longer pinpoint precisely where the river was forded.

But St Ciarán may not have been the first to recognise the significance of the spot as an important junction. The Irish life of the saint tells us that he got some Gaulish wine from Frankish merchants at Clonmacnois: the Irish have long appreciated a good drop of claret! These men would scarcely have come up the Shannon offering their wares had not some earlier trade-route existed to guide them on their way. In this respect, it is significant that a magnificent gold neck-ring of about 300 BC, found many years ago at Clonmacnois, turns out to have come from eastern Gaul or the Middle Rhine—possibly brought there to be deposited as an offering to a river god, like the prehistoric bronzes.

But if Clonmacnois may have been an important centre of some sort before it ever became a monastery, it became even more so after the death of its monastic founder. From the seventh to the nineteenth century, it was one of Ireland's most important centres of pilgrimage—an aspect of its activity often forgotten when compared to its monastic or artistic brilliance.

Another Shannon site famed for pilgrimage was Holy Island, or Inishcealtra, on Lough Derg. Like Clonmacnois, it has its Romanesque church and its round tower, both perhaps symbols of its pilgrimage trade. Like Clonmacnois, too, it had its collection of crosses and stone slabs, and they all combine to make these two ancient monasteries the most interesting of all historical sites to visit along the river's course. Before he founded his monastery of Clonmacnois, St Ciarán lived as a hermit on Hare Island in Lough Ree. Islands were favoured by early hermits as places where they could retreat from the cares of the world and concentrate on communicating with their Maker. Other islands in Lough Ree and Lough Key may also have been occupied by early hermits, around whose saintly graves small monastic communities may have grown up, later to build some of the pre-Norman churches which we find on some of the islands to this day.

A gold torc found at Clonmacnois

von Clonmacnois als Einsiedler gelebt hatte, eine interessante Klostersiedlung. Daneben gibt es noch eine Reihe von Inseln im Lough Ree und Lough Key, die von diesen frühchristlichen Einsiedlern und später von Mönchsgemeinschaften als Standorte ausgewählt wurden.

Die Wikinger, die auf dem Shannon ins Land eindrangen, verwüsteten sämtliche Klöster entlang seiner Ufer bis nach Norden hinauf zum Lough Ree. Schlimmer und anhaltender waren jedoch die Folgen der Eroberung durch die Normannen, die auf ihrem westlichen Feldzug am Shannon Brückenköpfe errichteten wie zum Beispiel in Athlone. Dadurch wurde Clonmacnois aus seiner führenden Position als Zentrumsort verdrängt. Faszinierend ist auch die normannische Siedlung in Rindoon am Lough Ree. Die Iren leisteten Widerstand und begannen ab dem 15. Jahrhundert, ihre eigene Vormachtsstellung durch die Errichtung von Turmschlössern und kleinen Burgen zu konsolidieren. Beispiele dafür sind diejenige der McDermotts auf einer Insel im Lough Key oder 1643 der Bau von Derryhivenny Castle – eines der letzten Turmschlösser – nördlich von Portumna. Das in den letzten Jahren wieder hergestellte Schloss Portumna zeigt in seinem Baustil den Übergang zwischen den befestigten Burgen des Mittelalters und den eleganten georgianischen Herrensitzen des 18. Jahrhunderts.

A silver "kyte broach" found at Clonmacnois

The Vikings

The Vikings, who penetrated up the Shannon, cannot have made life any easier for these religious communities. The Vikings, whose superior boat design had enabled them to cross the North Sea from Norway, started to make raids on the east coast of Ireland late in the eighth century. But even before they began to settle permanently at places like Dublin (c. 841), they devastated some of the monasteries close to the banks of the Shannon, such as Clonfert and Clonmacnois, reaching as far north as the islands of Lough Ree. We have yet to identify any bases they may have used for these free-booting expeditions, so they may well have sailed and rowed their boats upstream from Limerick, as their Russian counterparts had done from the Baltic, and they doubtless used the downstream flow of the river to make a quick getaway before the Irish could make a counter-attack. While fear must have entered every native heart at their very appearance, the Irish were even more horrified at one strange lady in their entourage who had the cheek to profane the high-altar at Clonmacnois by dispensing oracles from it!

The Normans

But more lasting were the effects created by those other descendants of the Norse Vikings, namely the Normans, who came to the Shannon at the time of their conquest of Ireland in the decades after their first arrival in 1169. From their bases east of the river, they crossed the Shannon and established bridgeheads on the other side in their campaign to conquer the western province of Connacht in 1235. One of these bridgeheads was Athlone, where stout remnants of the thirteenth-century Norman castle still survive by the quayside. It may have been the establishment of this castle c.1210 which caused the gradual decline in the use of the ford at Clonmacnois (where the Normans also built a castle), and set the seal on making Athlone the main crossing point along the middle reaches of the river, which it has remained to this day. There is, however, one other less well-known Norman fortification of importance on the western bank of the river, which makes for a fascinating voyage of exploration and discovery. This is Rindoon on Lough Ree, where the Normans literally dug themselves in on a promontory site, which they defended by cutting a water-course across the end of the peninsula to make it into an island.

In time, the Irish fought back against the Norman aggressors, and by the fifteenth century they had begun to establish their more personal hegemony by building tower houses and smaller castles. The MacDermot castle is still an imposing pile on an island not far from the Rockingham shore on Lough Key, and the intrepid visitor can leave his cruiser at Portumna and penetrate a few miles inland to Derryhivenny, where one of Ireland's last tower houses was built in 1643. But closer to the shore is a castle of a different kind—Portumna itself. Recently conserved, and with its eighteenth-century gardens partially restored, it gets away from the fortificatory idea of the medieval castle by broadening its windows to let in more light. This great manor was pivotal in paving the way for an age of enlightenment, and introducing us to a more gracious style of living which subsequently led to the building of the spacious Georgian mansions which grew up not far from the Shannon's banks in the eighteenth century.

Mac Dermot's castle on an island in Lough Key called 'The Rock'', now known as Castle Island, from an engraving in Grose's Antiquities of Ireland dated 1792

Early modern times

Harman Murtagh

The Shannon continued to influence Irish history from Tudor times when it was frequently used as an important line of defence. When more settled times gradually became established, some of the new ascendancy began to take up residence along its shores.

The sixteenth and seventeenth centuries were a period of upheaval and change in Ireland. Traditionally depicted in terms of military conquest, confiscations, colonisation and Reformation, what was taking place can also be viewed as the forceful modernisation of a highly conservative and even archaic society. The eighteenth century, in contrast was a more settled era, at least until its final decades were disturbed by the impact of revolution. These developments naturally influenced the contemporary history of the Shannon and the evolution of settlement patterns in its adjoining countryside, towns and villages.

Tudor Times

Tudor administrators were impressed by the potential of the waterway. Sir Francis Walsingham, secretary of state to Queen Elizabeth I, was told of 'the commodious havens and harbours, the beauty and commodity of this river of Shannon'. In 1571 a water bailiff was appointed and given two galleys to 'scour' the river, one to be based above and the other below Athlone; 'boats, cots, wherries and other vessels' were also mentioned at this time. By 1580 the navigation between Athlone and Limerick had been 'found out' and the Shannon was an important artery of communication in the savage conquest of Munster.

Even before this, Connacht was opened up to government control by the building of a new stone bridge across the river at Athlone and the old medieval castle there was adapted as a headquarters for the new provincial administration. The number of crossing-points increased as a succession of further stone bridges were erected in the centuries that followed: that at Shannonbridge, which has recently been renovated, dates from 1757.

Jacobite Wars

The concept of the river as a barrier between competing armies evolved during the confused wars of the confederacy and Cromwellian conquest, 1641–53, and reached its fullest expression a generation later in the Jacobite war when, in 1690–1, the Irish army doggedly defended Connacht and Clare from behind the line of the Shannon. Athlone and Limerick were each beseiged twice and smaller centres, such as Lanesborough, Jamestown and Boyle, were also the scenes of military engagement. The reverse strategy was

An early print of Athlone Castle

Der Shannon in der frühen Neuzeit

16. und 17. Jahrhundert in Irland waren eine Zeit des Umbruchs und des Wandels. Von der Geschichtsschreibung im allgemeinen mit den Begriffen der militärischen Eroberung, Beschlagnahmung, Kolonialisierung und Reformation gekennzeichnet, kann diese Epoche auch als Zeit der mit Gewalt durchgesetzten Modernisierung einer rückständigen, ja geradzu archaischen Gesellschaft angesehen werden. Das 18. Jahrhundert dagegen war bis auf seine letzten Jahrzehnte verhältnismässig ruhig. Diese Ereignisse hatten natürlich ihre Wirkung auf die modernere Geschichte des Shannon und das Siedlungsverhalten der Menschen in den umliegenden Landstrichen, Städten und Dörfern.

Die Verwaltungsbehörden der Tudorzeit waren von den Möglichkeiten der Wasserstrasse beeindruckt. Im 16. Jahrhundert wurde ein Wasserstrassenverwalter ernannt, der mit zwei Booten den Fluss überwachen sollte. Ausserdem werden andere Boote erwähnt, woraus man schliessen kann, dass der Fluss eine wichtige Verkehrsader war. Schon vorher war die Bezwingung Connachts durch den Bau einer Steinbrücke und die Umgestaltung der mittelalterlichen Burg von Athlone möglich gemacht worden. Steinbrücken an einigen der anderen Überquerungsstellen folgten.

Die Idee, den Fluss als eine Barriere

An axiometrical drawing and plan of Shannonbridge fortifications

Paul Kerrigan

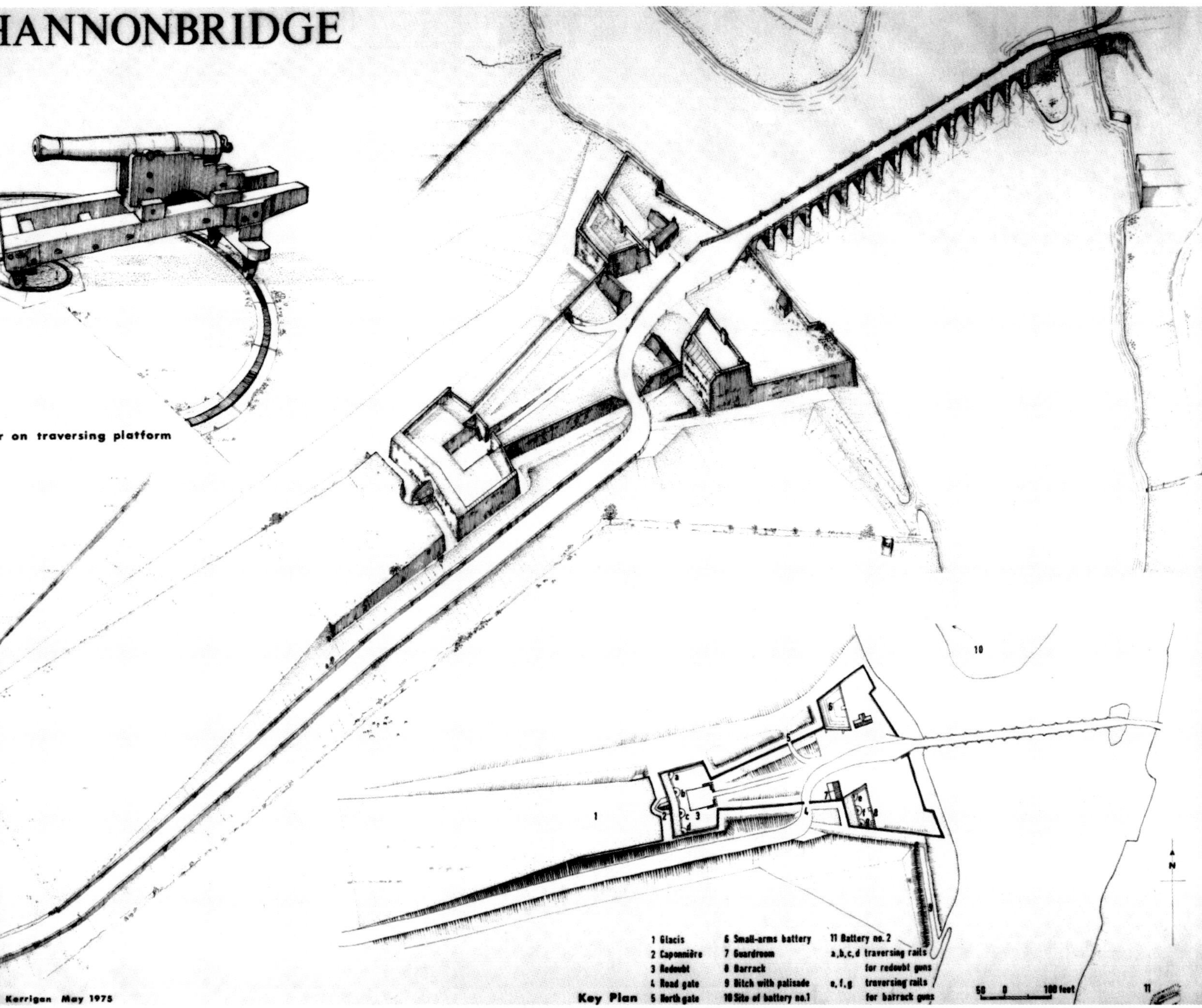

adopted during the conflict with revolutionary France, 1793–1815, when the government of the day strongly fortified the middle-Shannon crossings, with the idea of confining any newly landed French force in the west until the defending army could be mustered from its numerous garrisons east of the river to confront the invaders. Town wall fortifications of the seventeenth century can be seen at Jamestown, Athlone and Limerick, and the extensive defences of the Napoleonic era are still substantially intact at Meelick, Banagher and Shannonbridge.

The New Ascendancy

In the wake of conquest came settlement. In the 1620s there were formal plantation schemes in Leitrim, Longford and Offaly, which saw the development of new urban centres such as Jamestown, Lanesborough and Banagher. Older towns like Limerick and Athlone also revived and expanded. In general the new settlers preferred more comfortable and well-lit 'horizontal' residences to living in the grim vertical towers of late medieval Ireland, and the new styles they introduced were imitated by the older inhabitants. However, the insecurity of the times meant that the new houses were often fortified, so that they represent a transitional style. Examples can be seen at Cootehall, Athlone (Court Devenish) and, most spectacularly, Portumna. Two older tower houses,which were 'modernised', are Rathcline and Portlick on Lough Ree.

The Cromwellian and Williamite victories greatly consolidated the position of the new ascendancy and gave them the confidence and resources to erect on their estates numerous unfortified residences in the classical idiom. Two early examples, close to the Shannon, are at Eyrecourt and neighbouring Clonfert, both dating from the late seventeenth century and now sadly dilapidated. Rockingham, the magnificent Nash villa overlooking Lough Key, which was built for the King family about 1810, has been totally demolished. But, in nearby Boyle, an earlier house of the Kings, probably to the design of Sir Edward Lovett

zwischen kämpfenden Armeen zu benutzen, stammt aus dem 17. Jahrhundert. Es gelang der irischen Armee 1690/91, Connacht und Clare jenseits der Shannonlinie zu halten. Während des Krieges mit dem revolutionären Frankreich 1793-1815 wendete die damalige britische Regierung die gleiche Taktik an und befestigte den Fluss gegen eine Invasion der Franzosen von Westen her. Befestigte Stadtmauern und ausgedehnte Verteidigungsanlagen der napoleonischen Zeit können noch heute besichtigt werden. Der Eroberung folgten die Besiedlung des Landes, die Entstehung städtischer Ballungsgebiete und das Wachstum älterer Kleinstädte. Die hohen vertikalen Turmhäuser wurden allmählich durch horizontale Herrensitze ersetzt, aber selbst diese mussten noch angriffssicher gemacht werden. Beispiele dieser Übergangsarchitektur können in Cootehall, Athlone und Portumna besichtigt werden wie auch die modernisierten Turmhäuser in Rathcline und Portlick am Lough Ree. Erst die Siege Cromwells und Wilhelms von Oranien stärkten die Position der neuen herrschenden Klasse derart, dass unbefestigte Villen im klassizistischen Stil gebaut werden konnten. Zwei Beispiele dafür befinden sich in Eyrecourt und Clonfert.

Rockingham House am Lough Key ist jetzt leider völlig zerstört, aber in Boyle steht das

Shannonbridge: the bridge was constructed in the 1750s

Ruth Delany

Pearce or his assistant, William Halfpenny, survives from about 1730 and has recently been handsomely restored. Other notable examples of classical villas on the river are Drominagh, Castlelough, Bellevue, Belle Isle and Youghal on Lough Derg, and Killinure and the ruined Mount Plunkett on Lough Ree. In the centre of Carrick-on-Shannon, the well-maintained Hatley Manor, dating from about 1830, marks the transition to a new era: the street front is in the older classical style whereas the garden front is neo-Gothic. The handsome courthouse nearby, by the architect William Farrell, is slightly earlier in date and would benefit from conservation. The magnificent battlemented Castle Forbes, on the shores of Lough Forbes, dating from about 1830 is one of the finest examples of neo-Gothic romanticism in the country. Splendid mid- to late- nineteenth-century villas on Lough Derg are Tinarana, the Italianate Slevoir near Terryglass, and Kilteelagh, a well-maintained example of high-Victorian style. Of the Shannon towns, the city of Limerick has, after Dublin, the most important classical streetscapes in the country, and much of the architecture of the smaller centres retains a Georgian or Victorian flavour.

The End Of The Monastic Period

A direct consequence of the Reformation was the dissolution of the Shannon's numerous monastic houses. Their buildings were demolished, or simply fell into decay, and the remainder of their property (with much of the other endowment of the medieval church) passed to laymen. But the Counter-Reformation, which the Franciscans spearheaded in the midlands, ensured that the majority of the population kept the old faith. In 1631 the Poor Clare nuns founded the first post-Reformation convent in Ireland at a remote site, which they named Bethlehem, on the shores of Lough Ree. Shortly afterwards the Franciscans established a new house in the plantation town of Jamestown. In 1648 Cardinal Rinuccini, who was being rowed upstream from Shannonbridge to Athlone, broke his journey to view the ancient churches of Clonmacnois, where he was entertained to breakfast by the resident Franciscan bishop. A generation later, in the 1680s, the Franciscans commenced the building of a new church in Athlone, but the work had to be abandoned in the wake of the Williamite victory in 1691. However, Roman Catholic parish churches were erected in growing numbers from 1750 onwards and there are numerous nineteenth and twentieth-century examples, large and small, along the river.

For the Church of Ireland, the Board of First Fruits was responsible for the construction of many handsome parish churches and glebe houses, especially between 1800 and 1830. Of several on the Shannon, perhaps the most strikingly situated is Annaduff, near Drumsna, in Co Leitrim.

Early Pleasure Boating

The use of the waterway for recreation is recorded as early as 1731, when there is a reference to a regatta at Athlone and to musical evenings 'on the delightful River Shannon, which was made infinitely more so by the company of the ladies'. The date 1770 is claimed for the foundation of Lough Ree Yacht Club, which makes it the second oldest in the world. Lough Derg Yacht Club, dating from about 1836, is also amongst the most senior in the country. In the eighteenth and nineteenth centuries, prior to the invention of motor cars, an essential requirement of watersports enthusiasts was lakeside accommodation. One solution was the erection of lodges, around which the landscape was generally improved by the planting of trees. Today, these residences are among the most attractive on the great lakes.

Walter Borner

The ruined Abbey on Trinity Island, Lough Key

frühere Haus der Kings, in Banagher befinden sich die Reste von Cuba Court, und einige später gebaute klassizistische Landhäuser sind um Lough Derg und Lough Ree zu finden.

Als direkte Folge der Reformation lösten sich die Klöster entlang des Shannon auf, die Gebäude wurden zerstört oder verfielen. Bis zum Sieg der Protestanten unter Wilhelm von Oranien waren die Franziskaner die Vorkämpfer der Gegenreformation. Von der Mitte des 18. Jahrhunderts an wurden immer mehr katholische Kirchen gebaut. Die meisten der heutigen protestantischen Kirchen Irlands stammen aus der Zeit zwischen 1800 und 1830.

Schon 1731 wurde von der Wasserstrasse als einem Erholungsgebiet berichtet. Das Gründungsjahr des Lough Ree Yachtklubs (L.R.Y.C.) ist 1770, was ihn zum zweitältesten der Welt macht, während derjenige von Lough Derg von 1836 einer der ältesten des Landes ist. Eine weitere Entwicklung dieser Zeit war der Bau von Sommerhäusern an den grossen Seen und, gleichzeitig damit, die Pflanzung der herrlichen Bäume, die wir heute noch bewundern können.

The Shannon Navigation

Ruth Delany

From Battlebridge just south of Lough Allen to Killaloe at the southern end of Lough Derg, a distance of some 186 km, the Shannon falls only about 12 m; it meanders its way south, wide and slow-flowing with only a limited number of shallow stretches.

Since early times the River Shannon offered such a fine natural waterway that it was put to good use not only by the native population for the carriage of goods but also by Viking invaders who used it to penetrate deep into the country, hauling their long-boats up over the shallows. However, it was not until the eighteenth century that people began to consider ways of improving the navigation.

The Canal Age

Some of the early estimates for such works are an indication that the natural obstructions were not looked upon very seriously: Dr Bolton, Archbishop of Cashel, said he would undertake to make the river navigable for vessels of up to 30 tons for just £3,000; and a petition to the Irish parliament in 1697 spoke of a cost of £14,000 to make a navigation from Carrick to Limerick.

In fact, it was to prove a great deal more costly and difficult than these early waterway entrepreneurs suggested. Although legislation had been passed in 1715 authorising a number of navigation works including the Shannon, it was not until the 1750s that work actually began. In Britain waterway construction was left to private enterprise, but in Ireland the early navigation works had to be undertaken by a board of Commissioners of Inland Navigation funded by special levies. They did succeed in completing the first watershed canal in these islands, the Newry Canal, but progress in creating a waterway network would have been very slow had it not been for a fortunate set of circumstances. The Irish parliament found itself enjoying an annual surplus revenue and they determined that, rather than hand this money over to the English king, they would in future spend the money on public works and manufacturing enterprises. It was this financial bonanza in the 1750s which led to the first work on the Shannon.

Early Shannon Works

Work commenced at Meelick in 1755 under the engineer, Thomas Omer, who is thought to have been Dutch and who had been invited to come to Ireland by the commissioners. He made a canal with a lock to overcome the fall of 2 m. From Meelick he worked upstream making short canals with single pairs of gates, or flash locks, at Banagher and Shannonbridge where the fall was not so great. He reached Athlone in 1757 and here he had to construct a longer canal and a conventional lock with a fall of over 1 m. By the 1780s the navigation had been extended to Carrick with similar works at Lanesborough, Tarmonbarry, (where an alternative route using the River Camlin was used), Roosky and Jamestown (where a canal was constructed to bypass the great loop of the river). In the meantime work had begun at Limerick under another foreign engineer, William Ockenden. This was a much more difficult undertaking because the river fell about 30 m over a distance of 24 km and progress was so slow that this work was eventually handed over to a private company which did not fare much better. Omer's work was to

Die Schiffahrt auf dem Shannon

Der Shannon war seit frühen Zeiten eine Handelsstrasse. Den Wikingern ermöglichte er, tief ins Land einzudringen. Ihre Langboote schleppten sie einfach über die Untiefen. Erst etwa im 18. Jahrhundert begann man, den Ausbau der Schiffahrtsstrecke zu erwägen. Die ersten Kostenvoranschläge für diese Arbeit erwiesen sich als völlig unzutreffend.

Im Jahr 1715 wurde ein Gesetz erlassen, das Ausbauarbeiten am Shannon vorsah. Anders als in England wurden diese nicht der Privatwirtschaft überlassen, sondern einer durch Sondersteuern finanzierten Behörde für Inlandwasserwege. Obwohl diese erfolgreich den ersten Wasserscheiden-Kanal der britischen Inseln, den Newry Kanal, erstellte, wäre der Ausbau eines Wasserstrassennetzes nur sehr langsam voran gegangen, hätte sich das irische Parlament nicht im glücklichen Besitz eines jährlichen Steuerüberschusses befunden. Als es erfuhr, dass dieses Geld dem englischen König zu übergeben sei, wurde beschlossen, keinen Überschuss mehr entstehen zu lassen. Statt dessen finanzierte man viele staatliche Bau- und Manufakturunternehmungen. Aus dieser Quelle stammte auch das Geld für die Arbeiten am Shannon, die 1755 in Angriff genommen wurden.

Die Arbeit begann in Meelick unter der Leitung von Ingenieur Thomas Omer, der vermutlich ein Holländer war. In den 80er-Jahren des

The Avonmore- one of the early steamers which plied the river

Ruth Delany

Hamilton Lock, Meelick, one of the early Shannon Navigation locks built in 1755 and extensively restored in the early 1800's

prove equally unsatisfactory and when the directors of the Grand Canal Company had almost completed their canal to the Shannon, they were forced to take over the middle Shannon from Portumna to Athlone and reconstruct the works, putting in conventional locks to replace Omer's flash locks. In 1800 when the Union of the Dublin and Westminster parliaments took place, a new body, the Directors General of Inland Navigation, was created. They were obliged to complete the Limerick to Killaloe navigation and they also carried out some restoration work on the north Shannon. In the 1820s they extended the navigation into Lough Allen by means of a canal .

By this time many of the works had been allowed to deteriorate and the limited number of traders using the system were constantly suffering delays. The whole situation changed when steamers were introduced to the river in 1826 making movement much easier. Up to this time boats had to be sailed or poled when the wind was contrary. The government came under increasing pressure to improve the navigation and build larger locks to accommodate the steamers which had been brought to the river in sections and were reassembled at Killaloe. At a time of great unemployment and distress in the country, the government took over the entire system and authorised Shannon Commissioners to reconstruct the works completely to much larger dimensions.

18. Jahrhunderts reichte die schiffbare Strecke stromaufwärts bis Carrick mit Bauarbeiten in Banagher, Shannonbridge, Athlone, Lanesborough, Tarmonbarry, Roosky und Jamestown. Die Untiefen wurden durch Kanäle mit Schleusen oder, wo ein geringes Gefälle bestand, einem einzelnen Satz von Schleusentoren umgangen. Zur gleicher Zeit begannen unter der Leitung von William Ockendens, einem andern ausländischen Ingenieur, Arbeiten an der Fahrrinne von Limerick nach Killaloe. Diese Aufgabe war wesentlich schwieriger, da der Fluss auf einer Strecke von rund zwanzig Kilometern ein Gefälle von dreissig Metern hat. Die Arbeit machte so geringe Fortschritte, dass die Behörden froh waren, das Projekt einer privaten Gesellschaft zu überlassen. Dieser erging es kaum besser, und die Arbeiten mussten schliesslich mit öffentlichen Mitteln fertiggestellt werden. Omers Werk erwies sich ebenfalls als unbefriedigend, und als die Grand Canal Gesellschaft den Kanal von Dublin zum Shannon fast fertig gebaut hatte, wurde beschlossen, den mittleren Shannon von Portumna bis Athlone zu übernehmen, die gesamten Bauten umzugestalten und die Schleusen mit einem Paar von Einzeltoren durch die heute gebräuchlichen zu ersetzen.

The opening of the Shannon Commissioners' new bridge at Banagher on 12 August 1843 drawn by the contractor, William Mackenzie

James Scully

The Shannon Commissioners' Works

These works were carried out in the 1840s, at a total cost of £584,805 17s 9½d. The engineer was Thomas Rhodes and there was an average of 2,000 men employed at any one time. It is these works which form the Shannon Navigation which we still use today. Rhodes had to construct a completely new canal with the great Victoria lock at Meelick; he abandoned the short canals at Banagher, Shannonbridge and Lanesborough removed the shallows to make a navigation channel in the river at these places. At Athlone, Lanesborough, Tarmonbarry and Roosky he again used the river, making locks where necessary, and he had to widen and straighten the canal at Jamestown. He constructed weirs at each of the places where there were locks and he had to rebuild most of the bridges. He extended the navigation into Lough Key but virtually no work was carried out on the Lough Allen Canal or at the southern end between Limerick and Killaloe, where the smaller locks made it impossible to bring in larger boats from the sea.

The Railway Age

Ironically, the steam which had changed things so dramatically on the Shannon also heralded the Railway Age and by the time the navigation works had been completed there were lines in operation to Limerick and Galway and a line was extended to Sligo by 1862. The passenger traffic on the river rapidly declined and by the 1860s the fine steamers were laid up; those too large to be removed from the Shannon were eventually allowed to sink at Killaloe. The tonnage carried, which had risen to nearly 100,000 tons per year, fell away to half this figure by the 1880s. In 1897 the Shannon Development Company was set up and passenger steamers returned to the river but the service was not a success. It was reduced to a summer schedule in 1903 and

National Library of Ireland

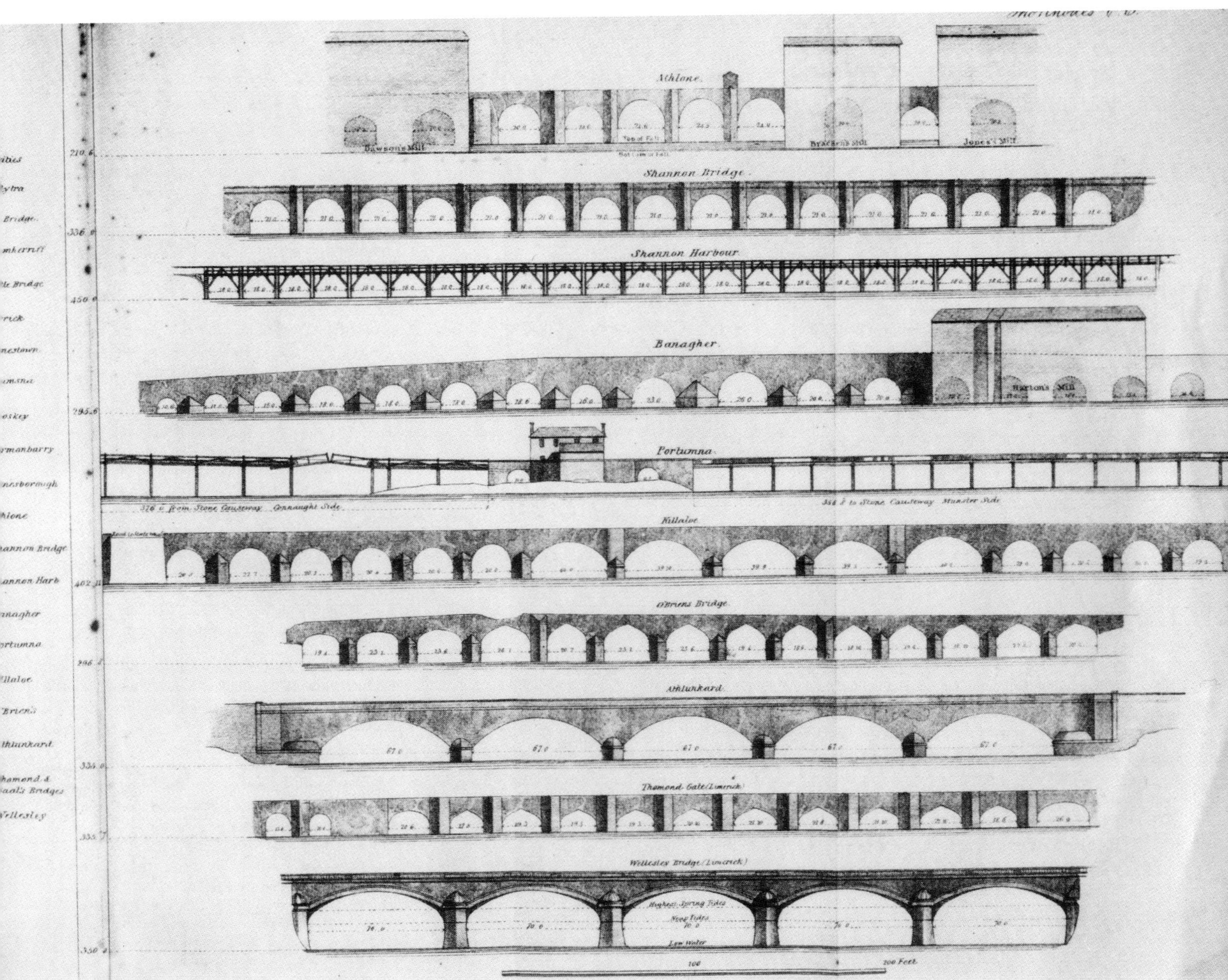

Elevations of all the Shannon bridges in 1833 before the work of the Shannon Commissioners took place

even this ceased in 1914. By this time the tonnage carried had stabilised at an average of 70,000 tons, most of which was between the Grand Canal at Shannon Harbour and Limerick, and a large proportion of this was Guinness stout, which was specially brewed to mature en passage. Pleasure traffic on the river fell to a low ebb in the 1950s following the war years and there was a threat to replace the opening spans with low fixed bridges. An Inland Waterways Association of Ireland was formed, modelled on the IWA in England, and CIE was persuaded to put passenger boats on the river which required a minimum clearance of 4.3 m, thus ensuring that the navigation was kept open with at least this headroom. It was only just in time: there had been a small increase in commercial traffic during the war years but when CIE withdrew the carrying service in 1960 only one trading boat continued to operate on the river.

The Shannon Fights Back

Despite the gloomy forecast of a well-known operator from the Norfolk Broads that the Shannon would have no future unless an umbrella could be erected over it, a few small operators began to offer boats for hire with success and soon the potential of the river came to be appreciated. The government made available a fund of £140,000 to improve facilities and encourage the setting up of larger firms. The number of private boats steadily increased. The IWAI runs two major rallies and a number of smaller Cruises-in-Company each year and the association continues to play an active role in ensuring that the unique quality of the river is retained in future development plans. It is interesting for the visitor to the Shannon today to trace some of the early works, and details of these will be found in the Gazetteer section.

Battlebridge, one of the few early Shannon bridges which was not replaced by the Shannon Commissioners

Ruth Delany

Im Jahre 1820 reichte die Schiffahrtslinie bis zum Lough Allen. Sie war jedoch lange vernachlässigt worden, und als die ersten Dampfschiffe auf dem Fluss erschienen, wurde an die Regierung appelliert, die Fahrstrecke zu verbessern und zu erweitern. Die Shannon Aufsichtsbehörde wurde eingerichtet, die in den 40er Jahren, einer Zeit grösster Armut und Verzweiflung im Land (Hungersnot), weitausgedehnte Bauarbeiten in Angriff nahm und dadurch vielen eine Beschäftigung geben konnte. Der leitende Ingenieur, Thomas Rhodes, verzichtete auf die alten Kanäle und liess statt dessen Fahrrinnen im Fluss ausbaggern und neue Schleusen und Wehre bauen. Er musste viele Brücken erneuern, verlängerte die schiffbare Strecke bis zum Lough Key, liess aber die Kanäle an beiden Enden nicht renovieren. Als die Arbeiten beendet waren, begann das Zeitalter der Eisenbahn. Die Passagierschiffe konnten nicht konkurrieren und stellten bald den Betrieb ein. Auch der Gütertransport auf dem Fluss ging zurück. Ein Versuch, die Dampfer 1897 wieder in Betrieb zu nehmen, scheiterte.

Nach dem Zweiten Weltkrieg, als wenig Verkehr auf dem Fluss war, bestand die Gefahr, dass diejenigen Brücken, die für Durchfahrten geöffnet werden konnten, durch niedrige, feststehende Brücken ersetzt werden sollten. Eine Vereinigung zur Förderung der Wasserwege wurde gegründet, die das staatliche Transportunternehmen CIE dazu überredete, zwei Passagierschiffe auf dem Fluss einzusetzen, die eine lichte Höhe von 4.30 Metern brauchten. Dadurch konnte der ganze Lauf des Shannon schiffbar erhalten werden. 1960 zog das CIE seine beiden Schiffe vom Fluss ab, aber mittlerweile waren dessen touristische Möglichkeiten erkannt worden. Die Regierung stellte die zur Verbesserung der vorhandenen Einrichtungen benötigten Mittel zur Verfügung und unterstützte die Gründung von Bootsverleih-Firmen. Heute gibt es immer mehr Boote auf dem Shannon, und die Vereinigung zur Förderung der Binnen-Wasserwege (Inland Waterways Association of Ireland – IWAI) ist streng darauf bedacht, den einzigartigen Charakter der Flusslandschaft zu erhalten. Es ist interessant, einige dieser frühen Bauwerke genauer zu betrachten. Im Ortsnamenverzeichnis findet man die entsprechenden Angaben.

Landscape of the River

John Weaving and Daphne Levinge

Ireland resembles a pie which has been baked without benefit of the necessary egg-cup to support the centre. The coastal areas are high and reasonably dry, whereas the centre of the country is low and extremely soggy. One-fifth of the land area of Ireland drains inward through various lakes, small streams and rivers, reaching the system known as the Shannon.

The river itself consists of a number of large and small lakes, mostly connected by sluggish river sections. In very few places does the river—or for that matter the lakes—produce anything resembling a valley, and as summer water levels over most of the area are only a few feet below the level of the surrounding fields, any rise in the water level produces very extensive flooding. Thus the Shannon remains the largest undrained river in Europe and the longest in Britain and Ireland.

Geological Formation

The landscape of the central lowlands of Ireland through which the Shannon flows reflects the underlying geology: this is predominantly carboniferous limestone (formed 350 million years ago), overlaid by varying thickness of glacial drift deposited during the Ice Age (which commenced two million years ago). Diversity in the landscape is provided by the small areas of higher ground formed from younger rocks on top of the limestone, such as the hills surrounding Lough Allen, or of older rocks of shale and sandstone, projecting through the limestone as a result of folding. Examples of the latter are Slieve Bawn, north of Lough Ree, a range of hills running southwest to northeast interrupted by the Shannon, and the Slieve Bloom mountains, or those mountains west and south of Lough Derg. Any other diversity in the landscape is the legacy of the last glaciation (100,000–10,000 years ago): the drumlins of South Leitrim; the moraines and eskers in the central Shannon area; the topography suitable for later bog formation; the major lakes, Lough Ree and Lough Derg, which were probably formed through chemical solution of the underlying limestone and denudation by ice and running water.

The source

Traditionally the Shannon rises in the Shannon Pot, a round pond on the slopes of Cuilcagh Mountain in Co Cavan, from which a small trout stream emerges, but there is no visible water support entering the pool. In recent years, however, pot-holers have discovered what is thought to be the true source of the river much further uphill, where a small stream disappears into a sink-hole. This, in fact, is across the Border in Co Fermanagh. The whole upper part of Cuilcagh Mountain consists of a porous limestone and is full of sink-holes and risers. From the Shannon Pot, the river receives a number of tributaries, some of which are larger than itself, and emerges into the head of Lough Allen.

Mineral Wealth

Lough Allen, the third largest of the Shannon lakes, lies between the heather covered Arigna hills and Slieve Anierin. These are Upper Carboniferous in age, made up of shales, flagstones and sandstones, and contain coal seams. Iron occurs in the form of nodules of ironstones within the shales—particularly on Slieve Anierin (the mountain of iron)—and small local smelting works existed in many places

Die Flußlandschaft

Irland hat die Form einer Schüssel. Die Küstengegenden sind höher gelegen und einigermassen trocken, während die Mitte tiefliegendes, mooriges Terrain ist. Das Shannongebiet entwässert ein Fünftel Irlands. Der Fluss selbst besteht aus einer Reihe von Seen, die durch träge dahinfliessende Flussabschnitte verbunden sind. Da er sich kaum irgendwo ein Tal geschaffen hat, bedeutet jeder Anstieg des Wasserstandes weite Überschwemmungen. So bleibt der Shannon der grösste nichtbegradigte Fluss Europas; er ist auch der längste in Irland und Grossbritannien. Die zentrale Tiefebene Irlands besteht in der Hauptsache aus von Gletscherablagerungen bedecktem karbonzeitlichem Kalkstein. Manche Anhöhen sind aus jüngerem Gestein wie die Hügel um Lough Allen, manche bestehen aus älterem Gestein, das sich durch den Kalkstein aufgefaltet hat. Dazu gehören die Slieve Bawn Hügel nördlich von Lough Ree und die Slieve Bloom Berge wie auch die Berge westlich und südlich vom Lough Derg. Die Drumlins im Süden Leitrims, die Moränen und Esker im zentralen Shannongebiet und die Topographie, die später die Moore und grösseren Seen schuf, entstanden alle während der letzten Eiszeit vor etwa 100'000 bis 10'000 Jahren.

Der Shannon entspringt im Shannon Pot, einem runden Teich an den Hängen des Cuilcagh Berges in der Grafschaft Cavan, der von höher gelegenen Quellen gespeist wird. Der aus dem Pot (Topf) fliessende junge Strom vereinigt sich mit andern Wasserläufen, bevor er in das Lough Allen fliesst. Dieser drittgrösste der Shannon-Seen ist von kohle- und eisenerzhaltigen Bergen umgeben. Hier gab es früher eine Eisenindustrie. Seit den 30er Jahren ist Lough Allen das Reservoir für das Flusskraftwerk Ardnacrusha.

Südlich vom Lough Allen entstanden während der verschiedenen Eiszeiten Drumlins, kleine runde Hügel aus Lehm und Schotter, die den Ablauf des Wassers blockierten. Es sammelte sich in Seen. Der vom Wasser angeschwemmte Blaulehm bildete auf beiden Seiten flache Sumpfwiesen. Die von Wellen erodierten Steilklippen am Südende von Lough Drumharlow sind ein Indiz für das Zurückdrängen des

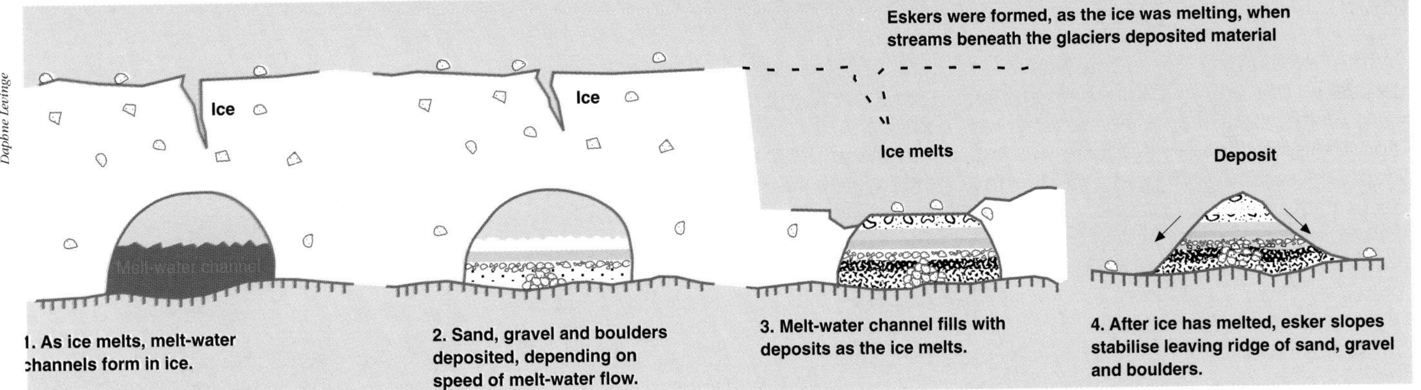

Formation of eskers

such as Arigna, Boyle, Dromod, Drumshanbo and Drumsna, utilising the coal seams and earlier charcoal from the forests around Lough Allen. Until recently the horizontal bands of coal were exploited almost exclusively in the nearby Arigna Power Station. Over the centuries, silt brought down by the Arigna river gradually blocked the Shannon's exit, raising the level of the lake. Since the 1920s it has been used as a storage reservoir for the Shannon hydro-electric scheme, causing variations in levels of up to 6 m.

Ice Age Influences

South of Lough Allen, the tremendous influence of the various ice ages becomes obvious. This is the area which is covered with drumlins, small rounded hills of blue clay, containing boulders of various sizes. These succeeded in blocking whatever drainage pattern existed prior to the ice ages, ponding back water into lakes. It has been suggested that Lough Allen at one time flowed into Donegal Bay. Further south, the evidence of blockage is very clear in many places: one of the most obvious is at Rosebank, just south of Carrick-on-Shannon, where the present high ground on either side of the river was obviously connected right across the river at one stage, ponding back the water right up to Lough Key. The water reaching these lakes carried a great deal of blue clay in suspension, and this was dropped in the still water to make very extensive, completely flat, boggy fields on either side of the river. The height of the flood water is clearly indicated by small cliffs on the southern shore of Lough Drumharlow, eroded by wave action when the lake was much higher than its present level. At Rosebank, immediately below this restriction, the river bottom has been scoured to a very considerable depth; this type of scouring could be evidence of a waterfall in the area at some time in the past. Where the restriction actually occurred the river bottom consists of very large boulders, which are too big for the current to move; this area had to be dredged in the course of constructing the present navigation.

These blockages occurred all the way downstream and were probably cleared one after the other, allowing plenty of time for the fine material from upstream erosion to be deposited on the bottom of the downstream lakes. The result is that the whole north Shannon between Cootehall and Lough Boderg is lined with low callow fields, with great depths of impermeable blue clay which grows nothing satisfactorily except field rushes. Here can be seen the typical drumlin landscape of south Leitrim, where 75% of farms are less than 12 hectares in extent, made up of small hedgerow-enclosed and ill-drained fields.

Wassers.

Das Flussbett des Shannon und die Seebekken sind sehr verschieden. Die Böden der kleineren Seen des Oberlaufs bestehen aus Ablagerungsschichten von weissem Muschelmergel, den Häusern von Millionen von Frischwasserschnecken. Die Felsen vom Lough Ree sind weich, da sie mit einer dicken Schicht von Kalkstein bedeckt sind. Wo immer die Strömung etwas stärker ist, ist das Wasser klar. Sonst ist es voll von Schlamm und Schlick und besonders von Torferde aus den maschinellen Torfstechereien. Die Versumpfung ist sogar bis zum Lough Derg fortgeschritten und hat verheerende Auswirkungen auf alle Arten von Lebewesen im See.

Die Esker des mittleren Shannongebiets entstanden, als Flüsse während der Eisschmelze unterhalb der Gletscher grosse Mengen von Sand, Kies und Felsblöcken mit sich schwemmten und in Form von langgestreckten Hügeln ablagerten. Aus seichten Seen zwischen diesen Hügeln bildeten sich Moore. Beispiele dafür sind in der Nähe von Clonmacnois und bei Shannonbridge zu finden.

Lough Dergs nördlicher Teil gleicht Lough Ree. Die Umgebung ist reiches Agrarland. Der südliche Teil ist völlig anders und wegen den auf beiden Seiten steil aufragenden Bergen von Arra und Slieve Bernagh sehr beeindruckend. Fast der ganze See wird von einem tiefen Graben durchzogen. Geologen rätseln immer noch darüber, warum der Fluss nicht den einfacheren Weg durch den Kalkstein von Scariff Bay zum Meer genommen hat. Man versucht es damit zu erklären, dass die zentrale Ebene einmal viel höher lag. Als sie immer mehr abgetragen wurde, behielt der Fluss seinen ursprünglichen, bis

Lough Key, one of the lakes formed by the ponding back of the water by the drumlin formation

Bord Failte

While excavating for a slipway near Drumsna, we dug through 2 m of blue clay, which contained neither sand, gravel nor stones. Underneath this there was 1 m depth of woodland peat, containing sections of pine. This lay directly above the limestone bedrock. As the top of the peat was over 1 m below the present summer water level, this would infer that, at some stage prior to the ice ages, the water level must have been considerably lower, or perhaps there might not have been a river in this area at all.

The Upper Shannon

The bed of the Shannon and its lakes is very varied. Lough Key has an even-chequered pattern of hard shoals and islands. The smaller lakes in the alkaline waters of the upper Shannon all have deep deposits of white shell marl, up to 9 m in depth in places which consist of the shells of myriads of small freshwater snails. The bottom depths are very even in these lakes, between 1.5 and 2 m, except where the incoming river has scoured it in places down to 18 m. Lough Forbes is peaty on the western side and alkaline on the eastern side, with a number of unexpected large rocks. The rocks in the shoals and on the shores of Lough Ree are reputed to be soft, being mostly covered with a very thick layer of lime. Some of the shoals on this lake are shown on the old maps as islands, but these have since been eroded away.

The Middle Shannon

Between Athlone and Portumna the landscape has changed. Here the Shannon is wide and sluggish and becomes extensively flooded in autumn and winter so that the river's course is no longer visible. The major feature of the landscape are the esker ridges which cross the river approximately east-west. Eskers were formed as the ice was melting, when streams beneath the glaciers carried and deposited large amounts of sand, gravel and boulders. The most spectacular eskers are those low-lying hills at Clonmacnois. Between the esker ridges shallow lakes remained after the Ice Age and rapidly filled with marl (a deposit of calcium carbonate). The lakes became shallower as the environment dried out. Reeds and sedges, rushes and willows grew and partly decayed—thus peat accumulated and bogs were formed. Good examples of bog can be seen near Clonmacnois and Shannonbridge and many bogs are now exploited for electricity generation as at Lanesborough and Shannonbridge. Over most of the river bed, where there is any strong flow, it is scoured to large stones or boulders, or down to bedrock. In the still-water sections it is filled with various silts. In the areas near the mechanised bogs the silt is largely milled peat and this peat has even encroached into the upper portions of Lough Derg, where it has seriously interfered with all forms of life in the lake.

Lough Derg

Lough Derg, in its northern section, resembles Lough Ree: headlands, islands and shoals composed of boulder-rich glacial drift appear, but the rocks in the lake are hard, with no protective coating of lime. On the mainland these soils support

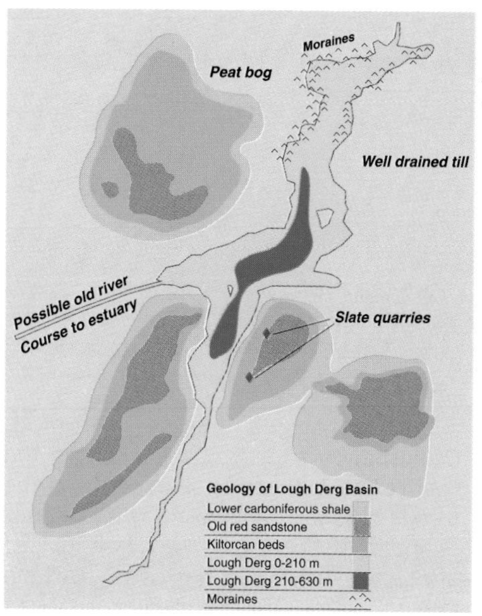

Daphne Levinge

Geology of Lough Derg basin

zur Felsenschwelle von Killaloe gegrabenen Lauf bei. Dieser natürliche Damm wurde während der Arbeiten am Wasserkraftwerk durch einen künstlichen weiter flussabwärts ersetzt.

Die Landwirtschaft hat im Lauf der Zeit die natürlichen Gegebenheiten des Shannongebiets verändert. Herkömmliche landwirtschaftliche Methoden sind noch in einem Grossteil der Region anzutreffen. Der durchschnittliche Bauernhof hat eine Grösse von zwölf Hektaren. Weni-

The "Fairy Bridge" over one of the canals at Rockingham, constructed with the stones taken from Lough Key which have been eroded into strange shapes

Ruth Delany

productive agriculture.

The southern end of the lake is different and very spectacular, with the Arra Mountains rising sheer on one side and Slieve Bernagh rising in the same way on the other side. The lake is of a considerable depth for more than half of its length: there is a continuous trench with depths of 24–30 m which runs almost to Killaloe. Geologically, there is some speculation on the reasons for the course of the Shannon in this region. Why did the river not enter the sea at Galway Bay or eastwards, rather than meandering south where it ignored the obvious exit at Scarriff Bay and instead left the limestone and cut through the sandstone and slate hills at Killaloe before reaching the sea at Limerick? One explanation is that at one time the central plain of Ireland stood much higher and when it was denuded the river retained its original course, having carved a way through to plunge over a rock sill at Killaloe. This natural dam was removed in the 1920s and a new artificial dam erected further downstream when the hydro-electric works were being carried out.

Farming Practices over the Centuries

Farming practices have changed the Shannon's natural landscape over time. Apart from the better drained and productive soils of the higher land around Lough Ree and Lough Derg, traditional farming methods are still found over most of the area. Here farm size is on average about 12 hectares. Less than 5% of the land is tilled. The farmland south of Athlone, winter-flooded and silt-enriched, is renowned for vegetable growing but summer flooding in some years causes problems. Geese are not uncommon, grazing in large flocks on the callows. These small farms cannot support a whole family and for most of them farming is now only a part-time activity. Additional income is sought from work in nearby towns, in

John Kenny

Banagher in flood

the few local industries or with Bord na Mona. For a few, and the signs are there on the landscape, expansion of the farm and more intensive agriculture seemed, for a time, the best way to derive an adequate income. But economic changes have halted agriculture's impact on the Shannon landscape. Surpluses within the EC and a growing realisation of the need for conservation of the rural landscape and way of life from within the EC itself, has meant a re-evaluation of modern agricultural practices. Introduced in the summer of 1994 the Rural Environment Protection Scheme (REPS) encourages farmers, through direct payments, to farm using environmentally sensitive methods. Whilst applicable throughout the country, this voluntary scheme, if taken up by farmers, should go a long way towards protecting the Shannon landscape and farming traditions. Diversification into other crops and farming methods, forestry, agri-tourism or direct financial support for the traditional farmer in environmentally sensitive areas must be discussed with a view to maintaining the richness of the Shannon's landscape.

ger als fünf Prozent des Bodens werden angebaut. Das im Winter überschwemmte Land südlich von Athlone ist angereichert mit Schlick. Überschwemmungen im Sommer können jedoch Probleme verursachen. Natürlich können diese kleinen Höfe nicht ganze Familien ernähren, daher sind sie für die meisten Bauern nur eine Teilzeitbeschäftigung.

Einige wenige allerdings begannen mit einer intensiven Bodennutzung. Die Anzeichen davon sind in der Landschaft nicht zu übersehen. Veränderungen der Wirtschaftsstruktur und EG-Überschüsse haben ihnen jedoch bereits Einhalt geboten. Aus diesem Grunde müssen moderne Anbaumethoden neu diskutiert und überprüft, eine abwechslungsreiche Nutzung gefördert beziehungsweise den traditionellen Bauern finanzielle Unterstützung garantiert werden. Sonst geht die Vielfalt und der Reichtum der Landschaft des Shannon verloren.

Flora of the River

Daphne Levinge

The Shannon provides many different habitats for a wide variety of species of flora including some rare and very interesting plants.

To the visitor stepping ashore along the river bank or at the lake edge, the shore can be wet and soggy or sometimes rocky and wave-swept. For most of the plants which inhabit these shores, the amount of water present is the determining factor as to whether they can establish themselves and survive successfully. Many of these plants have adaptations which enable them to cope with the water environment: some plants, like the microscopic algae, live rootless in the water; water lilies and pondweeds have large floating leaves; other plants live submerged in shallow water like the Canadian pondweed and water milfoils. Some plants prefer the sheltered waters of calm bays to the fast-flowing river sections.

Moving inland from the water's edge, other factors become important for the plant. Is the soil lime-rich or acidic? Is it shallow or deep to allow short grassland vegetation or rich woodland to develop?

Varied Habitats

Thus different Shannon habitats are found with a characteristic group of plants tolerant of or preferring the particular conditions of water, soil or climate. Of course, some plants are so tolerant of these conditions that they are found not only throughout the Shannon system but all over Ireland. These common species, because they are widespread and familiar, are not referred to in the list which can be found in the appendix.

Rare Plants

Some rare Irish plants can be found within the Shannon system. The origins of their presence here, and indeed in Ireland,

Ruth Borner

Die Flora des Flusses

Der Besucher, der am Fluss- oder Seeufer aussteigt, wird feststellen, dass die Ufer nass und sumpfig oder aber felsig und von Wellen beschlagen sein können. Für Pflanzen ist der bestimmende Faktor die Wassermenge, ob sie an einem Ort gedeihen und überleben können. Viele haben sich der wasserreichen Umgebung mit Erfolg angepasst wie zum Beispiel die mikroskopisch kleinen Algen, die wurzellos im Wasser treiben. Wasserlilien und andere Wasserpflanzen haben grosse, schwimmende Blätter. Andere wieder, wie das kanadische Laichkraut und die Wasserschafgarbe, leben unter der Oberfläche im seichten Wasser. Manche Pflanzen bevorzugen das geschützte Wasser einer stillen Bucht, andere die Flussabschnitte.

Neben den Uferrändern werden weiter im Landesinnern andere Faktoren wichtig. Ist der Humus kalkhaltig oder sauer? Ist er nur eine dünne Schicht oder tief? Kann nur eine Wiesenvegetation oder eine Bewachsung mit Waldbäumen gedeihen?

So findet man am Shannon ganz verschiedene Pflanzenhabitate nebeneinander mit charakteristischen Gruppen, welche die jeweiligen Wasser-, Boden- und Klimaverhältnisse tolerieren beziehungsweise bevorzugen. Natürlich gibt es ausserdem auch solche, die so anpassungsfähig sind, dass man sie in ganz Irland antrifft. Diese Pflanzengattungen werden wegen ihrer Verbreitung und Bekanntheit in der Liste, die im Anhang zu finden ist, nicht aufgeführt.

Es gibt einige sehr seltene irische Pflanzen, die im Shannongebiet zu finden sind. Wie sie hierher oder überhaupt nach Irland kamen, kann nur vermutet werden. Manche Gräser, Riedgräser und auch der Wacholder haben die Eiszeit wahrscheinlich im Hochland überlebt und besiedelten erst allmählich die tiefer gelegenen Gegenden. Als es nach der Eiszeit wärmer wurde, kamen Pflanzen aus allen möglichen Himmelsrichtungen nach Irland. So scheinen etliche der Orchideen aus dem Mittelmeerraum zu stammen. Das irische Flohkraut, in ganz Grossbritannien und Irland nur an den Ufern von Lough Derg anzutreffen, kam vom europäischen Konti-

Greater Spearwort
Yellow Loosestrife
Flowering Rush
Ragged Robin
Spindle Tree
Sedge
Buckthorn
Horsetail
Marsh Helleborine
Sneezewort
Purple Loosestrife
Hemp Agrimony
Marsh Pea
Bur-reed
Long Leaved Helleborine
Early Purple Orchid
Marsh Orchid
Mare's Tail
Birds Nest Orchid
Canadian Pondweed
Arrowhead
Grass of Parnassus
Bog Bean
Ivy Leaved Duckweed
Water Plantain
Irish Fleabane
Frogbit
Water Germander
Blue Eyed Grass
Daphne Levinge

is open to speculation. Some grasses and sedges and the juniper may have survived the Ice Age on high ground and later gradually colonised the lowlands. As the climate warmed up after the Ice Age, plants migrated into Ireland from all directions. Some of the orchids appear to have originated in the Mediterranean area; from continental Europe came Irish fleabane which is only found in Britain and Ireland at the edge of Lough Derg. The blue-eyed grass, which is also very rare, is a plant associated with the North American flora and this too may be found at the edge of Lough Derg. Other rare plants which can be found may have been introduced with man's help, such as the insect-eating North American pitcher plant. Many of these rare plants survive because they colonise conditions which they like and because they are under less competitive pressure than in Britain and Europe, with their richer flora.

Shannon Species

Exploring the Shannon flora is rewarding: the flora is rich and many of the rarer Irish species are easily found. Most species, except possibly the grasses and sedges, are easily identified from an illustrated flora (see bibliography). The list which can be found in the appendix includes most species characteristic of the Shannon, arranged by the habitats in which they are most likely to occur. The most striking Shannon habitats include the deep and shallow waters of the river and lakes, the reedbeds which develop from deposits of sediment in lakes and slow flowing river sections. Behind the reedbeds, fens are found where sedges, grasses and characteristic flowering plants, with willow trees, are dominant. Worth exploring too are the shores of Lough Ree and Lough Derg: characteristic plants of their rocky shores are described in the appendix.

nent. Ein sehr seltenes, eigentlich der amerikanischen Flora zugeordnetes Rispengras wächst ebenfalls um Lough Derg herum. Andere dieser seltenen Pflanzen, wie zum Beispiel eine insektenfressende nordamerikanische Pflanze, wurden von Menschen eingeführt. Viele überleben, weil ihnen die Lebensbedingungen zusagen und sie sich nicht gegen eine viel artenreichere Flora durchsetzen müssen, wie das in England und auf dem Kontinent der Fall ist.

Es lohnt sich, die Flora der Shannonregion zu erforschen. Sie ist vielfältig, und man kann die selteneren Gattungen leicht entdecken. Viele von ihnen, vielleicht mit Ausnahme der Gräser und Riedgräser, können anhand eines Pflanzenbuches ohne Schwierigkeiten identifiziert werden (siehe Bücherliste). Die folgende Aufzählung enthält die meisten für den Shannon typischen Pflanzen. Sie sind dem Gebiet zugeordnet, wo sie am wahrscheinlichsten vorkommen. Zu den bemerkenswertesten Lebensräumen gehören die tiefen wie auch die seichten Gewässer, das an schlickbedeckten Stellen vorkommende Röhricht und die träge fliessenden Stromstrecken. An das Röhricht schliesst sich Marschland voll Schilf, Gräsern und charakteristisch blühenden Pflanzen an. Hier ist das Weidengebüsch vorherrschend. Es lohnt sich auch, die Ufergebiete von Lough Ree und Lough Derg zu durchstreifen. Die für diese Gegend typischen Pflanzen finden sich bei den Beschreibungen im Anhang. Die Anmerkungen über die Verbreitung beziehen sich auf das Shannongebiet. Denken Sie daran, dass die beschriebenen Pflanzen nicht nur in einem einzigen Gebiet vorkommen können.

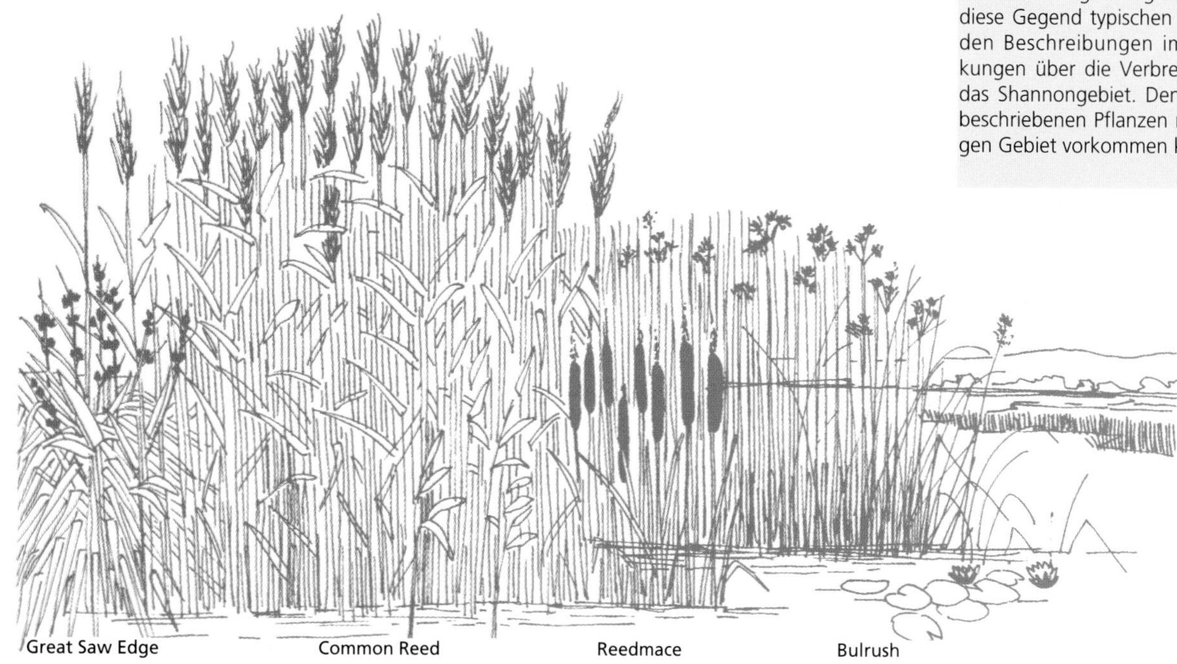

Great Saw Edge — Common Reed — Reedmace — Bulrush

Fauna of the River

Daphne Levinge

> ***The Shannon system contains almost every environment to be found in Ireland except those habitats exclusively marine and consequently offers a good cross-section of the fauna of the country.***

Because they move around and are not necessarily restricted to one habitat, most of our larger animals can be found throughout the Shannon system; the smaller invertebrates (e.g. insects, snails and crustaceans) which are not so mobile and tend to be dependent on certain vegetation or other physical conditions may only be found in specific areas. The identification of these smaller animals is a task for the specialist. In fact, the Shannon has not yet been comprehensively explored and frequently new and interesting species are discovered when new areas are studied in detail.

It is vital that this diversity of fauna and flora and the quality of the Shannon environment be maintained. Sadly, many habitats are under threat from man's activities. The large-scale arterial drainage of the Shannon is a controversial subject.

Brown hare

Office of Public Works

Office of Public Works

Fox

Water quality is deteriorating through increased fertiliser usage and farm effluents; sewage is still being discharged untreated from towns and villages; the working of peat bogs often produces an accumulation of silt from inflowing tributaries. In addition, poorly sited developments resulting from inadequate planning and development controls can despoil the landscape and destroy previously undisturbed habitats.

Notes and a checklist of the larger animals and butterflies likely to be encountered by the Shannon visitor are included in the appendix. A pair of binoculars and a quiet walk or row in a dinghy at dawn or dusk will often be rewarded with sightings of our larger animals. Butterflies and other insects prefer bright, sunny days. It is not possible to be comprehensive in the checklist of other smaller fauna because of the range and diversity of species whose identification is often difficult.

Die Fauna des Flusses

Im Shannongebiet sind fast alle in Irland vorkommenden Lebensbedingungen vertreten, ausgenommen diejenigen der Küstenregionen. Da die meisten der grösseren Tiere umherziehen und ihr Vorkommen nicht notwendigerweise auf einen Lebensraum beschränkt ist, trifft man sie überall an. Kleinere, wirbellose Tiere wie Insekten, Schnecken und Krebse, die nicht so mobil sind und manchmal von einer bestimmten Vegetation oder anderen Umweltbedingungen abhängen, treten oft nur in spezifischen Gegenden auf. Die Identifizierung dieser kleinen Tiere ist Aufgabe des Experten. In der Tat wurde das Shannongebiet bisher noch nicht völlig erforscht, und bei der genauen Untersuchung neuer Gegenden werden ständig noch unbekannte, interessante Gattungen klassifiziert.

Es ist von grösster Wichtigkeit, dass dieser Reichtum an Tier- und Pflanzenleben und die Qualität der Umwelt im Shannongebiet erhalten bleiben. Bedauerlicherweise sind viele Standorte von Menschen bedroht, immer wieder wird auch über die Drainage der Region diskutiert.

Durch Düngemittel und Abwässer von Bauernhöfen nimmt die Wasserqualität ständig ab. Die Kanalisationen von Städten und Dörfern münden noch immer – und oft ungeklärt – in den Fluss. Die Nebengewässer schwemmen Schlamm von den grossen Torfstichen mit und lagern ihn ab. Dazu kommt, dass durch unzulängliche Planung und Baukontrollen entstandene, schlechtplazierte Betriebe die Landschaft und damit noch ungestörte Lebensräume zugrunde richten können.

Nachfolgend findet man Angaben über die häufigsten grösseren Tiere und Schmetterlinge des Shannongebiets. Ein ruhiger Spaziergang oder eine Bootsfahrt in der Morgen- oder Abenddämmerung mit dem Fernglas wird sich sicher lohnen. Schmetterlinge und andere Insekten bevorzugen helle, sonnige Tage. Leider ist es nicht möglich, eine vollständige Liste aller kleineren Tiere in ihrer Vielfalt aufzustellen.

Irish Hare
Rabbit
Pine Marten
Stoat
Otter
Red Squirrel
Grey Squirrel
American Mink
Hedgehog
Pygmy Shrew
Common Lizard
Brown Rat
Black Vole
Frog
Common Newt

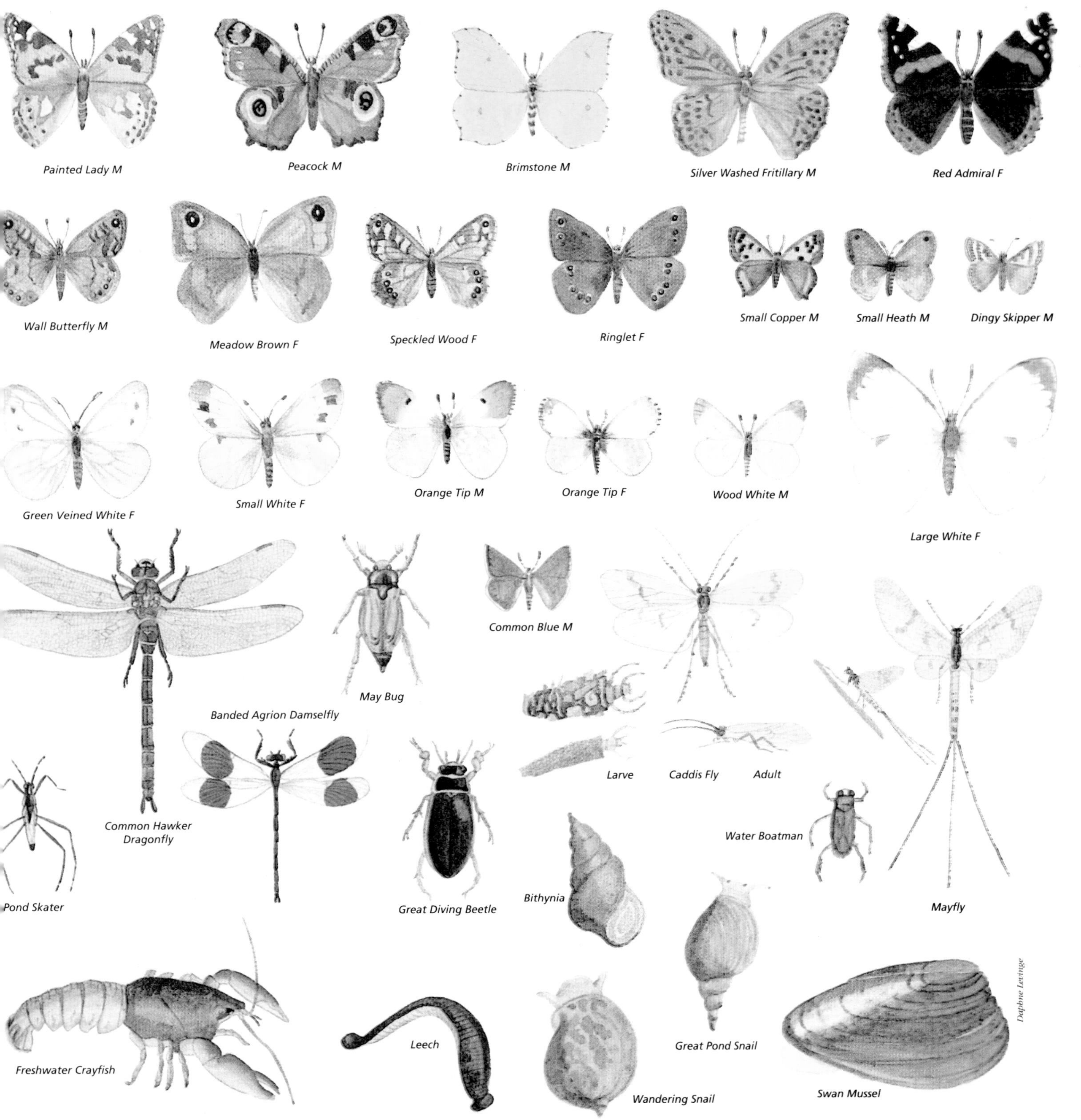

Painted Lady M
Peacock M
Brimstone M
Silver Washed Fritillary M
Red Admiral F
Wall Butterfly M
Meadow Brown F
Speckled Wood F
Ringlet F
Small Copper M
Small Heath M
Dingy Skipper M
Green Veined White F
Small White F
Orange Tip M
Orange Tip F
Wood White M
Large White F
Common Blue M
May Bug
Banded Agrion Damselfly
Larve
Caddis Fly
Adult
Common Hawker Dragonfly
Water Boatman
Pond Skater
Bithynia
Great Diving Beetle
Mayfly
Leech
Freshwater Crayfish
Great Pond Snail
Wandering Snail
Swan Mussel
Daphne Levinge

Birds of the River

John Weaving and Gerrit van Gelderen

The Shannon system is an area without equal in Europe for birds, some of them permanent residents and others summer or winter visitors.

Three main factors account for the importance of the Shannon as a habitat for birds. Firstly, the Shannon remains unaffected by large-scale drainage, unlike most other European river systems, so that in winter the river and some of its tributaries turn into vast, shallow flooded areas which support huge numbers of waders, swans and wildfowl. Secondly, the Shannon flows through or near a diverse range of habitats including marshland, fen, bog, woodland, grassland and hedgerow, all of which have their own characteristic bird population. Thirdly many of these habitats are undisturbed by man's activities: farming is less intensive than elsewhere in Europe, with low use of fertilisers and agricultural chemicals, so that there is plenty of food and undisturbed areas for breeding.

Permanent Residents

Many of the birds observed by the visitor to the Shannon are permanent residents and are commonly encountered throughout the river system. These include the coot, moorhen and little grebe or dabchick. whose 'whinnying' call, day and night, must earn the prize for the noisiest Shannon bird. The great crested grebe, also noisy at times, breed in smaller numbers and are also widespread. They win the prize for elegance: to watch, in the early morning, the ballet of their courtship is unforgettable. Of the duck, mallard and tufted duck must be the most common breeders, the former all over, and the latter liking the wide expanses of the large lakes. Teal are less numerous, at least in summer, and the status of the shoveller as a breeding bird is now uncertain. Keep a look-out for them in the Clonmacnois area and red-breasted mergansers on the islands of Lough Ree and Derg. Grey herons, also plentiful, are tree-dwellers and breed very early in the season. On the whole there is not much love lost between the anglers and the cormorants, the devil's black pigeons, accused of taking too much fish. However, they have little impact on fish stocks and are, in fact, an indication of piscine riches. The most abundant bunting is the reed bunting, almost every reedbed has its pair.

Die Vögel des Flusses

In ganz Europa existiert kaum ein für Vögel wichtigeres Gebiet als dasjenige des Shannons. Dafür sind drei Hauptfaktoren verantwortlich. Zunächst ist der Shannon zum grossen Teil noch frei von Drainagen im grossen Stil, so dass er, im Gegensatz zu anderen europäischen Flüssen, während des Winters gleich wie viele seiner Nebenflüsse weite Strecken des Landes überschwemmt. Hier leben grosse Mengen von Wildvögeln, Wasserläufern, Schwänen und Moorhühnern. Zweitens fliesst der Shannon durch verschiedene Landschaftsformen wie Marsch, Sumpf, Moor, Wald, Wiese und Heckenlandschaft, die jede ihre typischen Vogelarten besitzt. Drittens sind viele dieser Landschaften noch vom Menschen ungestört. Hier gibt es weniger Landwirtschaft als anderswo in Europa und dadurch auch weniger Kunstdünger und Chemikalien. Deshalb sind ausreichend Nahrung und

Walter Borner

Black-headed Gull in flight

Shannon Swans

The most obvious of all Shannon birds are the mute swans which breed all along the river. There is not a mile of waterway which does not fall within a mute swan's territory. Non-breeding birds, which make up a large section of the total swan population, flock together and feed on waterweeds in the shallows. As a swan cannot feed in water deeper than its neck is long, it makes a perfect indicator: never steer your craft into waters where swans are feeding, you're asking for trouble. The whooper and Bewick's swans are winter residents but for some reason single whoopers, easily recognised by the yellow on their beaks, sometimes stay over for the summer and have been known to mate with local mutes.

Gulls and Other Residents

Of the gulls, the black-headed one is the most common with large colonies on the lakes, ever increasing in number, at the cost of the common tern, which is a summer resident, and whose plunging dive for fish is a spectacular sight. Herring gulls and lesser blackbacks are to be seen in colonies on Lough Ree and common gulls more scattered in the same habitat. Our flying jewel, the kingfisher, is widespread and breeds in banks along the narrow tributaries. When the young have hatched and are flying, they can be met almost anywhere. Most common song bird is the meadow pipit. Pied wagtails and grey wagtails frequent the locks and weirs on the upper Shannon. Of the birds-of-prey, the kestrel and sparrow hawk are the most common. You may see a hen harrier or a marsh harrier, which is a summer resident, and even an occasional vagrant peregrine, osprey, merlin or buzzard. Don't be surprised to hear a pheasant calling from the riverside: they are plentiful even on the islands.

Summer Residents

Another group of birds which are of interest to the Shannon visitor are the summer residents: visitors themselves, they arrive in spring, stay to breed and depart again in the autumn. In reedbeds, scrub and wooded areas these include the many species of warbler; and in hay meadows between Athlone and Portumna the corncrake, declining in numbers throughout Europe, are easier heard than seen. They hang about the rough grass along the water margins to invade the meadows when these are starting to grow and provide cover. Swifts, swallows and house martins are widespread and also sand martins, frequently seen feeding low over the water, but they unfortunately are on the decline. The sedge warbler, the Irish nightingale, in all wet areas with thick

Family of Mute Swans

Walter Bonner

Walter Bonner

Mallard Duck

ungestörte Brutplätze vorhanden.

Viele vom Besucher beobachtete Vögel sind ständige Bewohner des Shannongebiets. Man trifft sie überall am Fluss. Dazu gehören Blässhuhn, Teichhuhn, Stockente, Höckerschwan, Reiher, Haubentaucher, Lachmöve und etwas seltener Zwergtaucher und Eisvogel. Die Weiden, Wälder und Hecken sind ebenfalls reich an Vogelarten, die überall in Irland vorkommen.

Eine weitere interessante Gruppe von Vögeln sind die im Sommer hier lebenden Zugvögel. Sie sind Gäste, kommen im Frühjahr, bleiben hier, um zu brüten und fliegen im Herbst wieder weg. Dazu gehören die vielen Arten der Grasmücken und in den Heuwiesen zwischen Athlone und Portumna die in Europa immer seltener werdende Wiesenknarre. Mauersegler, Rauchschwalben, Mehlschwalben und Uferschwalben sind häufig zu beobachten, wenn sie auf der Suche nach Nahrung oberhalb der Wasseroberfläche dahinjagen. Auch die gemeine Seeschwalbe ist ein Sommergast – ihr blitzschnelles Tauchen nach Fischen ist ein aufregender Anblick.

Im Winter, wenn das Flussgebiet überschwemmt ist, findet man grosse Mengen von Schwänen, Sumpfvögeln, Enten und Gänsen. Die Zahl der gewöhnlich hier ansässigen Vögel wird zu dieser Jahreszeit um zahlreiche Zugvögel vermehrt, die aus Nordosteuropa, Island und Grönland hierherkommen. Besonders interessant ist die grönländische Blässgans, von deren Gattung nur noch etwa 20'000 in der ganzen Welt existieren. Drei Viertel davon überwintern in Irland, zum Teil zwischen Athlone und Portumna.

Great Black-backed Gull
Morntelmöwe
Herring Gull Adult
Silbermöwe
Black-headed Gull
Lachmöwe
Lesser Black-backed
Gull/Heringsmöwe
Herring Gull Immature
Silbermöwe
Common Tern/Flußseeschwalbe
Chiffchaff/Zilpzalp
Reed Warbler
Teichrohrsänger
Willow Warbler
Fitis
Sand Martin/Uferschwalbe
Swift/Mauersegler
Reed Bunting
Rohrammer
Sedge Warbler
Schilfrohrsänger
Curlew/Großer Brachvogel
Swallow/Rauchschwalbe
House Martin/Mehlschwalbe
Tufted Duck/Reiherente
Kingfisher/Eisvogel
Snipe/Bekassine
Lapwing/Kiebitz
Mallard/Stockente
Teal/Krickente
Widgeon/Pfeifente
Grey Wagtail/Gebirgstelze
Little Grebe/Zwergtaucher
Winter
Summer
Great Crested Grebe/Haubentaucher
Grey Heron
Fischreiher
Mute Swan
Höckerschwan
Red-breasted Merganser/Mittelsäger
Whooper Swan
Singschwan
Pied Wagtail/Traverbachstelze
Coot/Blaßhühn
Moorhen/Teichhuhn
Berwick's Swan/Zwergschwan
Daphne Levinge

undergrowth, compete musically with the garden warbler, which has its main distribution over the islands of Lough Ree and the blackcap, an even sweeter songster than its cousin, the garden warbler, is found especially at the northern end of Lough Ree.

Walter Borner

Winter Residents

In winter, when the river system floods, large numbers of swans, waders, ducks and geese are found, the normal resident population being increased by numerous winter residents from north-east Europe, Iceland and Greenland with widgeon being the most numerous. Of particular interest is the Greenland white-fronted goose, with a world population of about 20,000 three-quarters of which over winter in Ireland and some of these can be found on the callows—the flooded water meadows—in the area between Athlone and Portumna. The Inner Lakes of Lough Ree and an area at the north end of Lough Derg are nature reserves where birds can feed undisturbed until they once more undertake the return flight to the tundras and lakes of the north. By the time the first angling tourist arrives, the whoopers will be on their way to Iceland, the white-fronts to Greenland and the golden plover back to Scandinavia. In spring when the waters are receding from the callows, they are invaded by the local breeding birds, the redshanks, snipe and lapwings and recently, the blacktailed godwit near Clonmacnois.

A full list of birds may be found in the appendix.

Fishing on the Shannon

Hugh Gough

The Shannon and its lakes offer a wide range of fishing to the enthusiast with conditions varying from stretch to stretch. Those cruising the river by boat can gain access to places which the bank angler can never hope to reach and to places which are seldom fished.

Rising in Cuilcagh mountain, the Shannon flows rapidly into its first big water, Lough Allen, and it is here that anglers sample the richness of fish that the great river produces. Pike over 15 kg come to the net every year, as anglers have learned to come to grips with the technique of fishing such a big water. Trolling in the area between the power station and the islands near Cormongan could produce a large pike. There are large stocks of roach and bream at the southern end of the lake where the bottom is soft and muddy. The lake also has some good brown trout.

The shallow, narrow Lough Allen Canal and Acres Lake have a plentiful supply of roach, small bream and some tench. But such a water calls for patient and skilful fishing, with blood worm as bait. In late May, huge stocks of roach move up to the stretch of the River Shannon at Battlebridge and this is a great place to fish from the boat, moored below the lock gate.

The Boyle River, 100 m above Drum Bridge, has small pools for roach and small bream, offering a pleasant change from the big waters. Lough Key has a good stock of coarse fish but is best fished for pike, which are mostly found near the islands and reeded shores in the summer months. Downriver at Knockvicar, bream and roach appear in the stretch between the lock and the bridge where the depth is 2–3 m. The serious bream angler will now find good fishing ground at Oakport Lake, to the right of the red marker coming downstream. Here, with the forest in the background and at other swims in the lake just off the marked channel, heavy ground baiting will bring on the bream, roach and rudd. At the jetty below the bridge at Cootehall, fishing for bream and roach is easy when the boat traffic is quiet.

At the marina in Carrick, catches to 45 kg of bream and roach may be taken, with hook baited with worm and caster. Downriver, the reeded lakes and river are seldom fished but stocks of fish here are very plentiful. The key to success for bream and roach is to bait the selected area heavily with cereal bait and to fish it for one or two days at least.

Below Albert lock and into Lough Boderg, stocks of the golden coloured rudd increase and the waters at the west end of Carnadoe are rich with specimen rudd. Try fishing on a summer's evening for them, as they cruise along the reeds. They will come to bread or maggots and will often take a

Angeln

Von seiner Quelle in den Cuilcagh Bergen fliesst der Shannon schon bald in Lough Allen, den ersten grossen See. Hier können Angler eine Kostprobe des Fischreichtums dieses mächtigen Flusses bekommen. Alljährlich werden über dreissig Pfund schwere Hechte an Land gezogen. Sehr gut für die Schleppangel ist die Gegend zwischen dem Kraftwerk und den Inseln in der Nähe von Cormongan. An der Südseite des Sees, wo der Grund weich und schlammig ist, hat es reichlich Plötzen und Brassen. Im ganzen See gibt es auch schöne Bachforellen.

Der seichte, enge Kanal zum Acres Lake hat einen guten Bestand an Plötzen, kleinen Brassen und Schleien. In einem solchen Gewässer muss man jedoch mit Geduld und Geschicklichkeit fischen und Blutwurm als Köder verwenden.

Gegen Ende Mai ziehen Mengen von Plötzen flussaufwärts in die Gegend um Battlebridge. Hier kann man sehr gut vom unterhalb des Schleusentors festgemachten Boot aus fischen. Hundert Meter oberhalb von Drum Bridge bietet der River Boyle mit seinen kleinen Tümpeln voll von Plötzen und kleinen Brassen eine hübsche Alternative zu den grösseren Gewässern. Lough

Lakeboat

Walter Borner

fly. Rudd are a shy fish, so approach your fishing quietly. It was here that the Irish record rudd, 1.4 kg was taken.

The thickly reeded Lough Forbes is sure to produce big pike, which find their food close to the reeds and lily beds. In the summer, pike will respond to spoon and plug baits. At Tarmonbarry, the river now offers a rich variety of fishing. Below the weir, there is an abundance of perch and roach, and big brown trout are caught here at the end of the season. The area near the canal at the black marker is good for bream and also pike, in September and October. Below the Lodge Cut, where the Feorish River joins the Shannon, bream and hybrid fishing is excellent in May and June. At Lanesborough, the hot-water effluent from the power station attracts big bream and tench in April, May and June. Bank fishing from the outflow to the small harbour along the left bank is rewarding for the serious angler who is prepared to fish during the day and night. Those big fish are again located at Ballyclare Cut, with lovely rudd in the islands of reeds behind the buoy.

Lough Ree is a rich reservoir of good quality fish, but finding those fish in such a large expanse of water is not easy. Bank conditions with rocks and shallow margins are also a problem for the angler. Fishing from a small boat can be rewarding after the selected area has been heavily ground baited, but many of those good areas are not near the recommended boating channels for big boats. The Inner Lakes, particularly Coosan Lough, hold tench and the best swims are at the old boat stakes close to the reeds. Rudd, bream and perch are also found in these reeded waters. In Athlone, there are fine rudd in the fast water in the channel at Charlie's Island beside the marina. Try floating bread through the weeds in the evening and a specimen rudd could be yours!

Between Athlone and Shannonbridge, there are many places holding superb stocks of bream, rudd, perch and pike. The slack waters behind the islands are always worth a try.

A feature of fishing on the entire river from Boyle to Athlone and increasingly downstream of Athlone as well has been the increase in the numbers of roach. They have now reached Shannonbridge but are not yet fully established downstream of here or on Lough Derg. At Shannonbridge, big rudd appear again at the end of Long Island just above the town bridge. At the confluence of the Rivers Suck and Shannon, the deep water is the home for specimen rudd/bream hybrids. Below the power station, there are good rudd to 1 kg and tench to 3 kg. The backwater behind Bullock Island above Banagher holds an abundance of all species and in the early season produces great catches of bream, rudd and tench. Once again the slack waters behind all the islands should be tried and with Meelick lock as a base, there is no better area for exploring. Behind Ballymacegan Island the Sheebeen Stretch is top class for bream where catches over

Walter Borner

Key hat einen grossen Bestand an Süsswasserfischen. Am besten fischt man hier nach Hechten, die während der Sommermonate in der Nähe der Inseln und an den schilfbewachsenen Ufern aufgespürt werden können. Flussabwärts gibt es bei Knockvicar zwischen Schleuse und Brücke in einer Tiefe von zwei bis drei Metern Brassen und Plötze. Der wirklich interessierte Brassenfischer findet im Oakport Lake westlich der roten Bojen ein gutes Angelgebiet. Hier, wo man den Wald im Hintergrund hat, aber auch an andern fischreichen Stellen des Flusses, kann man gleich neben der markierten Fahrrinne mit schwerem Grundköder Brassen, Plötze und Rotfedern fangen. Das gilt vor allem auch für den Abschnitt unterhalb der Brücke von Cootehall. Im Hafen von Carrick werden mit Angelhaken und Wurm Tagesfänge von Brassen und Plötzen bis zu hundert Pfund gemacht. Im verschilften Seen- und Flussgebiet weiter flussabwärts wird trotz reicher Vorkommen wenig gefischt. Ein Erfolgsrezept für Brassen und Plötzefang ist, am gewählten Angelplatz ausgiebig Getreideköder auszuwerfen und mindestens zwei Tage dort zu angeln.

Unterhalb der Schleuse von Albert Lock und im Lough Boderg hat es einen schönen Bestand an goldfarbenen Rotfedern. In den Carnadoe Waters gibt es Prachtsexemplare dieses Fisches. Versuchen Sie einmal, sie an einem Sommerabend auf der Fahrt durch das Schilf zu fangen. Sie beissen auf Brot, Maden und auch Fliegen. Da Rotfedern sehr scheu sind, muss man beim Angeln leise vorgehen. Hier wurde auch der irische Rekord gefangen, eine Rotfeder von drei Pfund Gewicht.

Im dicht verschilften Lough Forbes findet man grosse Hechte, die sich ihre Nahrung in der Nähe der Schilfufer oder Seerosen suchen. Hechte reagieren auf Blinker oder Fischköder. Unterhalb des Wehrs von Tarmonbarry gibt es Unmengen von Barschen und Plötzen. Hier werden gegen Ende der Saison auch grosse Bachforellen gefangen. Das Gebiet in der Nähe des Kanals bei der schwarzen Markierung ist gut für Brassen und Hechte, vor allem während der Monate September und Oktober. Unterhalb von Lodge Cut, wo der Feorish in den Shannon mündet, fängt man im Mai und Juni Brassen und Mischlinge. In Lanesborough zieht das warme Abwasser des Kraftwerks während der Monate April bis Juni grosse Brassen und Schleien an. Vom Abfluss bis

Walter Borner

A good pike catch at Athlone

90 kg have been taken.

The vast Lough Derg presents a challenge to the bank fisherman, but the boat user can anchor close to deep water in a bay or beside a reeded island and ground bait for the bream. This big lake holds huge stocks of fish.

Rossmore Bay beside the mooring is a first class place to fish for rudd, rudd/bream hybrids and perch. Bring the dinghy into the calm reeded area and up the small river for great fishing.

Tench to 3 kg come into the bays near Williamstown and can be fished in May and June by anchoring a small boat beside the reeds. Youghal Bay has a fine stock of pike around 5 kg and can be fished by trolling. The reeded inlets of Scarriff Bay and the islands near Mountshannon are again a great haven for all species and should be explored.

Along the east side of Lough Derg down from Scilly Island, there is very deep water close to the bank and it is here in the colder months that big pike are located.

zum kleinen Hafen am linken Ufer lohnt sich das Angeln vom Ufer aus, wenn man ernsthaft daran interessiert ist, Tag und Nacht zu fischen. Auch am Ballyclare Cut wurden diese Fische gefangen, und bei den Schilfinseln findet man Rotfedern.

Auch wenn Lough Ree einen grossen Bestand an Fischen von hoher Qualität hat, ist es nicht einfach, in einem so weit ausgedehnten Gewässer die Fischvorkommen festzustellen. Dies vor allem wegen der Beschaffenheit der Ufer, die oft felsig sind oder auch weit hinaus seicht bleiben. Man sollte von einem Boot aus angeln, nachdem die vorgesehene Stelle ausreichend mit Grundköder ausgelegt worden ist. Viele der fischreichen Stellen liegen nicht in der Nähe der empfohlenen Route für grosse Boote. Die Inner Lakes, vor allem Coosan Lough, sind reich an Schleien. Die besten Stellen finden sich bei den alten Bootspflöcken dicht am Schilfrand. Da gibt es auch Rotfedern, Brassen und Barsche. In Athlone hat es neben Charlie's Island gleich unterhalb des Jolly Mariner Rotfedern. Versuchen Sie es einmal abends mit einem Brotschwimmköder. Ein Prachtsexemplar von Rotfeder könnte der Lohn sein.

An vielen Stellen zwischen Athlone und Shannonbridge finden sich grosse Vorkommen von Brassen, Rotfedern, Barschen und Hechten. Auch das hinter den Inseln langsamer fliessende Wasser lohnt einen Versuch. Interessant ist, dass sich die Plötze unterhalb Athlone noch nicht sehr verbreitet haben. Grosse Rotfedern gibt es wieder am Ende von Long Island kurz oberhalb der Brücke von Shannonbridge. Das tiefe Wasser am Zusammenfluss von Suck und Shannon ist die Heimat von Rotfeder/Brassen-Mischungen. Unterhalb des Kraftwerks finden sich Brassen mit gegen ein Kilo und Schleien mit fast drei Kilo Gewicht.

Im ruhigen Wasser hinter Bullock Island oberhalb von Banagher gibt es eine Fülle von Fischen aller Art. In der Frühsaison kann man hier herrliche Fänge von Brassen, Rotfedern und Schleien machen. Wie schon gesagt, sollte man die stilleren Stellen hinter den Inseln nicht auslassen; mit der Schleuse von Meelick als Ausgangspunkt wird man kaum eine vorteilhaftere Stelle finden.

Die Grösse von Lough Derg macht das Fischen vom Ufer aus etwas schwierig. Aber der Bootsfahrer kann bei tieferen Stellen vor Anker gehen, zum Beispiel in einer Bucht oder neben einer Insel, und Grundköder für Brassen auslegen. Lough Derg ist voller Fische.

Ein guter Angelplatz für Rotfedern, Rotfeder/Brassen-Mischungen und Barsche befindet sich neben der Anlegestelle von Rossmore Bay. Grosse Schleien fängt man in der Bucht von Williamstown. Die beste Zeit sind die Monate Mai und Juni. In der Bucht von Youghal gibt es Hechte bis zu fünfeinhalb Kilo. Die Wasserläufe von Scarriff Bay und die Inseln von Mountshannon sind ebenfalls ein Paradies für alle Gattungen Fische und sollten vom Sportfischer unbedingt erforscht werden. Entlang der Ostseite von Lough Derg, in der Gegend von Scilly Island, finden sich nahe am Ufer sehr tiefe Stellen. Hier kann man in den kalten Monaten grosse Hechte sichten.

The following are the fish most commonly found with hints on how to catch them:

Brown trout (Salmon trutta)

These are found throughout the Shannon system, especially in the absence of predators such as the pike. They are fished for from March to the end of September, and are caught by trolling or fly fishing and also in May/June by 'dapping' using mayfly. *Irish/Shannon record: 9 kg*

Pike (Esox lucius)

Widespread and common throughout the Shannon system with large pike in the deeper waters of the lakes, they have a characteristic elongated body with dorsal and anal fins set well back. They are caught by trolling spoon or plug baits near the margins, particularly in the summer (silver spoon on bright days in clear water or copper fished deeper on dull days). In the early and late season, a wobbled dead bait is good (rudd or roach) and a static dead bait is most successful on cold winter days. Herring, mackerel or sprats are good as dead bait. *Irish record: 19 kg Shannon record: 17.2 kg*

Perch (Perca fluviatilis)

Widespread and very common but perhaps less abundant where roach are present, they are a rich greenish brown colour with five to seven dark cross-bands on their backs and bright red fins. They are caught by spinning a small bright bait or by float fishing with worm or maggot as hook bait. *Irish record: 2.5 kg Shannon record: 1.4 kg*

Hybrids-Rudd/Bream

These fish are commonly found throughout the Shannon system. *Irish/Shannon record: 2.6 kg*

Bachforelle Brown Trout

Kommt im gesamten Shannongebiet vor, besonders da, wo es keine Raubfische wie zum Beispiel Hechte gibt. Man fängt sie von März bis Ende September entweder mit Schleppangel oder Fliege oder Mai/Juni mit der Maifliege.

Irischer/Shannon-Rekord 9 kg

Hecht Pike

Im ganzen Shannongebiet verbreitet. Grössere Hechte leben im tiefen Wasser der Seen. Typischer langer Körper mit weit zurückliegenden Rücken– und Afterflossen. Man fängt sie, indem man besonders im Sommer Blinker vom Uferrand auswirft (Silberne Blinker bei gutem Wetter in klarem Wasser, kupferne in tiefem Wasser bei trübem Wetter). Früh oder spät in der Saison ist ein beweglicher toter Köder am besten (Rotfeder oder Plötze), während an kalten Wintertagen ein statischer toter Köder sich als am günstigsten gezeigt hat. Als toter Köder eignen sich auch Hering, Makrele und Sprotte.

Irischer Rekord 19 kg, Shannon Rekord 17,2 kg

Flussbarsch Perch

Weitverbreitet und sehr häufig besonders da, wo es wenig Plötze gibt. Er hat eine satte grünlichbraune Farbe mit fünf bis sieben Kreuzbändern auf dem Rücken und hellroten Flossen. Man fängt ihn mit hellem, kleinem, künstlichen Köder oder Angelhaken mit Wurm oder Made.

Irischer Rekord 2,5 kg, Shannon Rekord 1,4 kg

Mischung Rotfeder/Brasse

Hybrids-Rudd/Bream.Kommt im ganzen Shannongebiet vor.

Irischer/Shannon Rekord 2,6 kg

Rotfeder Rudd

Gewöhnlich bis zu 1 kg Gewicht. Lebt vor allem von Albert Lock an flussabwärts und bevorzugt verschilfte Seen oder langsam fliessende Flussstrecken. Sie hat einen sehr tiefgewölbten Körper mit roten Flossen. Sie ist sehr scheu, man fängt sie am besten während der

Rudd (Scardinius erythrophthalmus)

Commonly found to 1 kg particularly from Albert lock downstream, preferring weedy lakes and slow-flowing sections, they are a very deep-bodied fish with red fins. A shy fish, they are caught mostly in the summer months. In some waters, they are best in the evening and can be seen cruising along the reeds. A surface feeder, they are best taken by float fishing with bread or maggots as bait. *Irish/Shannon record: 1.4 kg*

Bream (Abramis brama)

Found in deepish water in muddy lakes and slow flowing water, they have a deep body with a very small mouth. Although common the angler must be prepared to bait heavily and to wait for at least one day for the fish to come on the feed. When they do, one can take over 45 kg with fish of 3–4 kg in a day. Worm with maggot is the most successful bait but bread or sweetcorn will also get results. *Irish record: 5.3 kg Shannon record: 5 kg*

Roach (Rutilus rutilus)

These fish are prolific breeders and can overrun a system, often quickly resulting in the reduction in size of other species, hence the bye-law prohibiting their transfer. Increasingly present in the Shannon system particularly from Shannonbridge north but will soon spread to the whole Shannon system. They resemble rudd but have slightly red fins and a body with a silver purple tinge. They feed all year and are caught by float fishing with maggot as bait. *Irish record: 1.3 kg Shannon record: 0.8 kg*

Tench (Tinca tinca)

Fairly widespread in rich weedy sections of lakes and in very slow flowing water especially near Lanesborough, a greenish-brown fish with very small scales and rounded fins and having a characteristic narrow mouth and barbel. They are a great

Sommermonate. In manchen Gegenden ist der Fang gegen Abend am günstigsten, wenn man sie am Schilf entlang ziehen sieht. Da sie sich ihre Nahrung an der Wasseroberfläche sucht, benützt man am besten Angelhaken mit Brot oder Maden als Köder.

Irischer/Shannon Rekord 1,25 kg

Brasse Bream

Man findet sie im tieferen Wasser verschlammter Seen oder trägen Flussabschnitten. Sie hat einen breiten Körper mit einem sehr kleinen Maul. Obwohl sie häufig vorkommt, muss der Angler darauf vorbereitet sein, viel Köder auszulegen und einen Tag lang auf das Anbeissen zu warten. Sobald sie beissen, kann man an einem Tag mit Fischen von 3-4 kg bis gegen fünfzig Kilo fangen. Am besten als Köder sind Wurm und Made, aber auch mit Brot oder Mais kann man Erfolg haben.

Irischer Rekord 5,3 kg, Shannon Rekord 5 kg

Plötze Roach

Diese Fische vermehren sich sehr schnell und können ein Flussgebiet völlig überlaufen, so dass andere Arten verschwinden. Das ist der Grund für die Verordnung gegen die Umsiedlung von Plötzen. Ihr Auftreten im Shannongebiet, besonders von Shannonbridge aus nach Norden, wird immer häufiger. Sie gleichen Rotfedern, haben aber leicht gerötete Flossen und einen silbriglila gefärbten Körper. Sie fressen das ganze Jahr über, als Köder verwendet man Angelhaken mit Maden.

Irischer Rekord 1,3 kg, Shannon Rekord 0,8 kg

Schleie Tench

Ziemlich verbreitet in dicht verschilften, bewachsenen Teilen der Seen und in sehr langsam fliessendem Wasser, besonders in der Nähe von Lanesborough. Ein grünlichbrauner Fisch mit sehr kleinen Schuppen und runden Flossen mit dem typischen schmalen Maul und Bartfäden. Sie sind grosse Kämpfer, die im Mai und Juni zum Fressen herauskommen. Am besten fängt man sie am frühen Morgen oder am Abend mit Wurm, Brot oder Made. Der Köder wird auf dem Grund ausgelegt.

Irischer/Shannon Rekord 3,5 kg

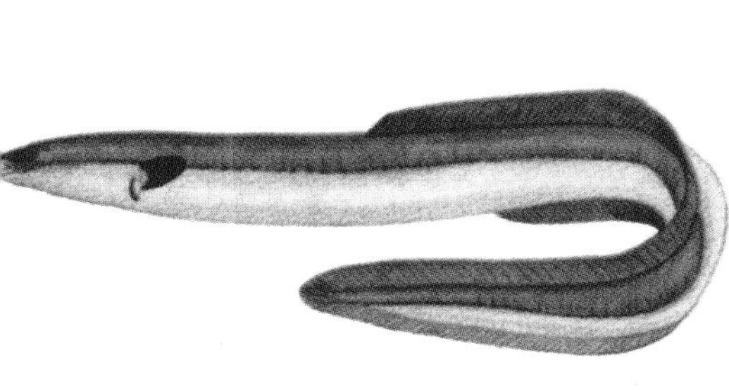

fighting fish which come on to feed in May and June and fish best in the early morning or evening. They respond to worm, bread or maggot bait, placed on the bottom. *Irish/Shannon record: 3.5 kg*

Eels (Anguilla anguilla)

Common throughout the Shannon system, they are caught by rod and line only with worms as bait (a special licence is required to fish for eels by any other method than rod and line). Evening fishing brings the best results. *Irish record: 3.1 kg Shannon record: 2.7 kg*

Other fish also occur and these include pollan (in Lough Ree and Lough Derg and very rarely caught), minnow, stickle-back and lamprey.

N.B. Maggots should always be kept in the dinghy and not brought aboard. They may be ordered in advance from the bait farm and collected at tackle shops in Athlone or Carrick-on-Shannon. Useful Fishing Notes may be found in the appendix identifying the best locations for catching each species

General Information

The River Shannon and its tributaries contain some game and an abundance of coarse fish. Game fish are salmon and sea trout but since the construction of the hydro-electric station at Ardnacrusha in the 1920s only an occasional salmon is caught. A licence is required to fish for salmon obtainable from Shannon Regional Fisheries Board, Thomand Weir, Limerick, Tel. 061-455171. (annual £12, annual juvenile £8, 21-day £10, one-day £3). No licence is required to fish brown trout or coarse fish at present but a share certificate system exists available through fishing tackle shops. There is a closed season for game fishing from 30 September to 1 March but there is no closed season for coarse angling. The following fishing laws should be noted:

1. It is illegal to have or to use live fish as bait. (Bye-law 592)
2. The only legal method to catch freshwater fish is by rod and line. (Bye-law 595)
3. A person may fish with not more than two rods at any time. (Bye-law 595)
4. It is illegal to transfer live roach from one water to any other waters. Offenders may be prosecuted. (Bye-law 561)
5. It is prohibited to take and kill a pike of more than 6.6lb (3 kilo). Specimen fish of over 20lb (9.1 kilo) fished in the river or 30lb (13.6 kilo) fished in the lake are exempt. It is prohibited for any person to have in their possession more than one dead pike. Bye-Law 667

NOTE– Penalties for breach of the above laws include confiscation of tackle and heavy fines.

Aal Eel

Häufig im ganzen Shannongebiet. Wird mit Angelrute und Schnur gefangen. Als Köder dürfen nur Würmer verwendet werden. Um Aale auf eine andere Weise fangen zu dürfen, braucht man eine Sonderlizenz. Am besten abends fischen.

Irischer Rekord 3,1 kg, Shannon Rekord 2,7 kg

Es gibt noch eine Anzahl anderer Fische, darunter die irische Muräne (Lough Ree und Lough Derg, wird aber selten gefangen), Elritze, Stichling und Neunauge.

Beachten Sie, dass Maden aus verständlichen Gründen im Ruderboot aufbewahrt und nicht an Bord gebracht werden sollten. Sie können in den meisten Fischereigeschäften entlang des Flusses gekauft werden.

Das Angeln im Shannon

Der Shannon und seine Nebenflüsse sind reich an mehreren Arten von Sportfischen und einer Fülle von Süsswasserfischen. Sportfische sind Lachs und Seeforelle, aber seit dem Bau des Wasserkraftwerks bei Ardnacrusha in den 20er-Jahren fängt man sie nur noch gelegentlich. Für den Lachsfang benötigt man eine Lizenz, die beim Shannon Regional Fisheries Board, Thomond Weit, Limerick, Tel. 061 455171 erhältlich ist. Für die übrigen Fische sind zur Zeit keine Lizenzen erforderlich. Für Lachs und Seeforelle gilt eine Schonzeit vom 1. März bis 30. September.

Es ist verboten, lebende Fische als Köder zu halten oder zu verwenden (Verordnung 592).
Die einzige gesetzlich erlaubte Methode, Süsswasserfische zu fangen, ist mit Angelrute und Schnur (Verordnung 595).
Man darf nicht mit mehr als zwei Ruten gleichzeitig fischen (Verordnung 595).
Es ist untersagt, lebende Plötze von einem Gewässer in ein anderes zu transferieren. Zuwiderhandelnde machen sich strafbar (Verordnung 561).
Das Gesetz Nr. 667 verbietet
a) das Fangen oder Töten von mehr als einem Hecht aus einem Gewässer pro Person und Tag; **b)** das Töten eines Hechtes mit einem Gewicht von mehr als 3 kg (6,6 lbs). Solche Tiere müssen zurückgesetzt werden. **c)** jeder Person den Besitz von wahlweise mehr als einem ganzen toten Hecht oder mehr als 1,5 kg (3,3 lbs) Hechtfilet oder Teilen eines Hechtes.

Verstösse gegen diese Vorschriften werden unter anderem mit der Konfiskation der Angelgeräte und hohen Bussen geahndet.

Ireland's Inland Waterways

Ruth Delany

Although the Shannon is one of the main areas for cruising in Ireland, there are a number of other waterways which have much to offer. You can travel back in time along the Grand Canal, visit the picturesque River Barrow or Lough Corrib, cruise along the beautiful Erne Navigation or Lough Neagh and the Lower Bann, or search out old waterways which are no longer navigable.

The Grand Canal and Barrow Navigation

Not only is the Shannon Navigation linked with the sea through Limerick but it is also possible to enter the Grand Canal system and travel across Ireland to Dublin or via the Barrow Navigation to Waterford. While most people holidaying on the Shannon will probably do no more than make a brief excursion up the canal to Shannon Harbour (see Gazetteer page 63), there may be some who will return one day to explore this waterway. The Grand Canal was Ireland's most successful waterway of the Canal Age; work commenced on it in the 1750s. A journey along it still evokes the past and you half expect to meet one of the old flyboats, surging along on its own bow wave, towed by a team of galloping horses. Leaving Shannon Harbour the canal wends its way through remote countryside between hawthorn hedgerows full of wild flowers and birds. There are not many locks and it is pleasant to be able to tie up to the bank at will and do a spot of fishing: there are good bream, rudd, tench, perch and roach in the canal. From the 32nd lock at Glynn there is a 10-km level across boggy terrain which affords an opportunity to observe the mechanised workings and the long mounds of dried peat dust ready for transporting to the power station at Ferbane. The twin towers

of the power station are visible to the south with the Slieve Bloom Mountains in the distance. The utilisation of the bogs has brought a new prosperity to this remote countryside. The canal passes through the little village of Pollagh and then climbs up through two locks to Rahan where there is a tempting quay beside the old canalside Thatch pub. Before quenching your thirst, you should visit the nearby churches of Rahan which have some interesting features. Ballycowan and Shra castles are worth looking at before continuing on to Tullamore, a bustling market town.

A flight of six locks brings the canal up to a long level of 30 km. Daingean makes a pleasant stopping place and then out across another great stretch of bog with a short detour up an attractive stretch of canal to the town of Edenderry. Lowtown is a busy centre these days with its marina and a large number of boats. The Main Line continues east through the canalside village of Robertstown. The local people have made great efforts to preserve the atmosphere of the past here by renovating the old canal hotel and attractive stable buildings. A pretty tree-lined stretch past Landenstown, which is a favourite place for fishermen, brings the canal to the Leinster aqueduct, across the River Liffey and to the Naas Line, a delightful stretch up to the town of Naas which was re-opened to traffic in 1987. The journey from Sallins into the city of Dublin is usually only undertaken by those who want to make their way out to the sea as there is a large number of locks. It is recommended that you moor in Ringsend Basin, Dublin, like all large cities, suffers from vandals.

The Barrow

The Barrow Line branches off to the south from Lowtown, passing through two small towns, Rathangan and Monasterevan, and the village of Vicarstown, a frequent winner of the Barrow Award, before entering the River Barrow at Athy.

This is a beautiful navigation, a series of river stretches interspersed with short canals which by-pass shallows. The coarse fishing is good and you might even catch a trout, particularly at dusk; local anglers

Grand Canal: a converted canal boat passing through Lowtown Lock

Ruth Delany

Die Schiffahrtslinie auf demGrand Canal und Barrow

Vom Meer her kommend kann man den Shannon bei Limerick oder auf dem Weg über den Grand Canal von Dublin aus erreichen. Eine weitere Möglichkeit bietet sich mit Barrow River von Waterford aus an. Früher einmal war der Grand Canal der belebteste Wasserweg Irlands, eine Fahrt auf ihm ruft Erinnerungen an die Tage der Passagier- und Frachtschiffe wach.

Von Shannon Harbour aus führt der Kanal durch abgelegene Landschaften mit wenig Schleusen und guten Angelmöglichkeiten. Hier sieht man die maschinell betriebenen Torfstiche, die der Gegend neuen Reichtum brachten. Der Weg führt durch die Dörfer Pollagh und Rahan mit ihren interessanten Kirchen, dann an zwei Schlössern – Ballycowan und Shra – vorbei, bevor die geschäftige Marktstadt Tullamore erreicht wird.

Über fünf Schleusen erreicht man eine offene Strecke von über dreissig Kilometern, die an der Marina der Celtic Canal Cruisers vorbeiführt. Das Dorf Daingean ist ein interessanter Anlegeplatz. Von da aus kann man einen Abstecher nach Edenderry machen. Lowtown hat sich zum grössten Bootszentrum am Kanal entwickelt, und Robertstown ist ein gutes Beispiel eines typischen Kanaldorfes. Auf dem Aquädukt von Leinster wird der River Liffey überquert. Man kann aber auch einen Umweg über den wiedereröffneten Naas Canal machen, bevor man nach Dublin weiterfährt. Normalerweise machen nur diejenigen Skipper den letzten Teil der Fahrt, die ans Meer gelangen wollen. In Dublin gibt es nämlich viele Schleusen und keine sicheren Anlegeplätze.

Von Lowtown aus führt die Barrowlinie des Kanals durch Rathangan, Monasterevan und Vicarstown, bevor sie schliesslich bei Athy in den River Barrow mündet. Diese Strecke ist sehr schön, eine einsame Landschaft und ausgezeichnete Fischgründe. Der Barrow fliesst durch Carlow, Milford, Leighlinbridge, Bagenalstown und Goresbridge nach Graiguenamanagh, wo die restaurierte Abtei von Duiske steht. Südlich von hier, ab St. Mullins, machen sich die Gezeiten bemerkbar. Für die hier beschriebenen Kanal- und Flussstrecken sind spezielle Führer erhältlich.

move along the towpath from the villages, but the boating fisherman can moor his boat in the more isolated stretches.

Carlow, like Athy, is a busy market town, and there is an interesting Norman castle dominating the river. Trees line the river to Milford, a picturesque place with its old mill and lifting bridge, and at Leighlinbridge another castle guards the oldest bridge on the river which dates back to 1320 and which is now superseded by a new bridge. Bagenalstown was designed in the grand manner by Walter Bagenal in the eighteenth century. He planned to make this an Irish Versailles and although little of what he planned came to fruition, it is an attractive town.

The fine old stone bridges and interesting lifting bridges are a feature of the Barrow.

Goresbridge dates back to 1756 and Ballytiglea Bridge carries the road high above the river. From here south, the river cuts an ever deepening valley for itself and the scenery becomes increasingly spectacular as you approach Graiguenamanagh. This is a fascinating old town and the original Duiske Abbey church has been lovingly restored. Below the town, Tinnehinch Castle guards the old fording place and the 20th lock from Athy. There are now three more locks before the navigation reaches the tidal waters at St Mullins. Hired cruisers are not permitted below this point but you can walk along the towpath and see the Scars, a shoal area which can only be navigated near high water. From there you can follow the road up to the village and the monastic settlement founded by St Moling in the seventh century. He is said to have set up a mill here to feed the poor, digging his own mile-long millrace, a task which took him eight years, and this legend forms the basis for part of the ceremonies attached to the annual pattern in July.

Ruth Delany

Grand Canal: Portobello on the Circular Line in Dublin during a rally in 1991

The Grand Canal System

The Grand Canal Main Line: 131 km from Dublin to Shannon Harbour with 44 locks including the sea-lock at Ringsend. The Naas Branch: 4 km with 5 locks. The Barrow Line: 46 km from Lowtown to Athy with 9 locks. The Barrow Navigation: 69 km from Athy to St Mullins with 23 locks. Tidal waters of Barrow, Nore and Suir: 88 km.

Maximum size of boat: 18.5 m x 3.9 m x 1.2 m (1 m in Dublin). In dry weather the depth is reduced, to as low as 0.76 m on the Barrow Navigation. Headroom under Carlow Bridge (the lowest on the system): 2.6 m over a width of 2.4 m on curved arches.

Speed limit: 4 miles per hour
6 km per hour

Slipways: Clondalkin, Lowtown, Edenderry, Tullamore, Rathangan, Monasterevin, Muine Bheag (Bagenalstown), Carlow, Athy, Graiguenamanagh, Goresbridge and Inistioge.

Charges: 50p per lock, payable for full journey in advance. Ringsend large sea-lock: £10. Bank mooring: £10 per month.

Naas Branch of the Grand Canal restored in 1987

Ruth Delany

Ruth Delany

Barrow Navigation: Milford with the canal in the foreground

Annual permit (unlimited lock passage and mooring): £100. All permits from Waterways Ireland, 17/19 Lower Hatch St., Dublin 2 or designated lock-keepers.

Boat Hire: Information from Bord Fáilte, Baggot Street, Dublin 2. Tel. 01–676 5871.

Publications: *Guide to the Grand Canal* Dúchas The Heritage Service in association with IWAI, 1999. A guide to the canal with maps showing the canal, road access and walkable towpaths.
Guide to the Barrow Navigation, Dúchas The Heritage Service in association with IWAI, 1998. A guide to the river and estuary, with maps showing the navigation and the trackway.

THE ROYAL CANAL

The Royal Canal: 145 km from Dublin to the Shannon at Richmond Harbour near Tarmonbarry with 46 locks. It was closed to navigation in 1961, but is currently being restored by Waterways Ireland. The eastern section from Dublin to Abbeyshrule in Co. Longford is now navigable. Work has already commenced on the western end, and many of the lock gates have been made and installed, and much of the dredging carried out. There are, however, eight culverted road crossings on this section, where the original hump-backed bridges were replaced during the years when the canal was closed to navigation, and these will have to be replaced by suitable alternatives.

Ruth Delany

The Royal Canal: The Deep Sinking, Clonsilla

Maximum size of boat: 18.5 m x 3.9m x 1.2 m. In dry weather the depth is reduced. Headroom: 3.0 m over a width of 2.4 m on curved arches.

Speed limit: 4 miles per hour.
6 km per hour.

Slipways: Leixlip, Maynooth, Enfield. Thomastown, Mullingar, Ballinea Bridge and Abbeyshrule.

Charges: 50p per lock, payable for full journey in advance. Bank mooring: £10 per month. Annual permit (unlimited lock passage and mooring): £100. All permits

Ruth Delany

Royal Canal: 12th Lock, Blanchardstown before restoration

from Waterways Ireland, 17/19 Lower Hatch St., Dublin 2 or designated lock-keepers.

Publications: *Guide to the Royal Canal,* Waterways Service in association with IWAI, 1997. A guide to the canal with maps showing the canal, road access and walkable towpaths.

OTHER WATERWAYS

The Corrib Navigation extends for 43 km from Galway to Maam Bridge through Lough Corrib giving 176 sq km of cruising waters. Lough Corrib is a beautiful lake with a backdrop of the Connemara mountains. It is studded with attractive islands but must be navigated with care because of many shoals.

Maximum size of boat: There is no access from the sea because the canal through Galway is obstructed by low bridges and the size of boat is restricted only by the dimensions of the slips.

Slipways: Galway, Maam and Oughterard.

Charges: None. Administrators: Corrib Navigation Trustees.

Publications: Semple, Maurice, *Reflections of Lough Corrib*, Semple, Galway 1973. Semple, Maurice, *By the Corribside*, Semple, Galway 1981.

The Lower Bann is navigable from Lough Neagh to the sea at Coleraine, a distance of 51 km with 5 locks. Lough Neagh, covering an area of 207 sq km, is increasingly being used for water activities. The lower reaches of the River Blackwater and Upper Bann are navigable.

Maximum size of boat: 36.6 m x 6.1 m x 1.5 m with headroom 3.2 m.

Slipways: Coleraine, Hutchinson's Quay (Kilrea), Portna (Kilrea) and The Cutts on the Lower Bann. Antrim, Ballyronan, Kinnego and Maghery on Lough Neagh. Blackwaterstown, Bond Bridge, Moy and Verner's Bridge on the River Blackwater. Portadown on the Upper Bann.

Charges: 5p per lock payable to the lock-keeper. **Administration:** Waterways Ireland.

There are a number of waterways which are closed to navigation and in some cases derelict but they are worth seeking out to follow them on foot:

Boyne Navigation from Drogheda to Navan.

Lagan Navigation, which linked Lough Neagh with the sea through Belfast, one of Ireland's most successful commercial waterways but closed since the 1950s.

Newry Canal, which linked Lough Neagh with the sea through Newry and was the first watershed canal to be completed in Ireland or Britain.

Strabane & Foyle Navigation, a short canal linking Strabane with the River Foyle, disused since the 1930s.

Tralee Ship Canal, linking Tralee with the sea closed in 1930 and currently under restoration.

Ulster Canal, which linked Lough Neagh and Lough Erne, subject to full feasibility study in 1998.

Corbally, Kilbeggan, Mountmellick and **Ballinasloe** branches of the Grand Canal.

Royal Canal: 12th Lock, Blanchardstown after restoration

Ruth Delany

Gazetteer - Limerick to Lough Derg

(See Appendix i for navigation notes)

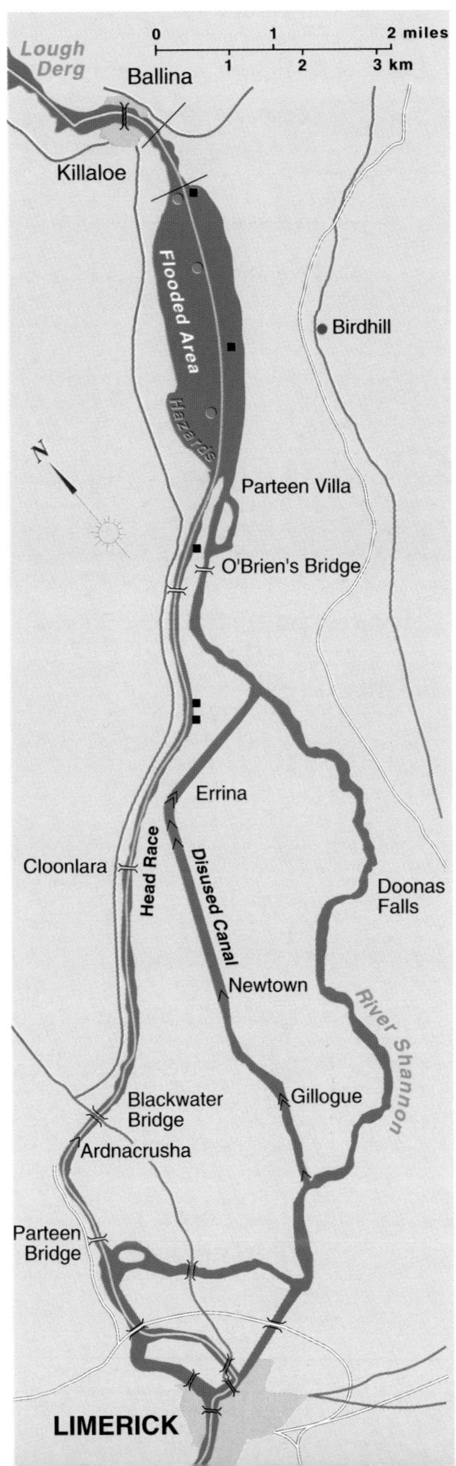

Limerick There are many interesting places to visit in Limerick and there are good guide books available. It was here that the Vikings established a settlement in the tenth century from which they launched their raids up the river. Commanding Thomond Bridge is King John's Castle, built by the Normans in 1200 as part of the town defences. At the other end of the bridge is the Treaty Stone, on which the treaty of surrender, entered into by Sarsfield in 1691, was signed which was subsequently violated by the Williamite victors. The C of I St Mary's Cathedral dates back to the twelfth century and has interesting architectural features. There are a number of other interesting churches and a museum in St John's Square.

Limerick to Killaloe The Shannon falls over 30 m between Killaloe and Limerick and for some years a scheme to harness this power was mooted. Eventually, in 1925 'The Shannon Scheme' was approved and became Ireland's first hydro-electric scheme. When it was completed the power station at Ardnacrusha supplied much of the country's electricity and was looked upon as an important step in establishing the economic freedom of the emerging Irish Free State. Today, however, it provides only about 5% of the national supply. The scheme involved considerable alterations in the navigation of this stretch of river. Formerly, the navigation was in three lengths of canal connected by river sections. The first stretch of canal from Limerick was about one and a half km long with two locks. The middle canal ran parallel to the new headrace; the locks along it, dating back to the late eighteenth century, have some interesting features. It can be approached by road at a number of places and the locks inspected by walking along the towpath. A trip by road to inspect this stretch of canal can include a visit to the Falls of Doonas: since most of the water is now diverted down the headrace, these Falls have been deprived of their former splendour and their once famous salmon fishing. The Falls may also be seen from the other side of the river at Castleconnell, which in the eighteenth century was famous for its spa water and was graced by the villas of the nobility from the Limerick area. The third canal was a short length at Killaloe which was by-passed when the weir was removed, raising the level below the bridge and creating an artificial lake.

The old Baal's Bridge over the Abbey River at Limerick which was later replaced by a single arch

Electricity Supply Board

Ardnacrusha

Bord Fáilte

King John's Castle, Limerick

Ortsverzeichnis mit Beschreibung

Limerick

Viele Sehenswürdigkeiten, gute Führer sind erhältlich. Die Wikinger gründeten hier im 10. Jahrhundert eine Siedlung. King John's Castle wurde um 1200 von den Normannen erbaut. Die Kathedrale von St. Mary stammt aus dem 12. Jahrhundert. Limerick erreicht man besten mit einem Taxi von Killaloe aus.

Von Limerick nach Killaloe

Das Kraftwerk von Ardnacrusha ist das erste Wasserkraftwerk Irlands. Sein Bau hatte beträchtliche Veränderungen dieses Flussabschnittes zur Folge. Früher bestand die navigierbare Strecke aus drei durch Flussarme miteinander verbundenen Kanälen. Castleconnell war ein im 18. Jahrhundert wegen seiner Mineralquellen berühmter Kurort.

Das Befahren dieser Strecke ist Mietbooten nicht erlaubt. Aus diesem Grund wird in der deutschen Fassung auf den Beschrieb weiterer Details verzichtet.

Gazetteer - Killaloe to Portumna

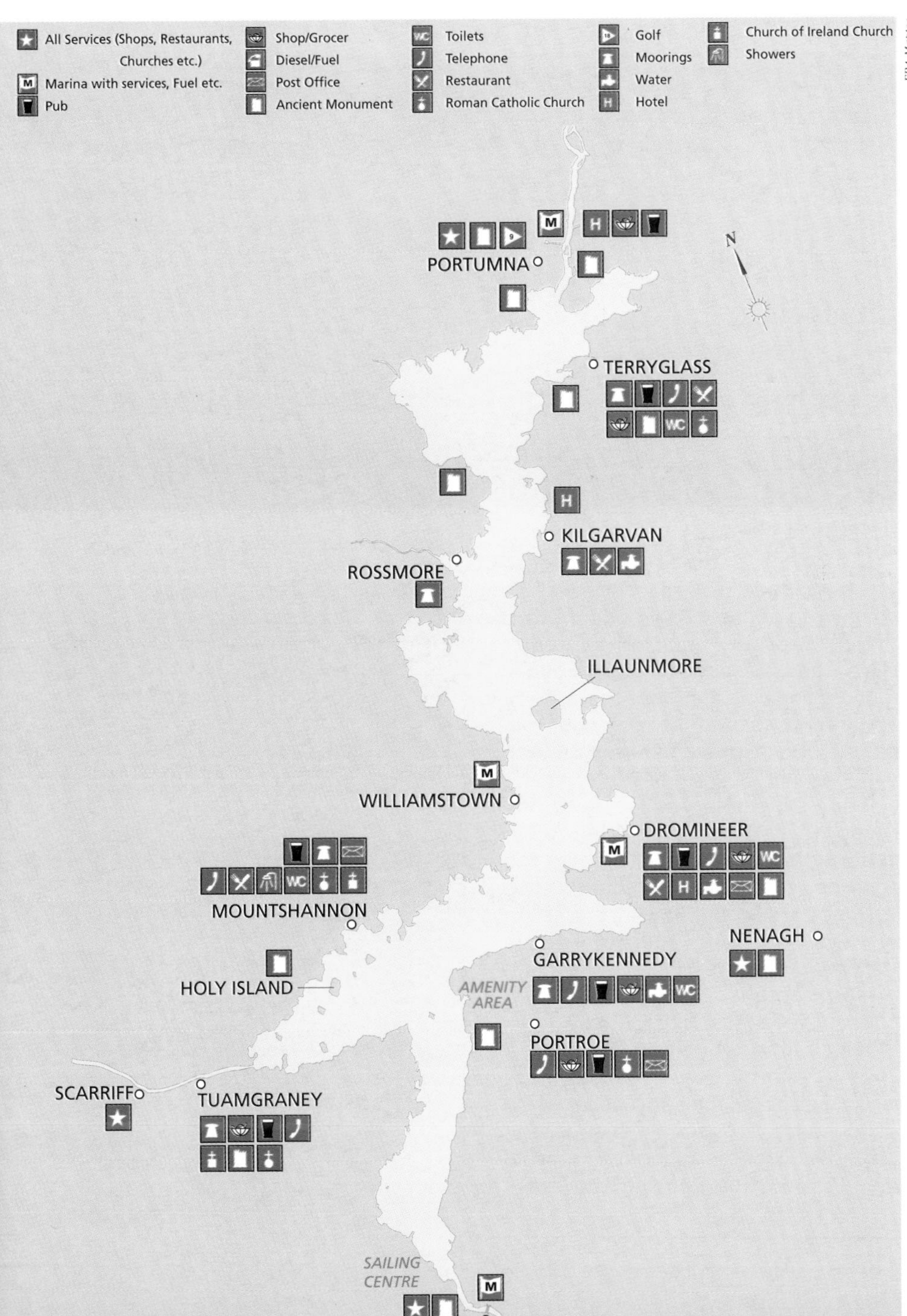

Lough Derg—Loch Dergdherc—the Lake of the Bloody Eye

The name Lough Derg recalls a tragic incident in ancient Irish legend. It is referred to in an old tale called Forbais Edair, or the Siege of Howth. In those days the poets and bards had almost unlimited influence. They were treated with mingled feelings of respect and dread by both the nobles and the people. Should a person happen to slight one, his name might be handed down to posterity in a manner far from flattering.

One harpist, particularly feared, was named Ahirny. He was a fine musician and a great hand at composing songs. If he liked a man he would compose a grand bit of poetry about his skill and courage, so that everyone would be wanting to go and pay him their respects. If he didn't like a man then woe betide him, for he had a knack of putting half-truths into his compositions in such a way as to make the poor fellow appear as the greatest villain unhung.

He once went on a journey through Ireland, a sort of collecting tour it was, for every chieftain buttered him with sweet words and loaded him with presents, hoping that he might give them a good 'sing up'. The more he was flattered the more haughty he became and the more outrageous and unreasonable were his requests.

At that time Eochy mac Luchta was king of South Connacht and Thomond. He had only one eye, the other having been poked out of his head in a battle. Although Eochy made a great fuss of the bard, the latter took an instinctive dislike to him. As he was saying goodbye, the king asked him what he would like as a gift, promising that he had only got to name the article and he would have it wrapped up and given to him. The malicious poet demanded the chieftain's eye. There was nothing the poor man could do about it so he plucked it out and pressed it into the harpist's hand. Then calling one of his attendants, he bade him lead the way to the nearby lake. There he bent down and washed the blood from the jagged socket.

Whilst the attendant was assisting him he noticed that the whole surface of the lake had suddenly become red. He remarked on its appearance to the king, as he guided him along the footpath to the fort. 'So let it be', said the chief: 'Loch Dergdherc will now be its name forever.'

Harry Rice, *Thanks for the Memory.*

Killaloe (cill da Lua–the church of Lua) is a place of great antiquity, best known for its connection with the great king, Brian Boru. Brian, a Dalcassian prince, probably took the name 'Boru' from Beal Borumha, at Ballyvally, on the west shore at the entrance to the lake. Here there is an ancient ring fort which appears to have been heaped up to form an uncompleted Norman motte at a later date. There is a legend that Brian tried to build a dam here to force the waters of the Shannon into Connacht but the less romantically inclined attribute the ridge of land here to glacial activity. At one time it was thought that this was the site of Brian's palace, Kincora, but it is now thought that the palace was at the top of the hill in Killaloe where the RC church stands today. It is recorded that there was a mile-long underground passage from the palace to the fort and two further passages leading from the banqueting hall to the kitchens, along which the food was passed by a continuous chain of servants with the empty dishes returning along the second passage. Brian died at Clontarf in 1014, fighting the Viking invaders, and a century later Kincora was destroyed, not by foreign invaders but by a great force of Connacht men.

Killaloe, which had enjoyed such prestige in the time of Brian Boru, gradually lost its position to nearby Limerick but it continued to be an important ecclesiastical centre. Beside the RC church on the top of the hill is St Lua's Oratory. St Lua was abbot here in the sixth century but this little church was built in the ninth or tenth century. It stood on an island, Friar's Island, just below the bridge, and was carefully transferred stone by stone to its present site in 1929 when the hydro-electric scheme raised the water levels and submerged the island. The nave originally would have had a timber roof and the stone-roofed chancel was a later addition.

Walter Borner

Derg Marina, Killaloe

Two centuries after St Lua St Flannan became abbot. St Flannan's Cathedral was commenced about 1180 by King Donal O'Brien, possibly replacing an earlier church. This building was destroyed by the raiding Connacht men and the present cathedral was built in the early thirteenth century when Gothic architecture with pointed arches was beginning to replace the rounded Romanesque style. It is cruciform in shape with the tower supported by four central arches. The original tower had a pyramid roof but this was replaced and the tower increased in height about 1800. There are some interesting features: inside the main entrance there is a richly ornamented Romanesque doorway (possibly part of the earlier church) which is serving as a window. Nearby is a cross fragment bearing ogham and runic inscriptions which was found in 1916 in a nearby wall. The ogham has been deciphered to read 'a blessing on Toroqrim' and the runes

Killaloe

Beziehung zu dem grossen König Brian Boru. In Ballyvally am Westufer befindet sich ein frühmittelalterlicher Ringwall, dessen späterer Umbau in eine normannische Motte wurde nicht vollendet. Kincora, der im 12. Jahrhundert zerstörte Palast Brian Borus, soll an der Stelle auf dem Hügel Killaloes gestanden haben, wo sich jetzt die katholische Kirche befindet.

Auf Friar's Island direkt unterhalb der Brücke stand früher die Kapelle von St. Lua aus dem 9. oder 10. Jahrhundert. Während des Kraftwerkbaus stieg der Wasserspiegel. So wurde 1929 die kleine Kirche sorgfältig Stein für Stein auf ihren jetzigen Platz gebracht. Das Kirchenschiff hatte ursprünglich eine Holzdecke. Der Altarraum mit Steindecke ist ein späterer Anbau. Der Bau der Kathedrale von St. Flannan wurde um 1180 begonnen. Sie wurde während eines Raubzugs von Eindringlingen aus Connacht zerstört. Die heutige gotische Kathedrale stammt aus dem 13. Jahrhundert, als die Spitzbögen begannen, die gerundete romanische Bauweise zu verdrängen. Sehenswert sind der reich verzierte romanische Torbogen sowie das Bruchstück eines Hochkreuzes mit Ogham- und Runeninschrift.

Die St. Flannans Kapelle stammt aus dem 12.

'Thurgrim carved this cross'. There is also a twelfh century high cross, which was brought from Kilfenora in Co Clare in 1821, an unfinished medieval font, a fine stained glass chancel window and some interesting memorial inscriptions, including one to John Grantham, a pioneer of steamers on the Shannon. The wooden screen dividing the nave was added later and, some would say, it is no great addition. In the adjacent old graveyard is St Flannan's Oratory, a twelfth century building with a barrel-vaulted inner roof over which there is a small loft and a very steep pitched stone roof, characteristic of Irish Romanesque. The old Bishop's palace, Clarisford House (perpetuating the name of the original ford here, Clare Ford), is set in behind the cathedral, and the deanery, across the road, is an attractive old house.

The village on the east side is called **Ballina** (Béal an átha—the mouth of the ford). Killaloe was an important fording place and, although there is evidence that there was a timber bridge built here in 1054, it is recorded that the river still had to be forded in the fourteenth century. Parts of the present stone bridge are very old. It was originally a nineteen-arch bridge but it has been much altered over the centuries and now has thirteen arches: the west end was altered for the canal in the early 1800s, the five central arches were rebuilt in 1825 and four more in the 1840s. Finally, a navigation span was inserted in the 1920s when the hydro-electric scheme led to the alteration in levels and the abandonment of the canal. The weir constructed here in the 1840s was removed at that time, raising the level of the water below the bridge; the black navigation marks keep boats clear of the weir site. The navigation between Killaloe and Limerick was greatly altered by these hydro-electric works.

The canal was completed in the early 1800s and an interesting feature of the lock is the provision for two sets of gates, making it a rising or a falling lock. This was made because at the time it was being built there was a suggestion that the level of Lough Derg might be lowered by removing the natural rock sill at Killaloe, which would have made this short length of canal a summit level, but this elaborate scheme was never carried out. On the east shore, near the bridge, is the old station of the former Birdhill branch railway. This railway extended behind the hotel to a quay upstream of the present marina and served the steamers which operated from the 1890s until 1914.

Lough Derg (Dergdherc—the lake of the bloody eye)

Derry Moving up the lake, on a small island near Deer Rock beacon there is a ruined castle. This was an O'Brien stronghold and is one of a number of fortified tower houses which ring the lake which were built from the fifteenth until well into the seventeenth century. The island is connected to the mainland by a

Jahrhundert. Das innere Dach hat die Form eines Tonnengewölbes, über das sich das sehr steile, für den irisch-romanischen Stil typische Steindach erhebt.

Killaloe war eine wichtige Furt. Im Jahr 1054 wurde eine Holzbrücke errichtet, die im Laufe der Jahrhunderte häufig umgebaut wurde. Einzelne Teile der Steinbrücke sind sehr alt. Der alte Kanal wurde in den frühen Jahren des 19. Jahrhunderts vollendet.

Lough Derg

Beim Marker von Deer Rock liegt die Ruine einer Burg der O'Briens. Sie ist eines der zwischen dem 15. und 17. Jahrhundert erbauten Turmhäuser, die sich rings um den See erheben. Der Hafen von Derry wurde gebaut, um den Transport von Schieferplatten aus den Steinbrüchen an den Hängen des Arra Gebirges zu erleichtern.

Am gegenüberliegenden Ufer steht Tinarana, ein im viktorianischen Stil von der Familie Purdon errichtetes Haus.

Castlelough ist ein sehr schönes Haus. Es wurde 1712 von der Familie Parker gebaut und 1860 beträchtlich vergrössert.

Cahir Island

Auf einer kleinen Insel in der Nähe von Cahir

Killaloe

Walter Borner

submerged causeway and there is a local tradition that it is haunted. Nearby is Derry harbour, built to facilitate the transport of slates from the quarries on the slopes of the Arra Mountains: these were a particularly hard, quality blue slate and were much in demand. The harbour is now privately owned and is much silted up.

On the opposite shore is Tinarana, a Victorian house built by the Purdon family who had lived on the property for some 200 years. It was sold in 1901 to the Gleesons who were originally owners of Athlone Woollen Mills. The Slieve Bernagh Mountains are known to have been forested in the Middle Ages with oakwood, some of which is reputed to have been used in the construction of Westminster Hall, London, and the Royal Palace, Amsterdam.

Castlelough and Castletown Castlelough Castle, a very ancient ruin, is on an island a short distance from the fine house of Castlelough. This house was built in 1712 by the Parker family and was considerably enlarged about 1860. The castle was probably the first stronghold built by the MacBriens of Arra on the east bank of the Shannon. Half a mile to the south are the extensive ruins of Castletown tower house, the principal residence of the MacBriens. Across the road is a ruined church and a graveyard with some interesting sixteenth and seventeenth century grave slabs.

Cahir Island The ruins of Ballykelly Castle stand on a small island near Cahir Island on the south shore of Scarriff Bay. It is surrounded by rocks and shoals and this seems to have made it an ideal place for illicit whiskey distilling. Eventually the revenue men asked the army to blow it up in 1827 to prevent its further use for this purpose.

Tuamgraney (tuaim Greine–the grave of Greine) The C of I church is one of the oldest churches in Ireland still in use today. The western portion with its lintelled doorway dates back to 969 and Brian Boru is reputed to have repaired the church around 1000. The eastern portion is twelfth century and it is thought that the two south windows may have been from an earlier church in Killaloe. The carved head at the east gable is said to be St Cronan who founded a monastery on this site in the sixth century which was plundered several times by the Vikings. Nearby are the remains of an O'Grady castle and in Raheen Wood on the opposite side of the road there are some very large and ancient oak trees. One of them known as Brian Boru's tree, is just 2 km from the entrance and is thought to be over 1000 years old.

Walter Borner

Holy Island

Scarriff (an scairbh—the shallow) has always been an important market town and there is an interesting old weighbridge in the market square. Originally, the river was navigable up to the shallows at Scarriff only in the winter when the level of the lake was high but in the 1840s the Shannon Commissioners dredged it and lined the banks. They formed a harbour by closing off one side of the small island. Where the river enters the lake, on the

Island steht die Ruine von Schloss Ballykelly. Es wurde als Schwarzbrennerei für Whiskey benützt, bevor es 1827 im Auftrag der Steuerbehörde von der Armee gesprengt wurde, um zu verhindern, dass es weiterhin zu diesem Zweck missbraucht wurde. Leider.

Tuamgraney

Das war eine der ältesten noch benutzten Kirchen Irlands. 1987 wurden die protestantischen Gottesdienste eingestellt. Der westliche Teil mit massivem Torsturz über der Eingangstür ist um 969 datiert. Der östliche Teil stammt aus dem 12. Jahrhundert. Der aus Stein gemeisselte Kopf am Ostgiebel soll den heiligen Cronan darstellen, der im 6. Jahrhundert an diesem Ort ein Kloster gegründet haben soll. In der Nähe sind die Überreste eines Schlosses der O'Grady's. Jenseits der Strasse, im Wald von Raheen, stehen einige sehr grosse, uralte Eichen. Eine davon, die unter dem Namen Brian Boru's Baum bekannt und etwas über zwei Kilometer vom Waldrand entfernt ist, soll mehr als tausend Jahre alt sein.

Scarriff

Scarriff war von jeher ein bedeutender Marktflecken. In den 40er Jahres des 19. Jahrhunderts liess die Shannon Aufsichtsbehörde die Fahrrinne des Flusses bis Scarriff ausbaggern und die Ufer begradigen. Am nördlichen Ufer, wo der Fluss in den See mündet, findet sich ein botanisch reiches Sumpfgebiet mit einigen seltenen

The following is John Colgan's version of the legend of Iniscealtra recorded by John O'Donovan in his **Ordnance Survey Letters** 1837.

Whilst St Caminus and St Cumineus, by surname The Tall, were on a certain day in the church, which St Camín founded on the island called Inis-Keltra situated on Lough Derg, conversing spiritually about matters concerning the soul with Guaire Aidhe, King of Connaught; St Camín among other discourses says to Guaire (his brother): 'With what things would you, O King, wish to have this church filled, which might be converted to use according to your desires?'Guaire replied saying: 'I would wish to have so great treasures of gold and silver, as that church could contain; not indeed led on by covetousness of worldly riches, but that I might lay them out for the use of the Saints of God, for the purpose of erecting churches and relieving the wants of the poor Christians.' The man of God, inspired by the Holy Spirit , says to the King: 'The Lord will benignly look to your pious wishes, and will give you much riches to be piously laid out for the salvation of your soul.' Guaire heartily embracing that prophetic promise, and giving immense thanks, said to St Cumín: 'And you, servant of God, with what things would you desire to have the church filled?' St Cumín replied: 'Would to God I had so many sacred volumes as this church could contain to bestow them on students of divine wisdom for the dissemination of the salutary doctrine of Christ among people, and for the purpose of withdrawing them from the service of the devil, leading them to a faithful observance of the commandments of God.' And when both afterwards enquired of St Camín, of what sort he would himself wish to have that church full, the follower of Evangelical perfection, and of true wisdom says, 'If this church were full of infirm affected with various kinds of languishments and sicknesses, I would wish, if it would please the Lord, that all the infirmities of all should come upon my little body alone, and that I should endure them patiently for the love of the Saviour who vouchsafed to suffer for mine and the infirmities of the whole world.' But everyone of them afterwards obtained through the most merciful indulgence of the Lord, the effect of his desire. For Guaire obtained earthly riches, St Cumín attained to the gift of knowledge and wisdom from the Lord; but St Camín as he wished, always afterwards laboured through the dispensation of God, under so many and so great infirmities which he bore most patiently for the love of Christ, that his whole flesh became utterly wasted, and the nerves of his body were loosed and his bones were hardly joined one to another, until he gave up his most pure spirit to his Saviour. And thus these three most pious men having obtained their different desires, which tended to the same end, purchased the Kingdom of Heaven, which they had purposed in fine.

northern banks, there is a botanically rich marshland area and this contains some rare species.

Mountshannon is an attractive little village which won the major award in the Tidy Towns competition some years ago. It has always been a popular fishing centre, particularly during the mayfly season. A small pier was erected here in 1845 principally for the landing of the rich marl dredged from the lake, which was much prized at that time for spreading on the land as a fertiliser. The harbour was extended in the 1970s and Mountshannon has now become a popular sailing centre.

Inishcealtra (inis cealtra–the island of the burial place) is sometimes referred to as **Holy Island**. The names of several early Irish saints are associated with it: St MacCreiche, the anchorite, St Colum of Terryglass in the sixth century and St Caimín who founded a monastic settlement here a century later. It suffered the same fate as the other Shannon sites at the hands of the Vikings in the ninth century. By the early seventeenth century the churches on the island had ceased to be used for worship and activity was limited to an annual pilgrimage which was held on Whit Sunday. This was suppressed in the nineteenth century because it was considered that abuses had developed. Some points of interest on the island are as follows:

1. The 'Confessional' is probably so called because it was used for this purpose at one time. It was thought to have been the cell of the anchorite MacCreiche but when it was recently dismantled and rebuilt and the area around it excavated, the indications were that it was more likely to have been a shrine, erected about 1700 and repeatedly rebuilt in the manner of a wooden original.

2. The Saints' Graveyard contains many interesting grave slabs, some of them dating back to the eleventh and twelfth centuries.

3. The Church of the Wounded Men is a small building within the graveyard, thought to be an eighteenth century mortuary chapel of the O'Grady family whose motto was 'Vulneratus non victus'—wounded but not vanquished. Its three doorways are puzzling and there is a local tradition that any woman who enters it

Pflanzenarten.

Mountshannon

Das kleine Dorf ist ein beliebtes Zentrum für Angler. 1845 wurde ein kleiner Pier gebaut. Der seither vergrösserte Hafen ist ein beliebter Ort der Segler.

Inishcealtra

Inishcealtra wird auch die Heilige Insel genannt. Die Klostersiedlung wurde im 7. Jahrhundert von St. Caimin gegründet. Im 9. Jahrhundert erlitt sie wegen der Plünderung und Zerstörung durch die Wikinger das gleiche Schicksal wie andere Klöster. Vom frühen 17. Jahrhundert an wurden die Kirchen nicht mehr benutzt. Im 19. Jahrhundert wurde die jährliche Wallfahrt am Pfingstsonntag verboten.

1. Der Beichtstuhl: Vor kurzer Zeit zerlegt und wieder aufgebaut. Ausgrabungen am Ort ergaben, dass es sich wahrscheinlich um ein Reliquiar handelt, das einem Original aus Holz nachgebaut wurde.

2. Der Heiligenfriedhof enthält interessante Grabsteine aus dem 11. und 12. Jahrhundert.

3. Die Kirche der verwundeteten Männer, im 18. Jahrhundert für die Familie O'Grady als Totenkapelle gebaut. Ihre drei Torbogen sind rätselhaft. Der Sage nach soll eine Frau, die diese Kirche betritt, nie wieder Kinder gebären.

4. Mittelschiff der Kirche des heiligen Caimin, im Stil der irischen Kirchen vor dem Jahr 1000 erbaut. Das romanische Gewölbe, der Chor

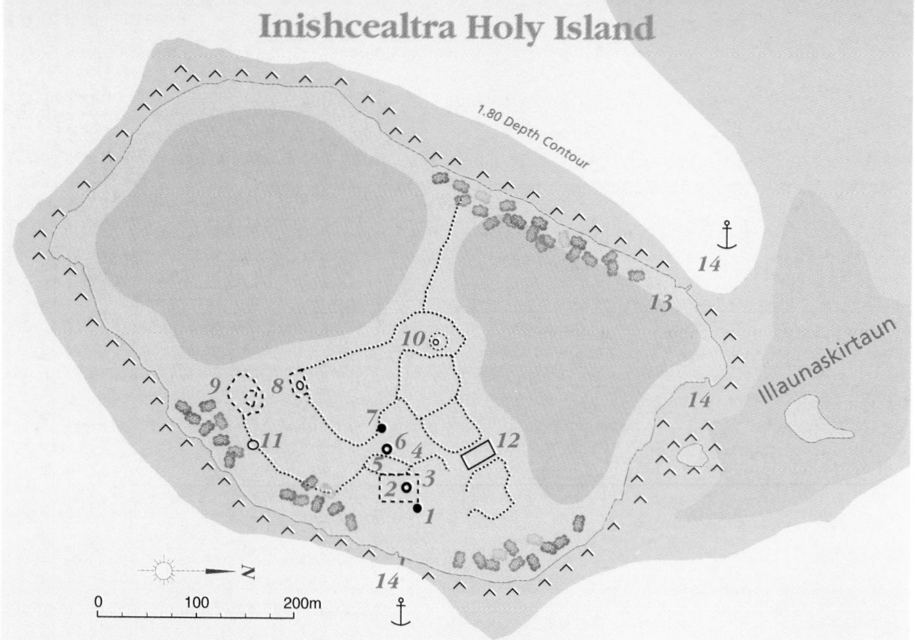

ERA Maptec

will never again bear children.

4. The nave of St Caimín's Church is built in a style found in Irish churches before 1000 and it is thought to be the church commissioned by Brian Boru for his brother who was abbot here. The Romanesque arch, chancel and west door were inserted in the twelfth century and suffered incorrect restoration in 1879 but the church is now being carefully restored using the correct stones. Inside the church are some eighth to eleventh century grave slabs and the remains of three separate high crosses, one of which has an inscription saying that it was erected by a man named Cathasach, who probably died in 1111.

5. Nineteenth century graveyard.

6. The round tower was probably built about the same time as St Caimín's Church. There is a local tradition that it was never completed.

7. The shaft of a ninth century cross is beside the round tower.

8. St Brigid's Church (sometimes called the Baptism Church) is a Romanesque church with a thirteenth century round-arched gateway leading into the enclosure. Recent excavations indicate that when it was replaced by the nearby St Mary's Church, this became a working area. Traces of bronze and iron workings, comb-making and bone-making have been found.

9. St Mary's Church is early thirteenth century and was the medieval parish church but it has been much altered and rebuilt. The 'altar' was originally the base for the O'Brien memorial on the south Wall: it was taken to the mainland and only returned to the island in the 1880s.

10. This enclosure. known as St Michael's Garden, was traditionally associated with miraculous cures. Recent excavations have revealed that this was a burial ground for infants, probably because they were unbaptised. There was a small stone church erected here in the eighteenth or early nineteenth century.

11. The Lady's Well, down near the shore, formed part of the pilgrimage walk and coins were thrown into it as a sign of repentance.

12. Some local families still enjoy burial rights on the island and this is the landing

und die westliche Türe wurden im 12. Jahrhundert hinzugefügt und haben 1879 unter einer unfachmännischen Restaurierung gelitten. Inzwischen wurde die Türe sorgfältig wiederhergestellt.

5. Friedhof aus dem 19. Jahrhundert.

6. Freistehender Rundturm, wahrscheinlich aus dem 11. Jahrhundert. Der Turm soll nie vollendet worden sein.

7. Kreuzschaft aus dem 9. Jahrhundert.

8. Die Kirche der heiligen Brigid (auch Taufkirche genannt) ist eine romanische Kirche mit Torbogen zur Einfriedung. Ausgrabungen zeigen, dass hier Werkstätten gewesen sein müssen. Reste von Bronze- und Eisenarbeiten sowie von Kamm- und Beinschnitzereien wurden gefunden.

9. Kirche von St. Mary aus dem fühen 13. Jahrhundert. Pfarrkirche im Mittelalter, vielfach umgestaltet und umgebaut. Der Altar war ursprünglich der Sockel eines Gedenksteins der Familie O'Brien.

10. Der Garten von St. Michael gilt als der Ort von Wunderheilungen. Ausgrabungen der letzten Zeit haben gezeigt, dass es sich um einen Säuglingsfriedhof handelt.

11. Brunnen Unserer Lieben Frau, der in der Nähe des Ufers steht. Ein Besuch gehörte zur Wallfahrt. Als Zeichen der Reue wurden Münzen

Holy Island: The thirteenth century gateway leading into St Brigids Church

Walter Borner

place and small modern mortuary where the coffins are brought ashore from the mainland.

The network of low banks are stone divisions and paved paths of the medieval period to cater for the annual pilgrimage. There are also several bullauns (stones with hollows used for pounding substances).

Garrykennedy was a stronghold of the O' Kennedys who built a castle here. The harbour was constructed in 1829, using some of the stones from the old castle, and it was another outlet for the slate quarries.

Portroe (port rua—red fort) is 2.5 km from Garrykennedy and owes its existence to the slate quarrying in the area.

The Mountaineer Rock bears the name of one of the earliest steamers on the river but there is no record of any incident which would account for the naming of the rock. A memorial to John Grantham in St Flannan's cathedral in Killaloe states that he introduced steamers to the river in 1825, but the records of the Grand Canal Company mention a neck-and-neck race between the Shannon Steam Navigation Company's Mountaineer and Grantham's Marquis Wellesley in November 1826 which was lost by the latter.

Lough Derg Flora and Fauna Sadly, the quality of the waters of Lough Derg has disimproved since an early study of the 1920s which showed that the lake was then unpolluted. This deterioration is reflected in the number and nature of planktonic algae, lack of water transparency and shoreline scums. This is because the lake is over-enriched with plant nutrients which enter the Shannon mainly due to the misuse of agricultural fertilisers, sewage disposal and other wastes. The characteristic plants of the Lough Derg shores are similar to those of Lough Ree and include the bog rush, bedstraw, hemp agrimony, gipsywort and sneezewort, and these can be found widely in the area. Particularly interesting areas are north of Williamstown, Rossmore Bay, Bellevue Point, Luska Bay and Kilgarvan.

Dromineer (Drom inbhir—estuary ridge) was always an important Shannon port. The castle quay dates back to the early 1800s and a pier was erected here in 1829 by the steam company which was later incorporated into the present harbour. Dromineer Bay has also been a sailing centre since the 1830s and the home of the Lough Derg Yacht Club. The club was formerly sited further around the bay at Kilteelagh, the site of an ancient Viking fort. In 1922 the yacht club amalgamated with the local boat club and moved to the latter's premises. The Shannon One Design, an 18 ft open centreboard boat which is still a flourishing class today, was designed

Garrykennedy drawn by Paul Gauci before the harbour was constructed

hineingeworfen.

12. Einige ortsansässige Familien haben noch immer das Recht, auf der Insel beerdigt zu werden. Das Netzwerk niedriger Wälle besteht aus ehemaligen mittelalterlichen Steinmauern und gepflasterten Wegen. Hier befinden sich auch mehrere Bullauns, die zum Mahlen benutzt wurden.

Garrykennedy

Hochburg der O'Kennedy's, die hier ihr Schloss errichteten. Einige der Steine wurden 1829 beim Bau des Hafens verwendet.

Mountaineer Rock

Hat seinen Namen von einem der ersten Dampfschiffe auf dem Fluss. John Grantham war der erste, der 1825 Dampfer in Betrieb nahm. 1826 gewann die Mountaineer eine Wettfahrt.

Dromineer

Wichtiger Hafen am Shannon. 1829 wurde ein Pier errichtet, der später dem heutigen Hafen angegliedert wurde. Seit den 30er Jahren des 19. Jahrhunderts ist Dromineer ein Segelzentrum und Heimat des Lough Derg Segelklubs. Die 'Shannon One'-Jolle ist ein noch heute bei Wettsegeln äusserst beliebter Bootstyp. Am Nordufer der Bucht steht St. David's. Das Haus wurde Mitte des 19. Jahrhunderts vergrössert und ausgebaut. Kilteelagh ist ein schönes Beispiel viktorianischer Architektur. Kleine Ruine einer romanischen Kirche aus dem 12. Jahrhundert, von Mönchen von Inish Cealtra angefangen, aber nie vollendet. Die auf Befehl der Williamitischen Regierung zerstörte Burg wurde wahrscheinlich im 16. Jahrhundert gebaut.

Nenagh

Die Burg stammt etwa aus dem Jahr 1218. An der Nordecke einer bewehrten fünfeckigen Festung befindet sich ein kreisrunder Turm. Zwischen dem 15. und dem 17. Jahrhundert wechselte die Burg mehrmals den Besitzer. 1692 wurde sie auf Befehl der Regierung zerstört. Die oberen Zinnen des Burgfrieds wurden erst 1860 angebracht. Auf der andern Strassenseite befindet sich im ehemaligen Gefängnis ein Museum.

Williamstown

Früher wichtiges Zentrum für Angler. In den späten 20er Jahren des 19. Jahrhunderts wurden ein Hafen und ein Hotel gebaut, das etwa 1860 geschlossen wurde. Es brannte 1920 nieder.

Castletown Bay

Schloss Annagh ist ein weiteres Beispiel der typischen befestigten Turmhäuser. Am Ende des Wasserwegs von Annagh Lough findet sich ein Crannog, ein frühmittelalterlicher Pfahlbau auf

by Morgan Giles in 1921. On the north side of the bay is St David's which was originally a fishing lodge for the Holmes family of nearby Petersfield (later called Johnstown). The house was enlarged in the mid-ninteenth century by the Very Rev. Gilbert Holmes, Dean of Ardfert. The Holmes family were great supporters of sailing and one of them, Traherne Holmes, a legendary figure in the late nineteenth century, was famous for his exploits. Kilteelagh on the south side of the bay is a fine Victorian house built by the Gason family.

There is a small ruined Romanesque church in the old graveyard at Dromineer which, according to local tradition, was begun in the twelfth century by some of the monks from Inishcealtra who intended forming a new settlement here but it never materialised and the church was not completed. The castle was probably built in the sixteenth century by the Cantwells, who were tenants of the manor of Dromineer from the Butlers, earls of Ormond. It is larger than most tower houses and stood four storeys high. It was taken by the Cromwellian General, Ireton, in 1650, its garrison of a lieutenant and 50 men surrendering when cannon were set up nearby. It was subsequently returned to the Duke of Ormond but was dismantled together with all the larger castles in Ormond on the orders of the Williamite government. Illaunagore Marina is located in the south east corner of Dromineer Bay.

Nenagh (9.6 km away) The castle here was built about 1218 as the stronghold of Theobald Fitzwalter, the first Butler of Ormond who had received a grant of some 500,000 acres of land from Prince John. It remained the principal residence of the Butler family until 1380 when they moved to Carrick-on-Suir. The circular keep is a unique structure and was the north point of a compact pentagon castle with the main residence inside the gate on the south side. The castle changed hands several times in the fifteenth to seventeenth centuries and was demolished by government order in 1692. The upper crenellations were added to the keep in 1860 by the Bishop of Killaloe. There is an interesting museum in the old gaol buildings across the road.

Williamstown was another popular fishing centre in the past; the Inland Steam Company made a harbour here in the late 1820s and built a hotel. In those days there

Walter Borner

Cregg Point

einer künstlichen Insel. Ausser bei Niedrigwasser ist er meist überflutet.

Illaunmore

Grösste Binneninsel Irlands. Reste einer Klostersiedlung mit Kirchenruine am Nordostende der Insel.

Benjamin Beacon

Die Büsten auf diesem Marker und demjenigen von Horse Island wurden vor über dreissig Jahren aus Spass aufgestellt und haben bis heute

Mountshannon

Walter Borner

was salmon and trout fishing as well as coarse fishing but the former declined greatly when the river was harnessed for electricity. When the steamers ceased to trade in the 1860s the hotel closed down and became the private residence of General Cooper who added the crenellated pier. The house was burnt down in the 1920s and some of the outhouses have now been converted into holiday apartments by Shannon Castle Line who have restored the harbour as a base. The new Dromaan harbour is in the next bay to the south.

Castletown Bay The ruins of Annagh Castle, another of the typical fortified houses ringing the lake, dominate the bay. There is a crannóg (an ancient dwelling place built on piles on an artificial island) at the end of the channel from Annagh Lough which is submerged unless the water level of the lake is particularly low.

Illaunmore (oileán mór—big island) is the largest inland island in Ireland and is privately owned. There are indications of a monastic settlement here but little is known about it and the only visible remains are the ruins of a church at the north-east end and a few small grave slabs dating back to the seventh and eighth century.

Benjamin Beacon The busts on this beacon and on the Horse Island beacon were placed there over twenty years ago as a prank by some members of the Tottenham family. They have survived many winters and have become a feature of the lake, if somewhat puzzling to the visitor. 'The Goat's Road', a line of rocks which led out to Goat Island, is another prominent feature, extending out across the narrowest part of the lake.

Kilgarvan used to be one of the principal barley exporting stations in the days of commercial traffic: the barley was shipped from here to the maltings at Banagher. To the south is Waterloo Lodge, a former fishing lodge, and Bellevue and Brookfield houses, and to the north Gurthalougha, a nineteenth century house built by the Farrar family which is now a popular country house hotel. Drominagh, formerly Castle Biggs, is a fine three-storey, seven bay Georgian mansion built by the Biggs family, which passed in the mid-nineteenth century to the Esmonde family, who lived there until the 1940s. Eugene Esmonde played a part in the sinking of the Bismarck and was awarded a posthumous VC for the daring attack which his squadron made on part of the German fleet during the 1939–45 war. The ruins of an O'Kennedy castle are down by the shore.

Rossmore There are no facilities here but it is a good fishing bay. In the past boats of up to 20 tons went up the

Walter Borner

Dromineer

überdauert. Dem Betrachter geben sie einige Rätsel auf. Auffällig ist auch Goat's Road, die Ziegenstrasse, eine Reihe von Felsen, die sich quer über die schmalste Stelle des Sees erstrekken.

Kilgarvan

Früher einer der bedeutendsten Umschlagplätze für Gerste. Südlich davon liegt Waterloo Lodge, ein ehemaliges Landhaus für Angler. Gurthalougha, nördlich davon gelegen und heute ein beliebtes Hotel, ist ein Landhaus aus dem 19. Jahrhundert. Drominagh, im georgianischen Stil erbaut, war früher das Schloss Biggs. Am Ufer stehen die Überreste eines Schlosses der O'Kennedy's.

Rossmore

Bucht mit guten Angelmöglichkeiten, aber den Ost- bis Südwinden sehr ausgesetzt.

Cloondagough Castle

Vor einigen Jahren restauriertes und mit ei-

Woodford River to serve the mill at Rossmore Bridge and recently the mouth of the river was dredged by John Weaving and the river opened up again to boats up to a pool where the river widens out and boats can be turned.

Cloondagough Castle is a tower house on the south shore of Cloondavaun Bay. Some restoration work was carried out and it was re-roofed some years ago but it is not safe to venture inside now. It was the scene of one of the last evictions in Ireland in 1906 when the agents of the infamous landlord Clanricard overcame the locals' attempts to resist.

Terryglass (Tír dhá ghlas—the land of the two streams). A monastery was founded here by St Colum mac Cremthain, who died in 549. It soon became a prominent centre of learning and was visited by the great St Columba or Colmcille. In 845 the Vikings burned the church and slew its abbot and the monastery fell into oblivion after a disastrous fire in 1162. There is a ruined Norman church here, which shows signs of fifteenth century alterations. Beside it the abandoned C of I church has now been restored and is used as a craft shop. There are some other medieval fragments in the churchyard of the RC church on the hill. This church was built in 1910 with a grant from Mrs Hickey of nearby Slevoir House who was Spanish; she stipulated that all the gravestones should be exactly alike. Slevoir was built at the end of the eighteenth century by the Synge family and was bought in 1870 by Lt Col James Hickey who had married the Spanish heiress. They enlarged the house, adding the four-storey high campanile tower. In the 1950s it became a novitiate of the Salesian Sisters of St John Bosco. The mooring facilities at Terryglass were greatly improved in the mid-1990s by the construction of a fine new harbour.

Oldcourt Castle, access to which can be obtained from the village of Terryglass, is a fine quadrilateral Norman castle with towers in each corner, a type not very often found in Ireland. It dates from the late thirteenth or early fourteenth century and the experts say that it was more likely to have been built by the Butlers of Ormond than the de Burghs, from whom the

Walter Borner

Sailing on Lough Derg

nem neuen Dach versehenes Turmhaus. Das Betreten ist gefährlich. Es war 1906 Schauplatz einer der letzten Zwangsräumungen Irlands.

Terryglass

Das Kloster wurde durch den heiligen Colummac Cremthain, der 549 starb, gegründet. 845 wurde die Kirche von den Wikingern nieder-

Terryglass

Walter Borner

Walter Borner

Lecarrow Band, an Irish and Swiss jam Session

Clanricards of Portumna Castle are descended. It has a strangely truncated appearance and looks as if it might have been originally several storeys higher but the evidence suggests that it was in fact never built any higher. A wall divided the central area and there are puzzling outside steps giving access to the north east tower.

Portumna (port omna—the harbour of the tree trunk) Portumna Castle Harbour is a good place from which to visit Portumna Castle and Priory. The opening times are: mid-June - mid-September 09.30-18.30 every day, last admission 45 minutes before closing (tel. 0509-41658). The former Clanricard estate is now administered as a Forest Park by the Forest & Wildlife Service and the castle has undergone some partial restoration. It has a long and interesting history and a guide book is available in the town. The Clanricards were descendants of the de Burghs, a Norman family which had been granted extensive lands in Connacht in the thirteenth century. The castle, built shortly before 1620, is of great architectural importance because it represents a transitional style between the vertical tower houses, which encircle the lake, and later manor houses, which were laid out horizontally. Conditions at the time dictated that it must be easily defended and it was built with strong exterior walls, which have a slight batter, and two massive interior walls running the entire length support the roof. It had other defensive features: small inaccessible windows, only two entrances and projecting corner towers with musket loops. The front door was fortified by an iron grille (the chain holes can be seen and have been confused with pistol loops) and above it there is a machicolation, an opening in the parapet through which the defenders could drop things on the intruders. The castle was set inside the traditional fortified enclosure, or bawn: one side of this is still intact, covered by flanking towers with an attractive classical gateway dividing it from the outer enclosure. The gothic main gateway, which

gebrannt. Nach einem weiteren Brand im Jahre 1162 geriet sie langsam in Vergessenheit. Ruine einer normannischen Kirche mit interessanter Horizontalbalkentüre, die wahrscheinlich im 15. Jahrhundert verändert wurde. Daneben steht eine ehemalige protestantische Kirche, in der sich heute ein Kunstgewerbeladen befindet. Die katholische Kirche wurde 1910 erbaut, auf dem Friedhof stehen nach wie vor die alten Grabsteine.

Oldcourt Castle

Prächtige vierseitige Normannenburg mit vier Ecktürmen aus dem späten 13. oder frühen 14. Jahrhundert. Sie macht einen merkwürdig niedrig geratenen Eindruck. Alle Anzeichen sprechen jedoch dafür, dass sie nie höher gebaut war. Eine bemerkenswerte Treppe führt von aussen zum Nordostturm.

Portumna

Der Hafen vom Schloss Portumna ist ein guter Ausgangspunkt für die Besichtigung von Schloss und Abtei. Ehemaliges Landgut der Clanricards, heute ein Naturpark unter der Verwaltung des Amtes für Forstwirtschaft. Das Schloss wurde restauriert. Führer zur Geschichte sind in der Stadt erhältlich. Das kurz vor 1620 errichtete Schloss ist von grosser architektonischer Bedeutung, es repräsentiert den Baustil der Übergangszeit von vertikal angelegten Turmhäusern zu den späteren Herrenhäusern mit horizontaler Bauweise. Zwei massive Innenwände tragen das Dach. Das Gebäude steht innerhalb des traditionell bewehrten Schlosshofs. Ein schönes klassizistisches Eingangsportal führt in den Innenhof. Das gotische Haupteingangstor stammt aus dem 18. Jahrhundert. 1826 wurde das Schloss durch einen Brand zerstört. 1864 erfolgte der Neubau eines Schlosses etwa anderthalb Kilometer südlich. Es wurde nie bewohnt und fiel in den 20er Jahren einem Feuer zum Opfer.

Der Naturlehrpfad ist ein äusserst interessanter Spaziergang. Mehrere Turloughs (Polje), Brunstplätze von Rotwild, Aussichtsturm mit Vogelwarte, Uferland und Inseln von grossem botanischen Interesse.

Die Dominikanerabtei, eine ehemalige Zisterzienserkapelle, wurde im frühen 15. Jahrhundert von den Dominikanern übernommen. Die Nord- und Südwände stammen noch von der alten Kapelle, der Rest aus dem 15. Jahrhundert. Der Altarraum war überdacht und diente als prote-

is attributed to Richard Adam, was added in the eighteenth century. The foundations of the bawn on the side facing the lake can be traced. The castle was built by the 4th earl and its defences were put to the test in the confederacy wars in 1651. Patrick Sarsfield, the famous Irish general, lodged here while defending the Shannon in 1690–1 and married Honora de Burgh, the daughter of the house. It was undergoing major alterations when it was destroyed by fire in 1826. A new castle was built in 1864 about one mile to the south and, although completed and furnished, it had never been occupied by the absentee landlord, when it too was destroyed by fire in the 1920s. The Clanricard title died out with the infamous 15th earl and the estate passed to the Lascelles family who eventually sold it to the Land Commission in 1948 for £12,000.

A nature trail has been laid through the estate commencing at the car park (the site of the second castle) about 1.5 km from the harbour. It is a most interesting trail with a number of turloughs (dry lakes), the rutting stands of the fallow deer and many other features, including an observation tower for viewing the birds on the nearby islands, which are a nature reserve. The foreshore and islands here are of considerable interest botanically. Juniper, one of Ireland's two native conifer species, can be seen abundantly on the shore. The Irish fleabane is found in this area and also across the lake at Slevoir Bay. It is found only on the shores of Lough Derg and is absent from the rest of Ireland and Britain.

Close to the harbour, beside the old farm buildings, are the ruins of the Dominican Priory. There was formerly a Cistercian chapel here but it fell into disuse and was taken over by the Dominicans in the early fifteenth century. The north and south walls of the main church with their pointed windows date back to the earlier chapel and the rest of the church is fifteenth century; the chancel was roofed

Office of Public Works

Portumna Castle

Plan of Portumna Castle drawn by Maurice Craig with identification of rooms after J. Bilson, architect. The servants' quarters were in the basement and on the top floor a gallery extended the entire length of the building looking out over the lake

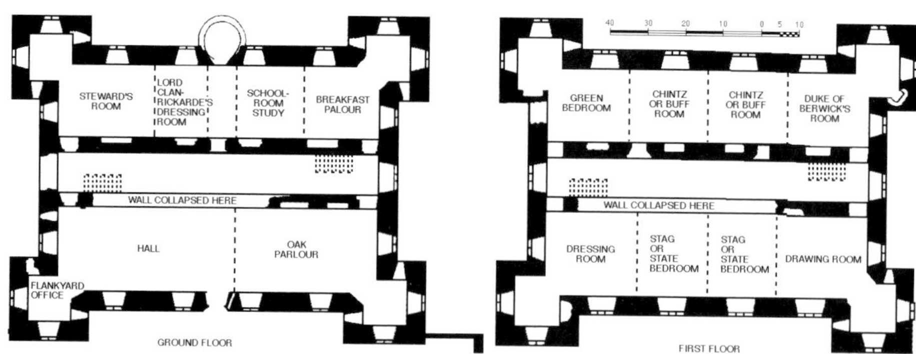

and used as a C of I church up to the early nineteenth century. There are some fine windows: a four-light east window, an ornate window in the south transept, with the initials of the sculptor visible from the outside, and an unusual quatrefoil window in the sacristy to the north of the chancel. An interesting feature in the sacristy is a strange upside-down head at the base of the doorway. Some of the cloisters were re-erected in the 1950s and there are some remains of domestic buildings including a refectory at the north east end.

Ballynasheera Castle, sometimes known as Ireton's Castle or Derrymacegan Castle, is upstream of Derry Point, on the east shore, near Belle Isle house. It was completed about 1654 just at a time when advances in artillery made castles more vulnerable, and it must be one of the last surviving castles to be built in Ireland. It is of a unique design: the two circular turrets at opposite corners have projecting bastions, enabling the defenders to command all the approaches to the walls. Cromwell's General, Ireton, is said to have lodged here in 1651 and launched his attack on the 5th earl of Clanricard in Portumna Castle from here. He forced him to surrender and the Clanricard estate was confiscated and handed over to Henry Cromwell for a short time before being restored to the Clanricards. Belle Isle is an eighteenth century house built by the Yelverton family which passed in marriage

Ruth Delany

Portumna Priory

Ruth Delany

Some of the cloisters of the Dominican Priory, Portumna which were re-erected in 1954

stantisches Gotteshaus. Einige schöne Fenster. Teile des Kreuzgangs wurden vor rund fünfzig Jahren restauriert.

Ballynasheera Castle

In der Nähe vom Haus Belle Isle, 1654 vollendet. Eine der spätesten Burgen Irlands. Aussergewöhnlicher Bauplan: Zwei runde, einander gegenüberstehende Türmchen über vorspringenden Bollwerken gewähren Überblick über sämtliche Zugänge zur Festung.

Wann die erste Brücke in Portumna gebaut wurde, steht nicht fest. Bis 1796 gab es eine Fähre. Danach wurde eine Holzbrücke errichtet. 1840 liess die Shannon Aufsichtsbehörde eine neue Brücke bauen, die 1911 von der heutigen ersetzt wurde. In den 60er Jahren des 19. Jahrhunderts legte die Parsontown Portumna Bridge Railway Company eine Eisenbahnlinie, von der heute kaum noch etwas zu sehen ist.

Portland House

Der Sitz wurde von der Familie Stoney gebaut. Er brannte vor rund achtzig Jahren aus nie geklärten Gründen nieder.

to the Avonmores. The 4th viscount played a prominent role in the introduction of yacht racing on Lough Derg. Sir Henry Seagrave, who died attempting to break the world water speed record, lived here and from 1925–35 it was the home of Major Bertie Waller, a well-known hunting and sailing sportsman .

Portumna Bridge One of the Emerald Star bases is sited up the short canal above the bridge. There is some doubt as to when the first bridge was erected at Portumna but it seems to have been replaced by a ferry until 1796 when Lemuel Cox, who also built bridges at Derry and Waterford, built a wooden bridge here. He made use of Hayes' Island in the middle of the river and fitted a drawbridge close to the west of the island. The Shannon Commissioners replaced the opening span of the bridge in the 1840s using a cast iron swivel. This was replaced by the present bridge in 1911.

Ruth Delany

The bridge at Portumna

Ruth Delany

The old gate which used to be on the original toll bridge at Portumna

The Parsonstown & Portumna Bridge Railway Company constructed a line to connect with the GS&WR at Birr in the 1860s, encouraged by the Marquis of Clanricard. It was never a commercial success and went into receivership in 1871. It earned the title of The Stolen Railway because in 1883 the creditors moved in and took what they could: rails, sleepers and the Portumna Bridge railway station are all said to have disappeared in one night. There is very little evidence of this railway to be seen today.

Portland House is on the east bank before reaching Portland Island. This house was built by the Stoney family. When Butler Stoney died in the 1920s, he left it to a Protestant orphan society. Before they could take posession the house was mysteriously burnt down and it was suggested that there were fears that it would have been used to proselytise Roman Catholic children. A hotel has now been built adjoining the old house.

Gazetteer - Portumna to Athlone

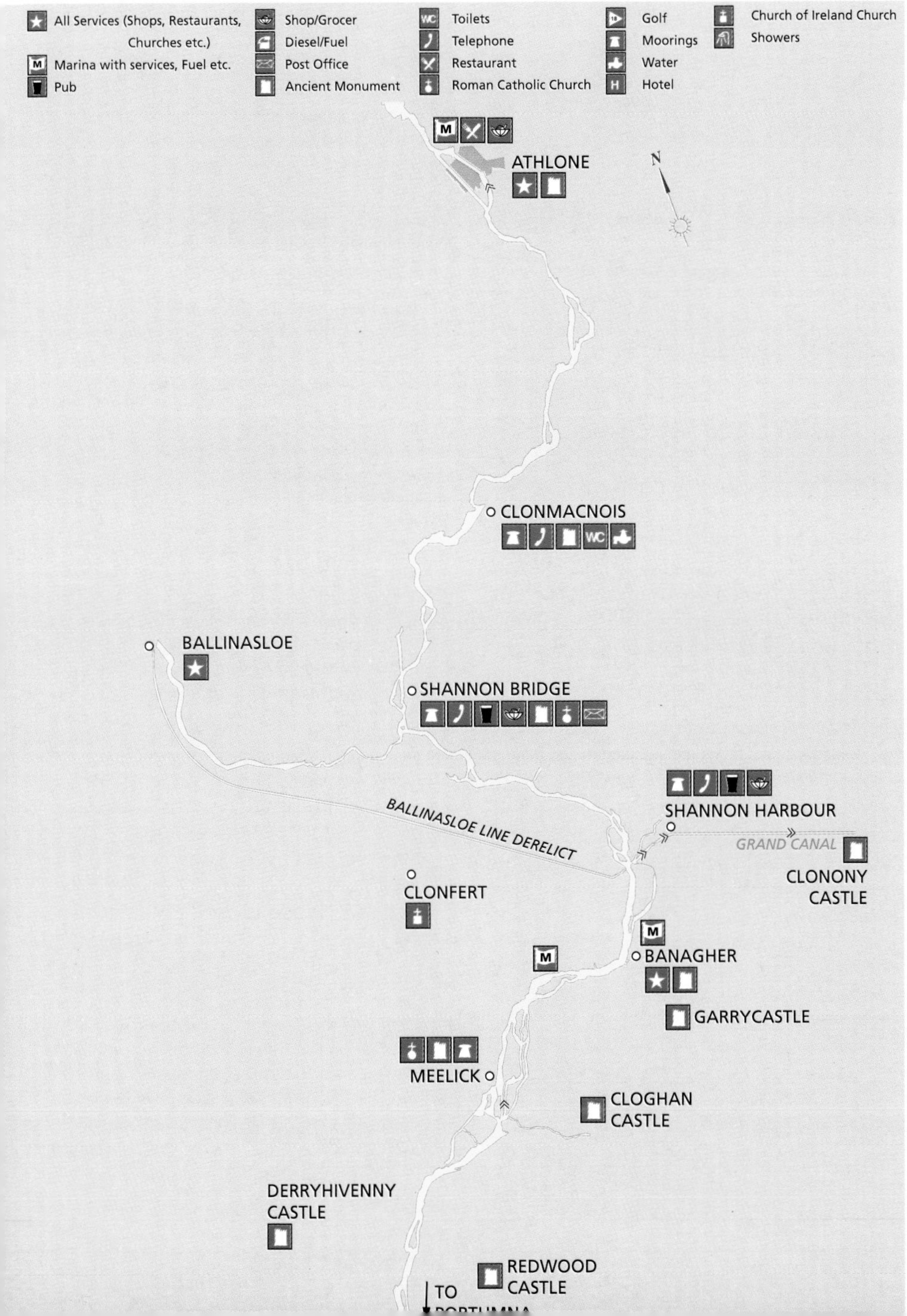

All Services (Shops, Restaurants, Churches etc.)
Marina with services, Fuel etc.
Pub
Shop/Grocer
Diesel/Fuel
Post Office
Ancient Monument
Toilets
Telephone
Restaurant
Roman Catholic Church
Golf
Moorings
Water
Hotel
Church of Ireland Church
Showers

ATHLONE
CLONMACNOIS
BALLINASLOE
SHANNON BRIDGE
SHANNON HARBOUR
BALLINASLOE LINE DERELICT
GRAND CANAL
CLONONY CASTLE
CLONFERT
BANAGHER
GARRYCASTLE
MEELICK
CLOGHAN CASTLE
DERRYHIVENNY CASTLE
REDWOOD CASTLE
TO PORTUMNA

ERA Maptec

Portumna to Meelick Leaving behind the hill of Portland, the river between here and Meelick is wide and the channel divides around a number of large islands. The navigation is on the west side to the head of Long Island and then it follows the east shore to Meelick. The still water in the channels behind the islands may look deep but there is a build-up of silt from the bog workings which make them very shallow in places. In order to prevent the river extending out over the low-lying land to the west when it is in flood, an embankment was erected all the way from Portumna to Meelick in more recent years with pumping stations at intervals.

Derryhivenny Castle While passing Long Island, Derryhivenny Castle can be seen about 1.5 km away to the west. This is a well preserved four-storey tower house with interesting fireplaces on the three upper floors. The tower forms part of an L-shaped bawn with rounded turrets at opposite corners. On the corbels of the machiolation at the north east corner is the inscription 'D:OM ME:FIERI: FECIT: 1643. It is one of the few dated castles in Ireland although it was common for the builder to leave his mark on a stone. It indicates that the castle was built by Daniel O'Madden in

Dundalgan Press

Derryhivenny Castle

1643, one of the last to be built, a few years before Ballynasheera Castle further downstream. The idea of dividing the windows with an upright stone, or mullion, and the Jacobean style chimney stacks, may have been copied from Portumna Castle which had been completed some twenty-five years earlier.

O'Sullivan Beare's Crossing At the upper end of Long Island, before the days of the navigation works, there was a ford called White's Ford. This was the place where O'Sullivan Beare crossed the river on his epic march to Leitrim on a cold January day in 1603. He had set out from Glengarriff in Co Cork with one thousand of his followers on 31 December, after defeat at Kinsale, in an effort to link up with Hugh O' Neill in Ulster. Harassed all the way, they reached Portumna to find the ferries closely guarded. Making their way up the east shore, they reached the ford and slaughtered some of their horses to provide themselves with much needed food and skins to form makeshift boats for the crossing. The river was in flood, extending out over the low land on the west side and it took many journeys to ferry his people across. Nearby, in Redwood Castle, the Queen's sheriff, MacEgan, learnt of their presence and attacked when the group was divided. There was great slaughter on both sides and MacEgan himself was killed. The depleted force continued northwards and thirty-five of them, sixteen armed men, eighteen non-combatants and one woman staggered into Leitrim Castle on 14 January. Passing under the modern power lines here today in this quiet spot it is hard to visualise the scene.

Redwood Castle To the east abreast of Ballymacegan Island, you may see a flag flying from the battlements of Redwood Castle; the present owner, himself a MacEgan, has restored the tower house and it is open to the public. Although only about 1.5 km from the river, it is not feasible to approach it over the marshy ground and it is easier to visit it by road from Portumna.

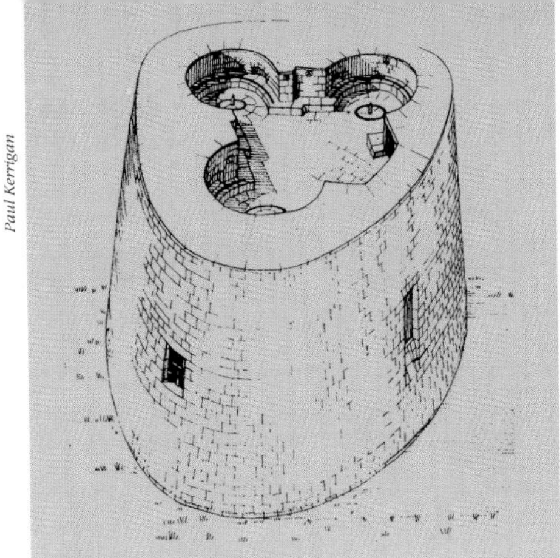

Paul Kerrigan

The cam-shaped martello tower on the island near Meelick lock

Cloghan Castle (approached on foot, about 3 km from Victoria lock, Meelick or by dinghy up the Little Brosna) is a fine five-storey towerhouse near the banks of the Little Brosna, strategically placed on the route along the esker ridge to the fords at Meelick, which was held at different periods by the MacCoughlans of West Offaly and the O'Maddens of East Galway. It was extended in the early nineteenth century and retains many of its late medieval defensive features.

Meelick (mí leac—low marshy place) is a complicated place with its canals, river channels and islands and it is necessary to consult the map to work it out. Below the lock the Little Brosna, the old canal and an overflow channel all enter on the east side while on the west side, around the top of Friar's Island, there is a strong flow from the weir. The large Victoria lock was constructed in the 1840s to cater for the steamers which had arrived on the river and which were too large for the old canal. It is worth walking across to look at this old canal and Hamilton lock, which is the site where the very first lock on the river was constructed in the 1750s. The lockhouse,

Ruth Delany

The martello tower at Meelick

Von Portumna nach Meelick

In neuerer Zeit wurde auf der Strecke von Portumna nach Meelick ein Deich errichtet, der Überschwemmungen des westlichen Flachlands verhindern soll.

Derryhivenny Castle

Gut erhaltenes, vierstöckiges Turmhaus. L-förmiger Burghof mit runden, einander gegenüberliegenden Türmen. 1643 von Daniel Madden gebaut.

O'Sullivan Beare's Übergang

Am oberen Ende von Long Island, wo O'Sullivan Beare 1602 auf seinem dramatischen Marsch nach Leitrim den Fluss überquerte. Er war mit tausend seiner Gefolgsleute aufgebrochen und wurde von MacEgan von der Burg Redwood überfallen. Nur fünfunddreissig zerschlagene und müde Krieger erreichten die Burg in Leitrim.

Redwood Castle

Der jetzige Besitzer, auch ein MacEgan, liess die Burg restaurieren. Sie ist für Besucher geöffnet.

Meelick

Abwechslungsreiche Gegend voll von Kanälen, Querverbindungskanälen und Inseln. Die Viktoria-Schleuse wurde um 1840, der alte Kanal und die Hamilton-Schleuse etwa um 1750 erbaut. Meelick war einst eine bedeutende Furt und wurde anfangs des 19. Jahrhunderts von den Briten zu einer Festung gegen eine mögliche französische Invasion von Westen her umgebaut. Auf der Insel westlich der Viktoria-Schleuse stehen ein Martelloturm, die Artilleriegebäude von Keelogue und eine von Wassergräben umgebene Steinfestung. Die Anlage wurde nie benutzt und gegen 1870 demoliert.

which bears the date over the door inside the porch, was built at this time but the lock was rebuilt in the early 1800s, leaving some traces of the original lock to be seen.

Meelick was an important fording place in the past and was the site of a medieval castle and a seventeenth century fort. This is one of the places that was strongly fortified in the early 1800s by the British who feared a French invasion from the west. Three earthwork batteries were erected here and another on Incherky Island further upstream which was replaced by a stone fortification about 1811. A martello tower was erected on the island to the west of Victoria lock; it is best approached on foot from the lock. It was one of the few cam-shaped towers erected in Ireland. A massive central pillar supports the roof on which three guns were mounted, probably one 24-pounder cannon and two howitzers firing an explosive iron shell. Some of the iron pivots, tracks and ring-bolts for handling the guns are still in position, also the original iron sheeted door raised high above the ground.

From the new quay above the weir it is possible to row across to Incherky Island to visit the Keelogue battery. This stone fort was surrounded by a moat and had a bomb-proof barrack at the rear with two howitzers on the roof. In the enclosure were seven 18-pounder or 24-pounder guns on traversing platforms, firing over the parapet to the north and west. The remains of one of the earlier earthwork batteries is at the north end of the island. The Keelogue battery looked out on the shallows of Keelogue which were subsequently removed by the Shannon Commissioners in the 1840s. This must have been one of the principal fording places on the river because when the shallows were being excavated, many interesting items were recovered at various levels including stone hatchets from prehistoric days. The Meelick fortifications were never needed and were dismantled in the 1870s when the development of rifled artillery had rendered such defences obsolete. They remained, however, in the hands of the military authorities and were garrisoned occasionally in times of crisis.

It is a short walk south along the river from the new quay to Meelick church. This is a medieval church which is still in use today. A Franciscan settlement was established here about 1414 and the main walls, the two aisle arches (with the figure of St Francis inserted later between them), the west doorway and a door that once led

Paul Kerrigan

Keelogue battery on the east shore above Meelick lock

Franziskanerkirche: Die tragenden Wände, zwei gewölbte Seitenschiffe und das Westtor sind Teil der ursprünglichen Klosterkirche. Das westliche Fenster und die Sakristei wahrscheinlich aus dem 17. Jahrhundert. Seit 1852 ist die Klostersiedlung verlassen. 1986 wurde die restaurierte Kirche wieder eröffnet. Die Landschaft um Meelick mit ihrer Hochwasserebene ist von internationaler Bedeutung als Überwinterungsgebiet für viele Arten von Wild- und Sumpfvögeln.

Von Meelick nach Banagher

Stromaufwärts von Meelick verändert sich der Fluss. Die Fahrrinne wird enger, der Shannon fliesst zeitweise in mehreren Flussarmen.

Victoria Lock, Meelick, built to accommodate the large steamers in the 1840's

Ruth Delany

into a south transept are part of the original friary church. The west window and sacristy probably date from the seventeenth century and there are also some remains of the domestic buildings. The settlement was abandoned in 1852 but the church was later renovated, and again extensively refurbished in 1984–5 including the erection of an interesting wooden altar-screen and Stations of the Cross by Ray Carroll. The area around Meelick and the Little Brosna, which enters the Shannon at this point, with its flood plain is of international importance for wintering wildfowl and waders.

Meelick to Banagher Upstream from Meelick the river changes in character. The banks are higher on each side and the river channel constricted. When the river is in flood, the great waters strain to pass through here and the back-up causes flooding upstream. There are two attractive houses on the west bank below Banagher, Shannon Grove and Shannon Lodge and Shamrock Cruisers base is located on the west shore in behind Inishee.

Banagher (beann char—pointed rocks).Carrick Craft and Silver Line have bases here and the Office of Public Works has made a fine new harbour here above the bridge. The town dates back to the seventeenth century plantation of Offaly but it must have been an important fording place from early times and there is evidence that there was an 18-arch bridge built here in 1049. It is not known how long this bridge survived but a medieval bridge of 27 arches was later erected and in 1685 a 17-arch bridge was built which the Shannon Commissioners replaced with the present bridge, completed in 1843. At that time there was a short length of canal with a lock by-passing the shallows here but the commissioners decided to abandon the canal and make a navigation channel up the river. The old canal with the lock at the downstream end and the harbour and lockhouse near the bridge can be seen on the west bank.

In the Napoleonic period Banagher was one of the Shannon crossings fortified against a French invasion from the west. On the west shore, beside the old canal, Fanesker martello tower was built about 1812. It is a smaller tower than the one at Meelick and is ellipitical in plan with a mounting on the roof for a 24-pounder cannon. Nearby on the river bank is an old MacCoghlan castle, known as Cromwell's Castle, which was strengthened at this time and used as a magazine with a second 24-pounder mounted on the roof. At the east end of the bridge can be seen the walls of a barracks, erected at the same period, which had three guns mounted on a platform firing directly along the old bridge, which was a short distance downstream of the present bridge. This barracks replaced an earlier fortification of the 1620s called Fort Falkland. Downstream of the town, on the east bank, there is a five-sided battery also dating from the Napoleonic period called Fort Eliza with mountings for four guns and

Banagher

Der Ort wurde während der Besiedlung von Offaly im 17. Jahrhundert gegründet, war aber schon lange vorher eine wichtige Furt. Im Jahre 1049 existierte bereits eine Brücke mit achtzehn Bogen, eine spätere hatte sogar 27 Bogen. 1685 wurde eine Brücke mit siebzehn Bogen gebaut, die 1843 der heutigen Platz machen musste. Damals führte ein kurzer Kanalabschnitt mit Schleuse an den Untiefen vorbei. Am Westufer sind noch der Hafen und das Schleusenwärterhaus zu sehen.

Banagher war ein Übergangspunkt über den Shannon, der gegen eine französische Invasion befestigt wurde. Der Fanesker Martelloturm stammt aus dem Jahr 1812. Die alte MacCoghlan-Burg wurde ebenfalls in dieser Zeit zu einer Festung ausgebaut. Am Ostende der Brücke stehen noch Mauern einer Kaserne. Das etwas stromabwärts gelegene fünfseitige Artilleriegebäude Fort Eliza aus napoleonischer Zeit ist am besten auf einem kurzen Weg, der ausserhalb des Dorfes abbiegt, zu erreichen.

Banagher bietet eine Reihe weiterer Sehenswürdigkeiten. Im Ort sind mehrere gute Führer erhältlich. Empfehlenswert ist eine Fahrt mit dem Torfbähnchen.

Shannon Harbour

Ende und letzter Hafen des Grand Canal. Die Ruinen von alten Gebäuden, unter anderem von

James Scully

An interesting engraving of Meelick Abbey, dated 1833, which indicates that it was in a ruinous state at that time

a strongly built magazine set in the centre. It is not possible to approach it from the river but it is only a short walk from the town down the first turn on the right.

Banagher has a number of other interesting features and there is a good local guide book. There are the ruins of St Rynagh's Abbey and 'Trollope's house', the little cottage in which the author lived when he was stationed here as a deputy postal surveyor in I841. Little remains of Cuba Court nearby which was built for George Frazer, a former governor of Cuba, in about 1730. Sir Edward Lovett Pearce was said to have been its architect and the local Royal Free School moved into it in 1818. Charlotte Brontë spent part of her honeymoon there with her husband, the Rev. Arthur Bell Nicholls, just nine months before her death and he is buried in the Church of Ireland graveyard here.

Garrycastle (about 2 km) was the chief castle of the MacCoughlan clan. The tower house itself is mostly in ruins but the surrounding bawn wall is mostly intact and includes a fine gateway.

Shannon Harbour It is well worth visiting the terminus of the Grand Canal by locking up through two locks from the river or lying below the locks and walking up along the towpath. The old buildings here evoke the past when it was a busy centre. The old hotel, now in ruins, was opened in 1806 and many emigrants passed through here in the 1820s–40s on their way to seek new lives. The two locks leading up to the harbour from the river were built to the same size as the original Shannon Navigation locks and are larger than the rest of the locks on the Grand Canal. They were further enlarged in 1946 to accommodate new motor barges by the rather crude process of paring off the stone with pneumatic drills.

Clonony Castle About 1.5 km from Shannon Harbour there is a fine sixteenth-century tower house, Clonony Castle. It has a well preserved fortified enclosure, or bawn. It was restored and inhabited in the last century by an eccentric lawyer but is now in bad repair. There is an interesting grave slab here of the Boleyn family which was unearthed by workmen digging clay for the canal.

The Ballinasloe Line Across the river from the entrance to the Grand Canal is Fanning's lock, the first of two locks on the extension of the canal to Ballinasloe. This canal was completed in 1828, closed to navigation in 1961 and has virtually disappeared in bog workings today. It is surprising that the Grand Canal Company

An engraving of the old bridge at Banagher

einem Hotel (1806 in Betrieb genommen), machen die Vergangenheit lebendig. Von 1820 bis 1840 war Shannon Harbour ein wichtiger Durchgangspunkt für Auswanderer auf ihrem Weg nach Amerika.

Die Ballinasloe-Linie

Dieser Kanalabschnitt wurde 1828 fertiggestellt und 1961 für die Schiffahrt geschlossen. Heute ist er in der Torf- und Moorlandschaft praktisch verschwunden, als Relikt steht mitten in der Wiese eine Schleuse. Bis gegen 1840 überspannte hier eine Holzbrücke den Shannon, auf der Pferde auf die andere Flussseite gebracht werden konnten. Dann wurde sie von einer Kettenfähre ersetzt. Reste der Holzbrücke und der Anlegestelle der Fähre sind noch zu sehen.

Ruth Delany

Shannon Harbour, the terminus of the Grand Canal during a rally in 1975

Clonony Castle, near Shannon Harbour, a tower house with a very well preserved bawn

did not make use of the River Suck instead of making a canal but the reason for this was that the boats were still horse-drawn at that time and the additional expense of making towpaths from Shannon Harbour to the Suck and along that river to Ballinasloe made it less expensive to build a canal. Ironically, by the time the canal was finished, steamers had arrived on the river and towpaths would no longer have been needed. The Shannon was spanned by a wooden bridge for bringing the horses across until the 1840s when it was replaced by a chain ferry, which in turn was abandoned when the boats became mechanised. Some remnants of the wooden bridge can be seen on the east side connecting the mainland to Bullock Island and the terminal points of the ferry can also be seen.

Clonfert (cluain fearta—the meadow of the grave)It is difficult to approach from the river but there are plans to build a jetty at the bend in the river where it is only about 1.6km distance. It can also be visited by car from Banagher or by walking along the line of the old Ballinasloe Line to the first bridge. From this bridge it is possible to see the extent of the bog workings. After many years of experimentation it was found that the best way to dry turf was to mill it finely and allow it to dry naturally over the summer months. Machines were devised to scrape the surface of the bog and the milled peat is then heaped up into ridges when it is dry. A light railway uses the bed of the old canal for part of the way to transport the milled peat to the power station at Shannonbridge.

St Brendan founded a monastic settlement here in the sixth century and is reputed to be buried under the large slab near the church. He was the famous navigator who has been credited with the first discovery of America; the tale of his travels, the *Navigatio Brendani*, was one of the best known pieces of travel literature in the Middle Ages and a translation of it is in print. In the twelfth century the Irish monastic church gave way to a diocesan church and Clonfert was chosen as the centre of one diocese. It is from this time that the facade of the cathedral dates with its famous doorway which is one of the supreme examples of Irish Romanesque architecture. The doorway is in six orders with an amazing variety of carvings surmounted by a triangular pediment. The slope of the jambs of the door is accentuated by the inner order which is vertical and was a later addition. This slope had been necessary in earlier church buildings to support the heavy lintels but although not necessary here, this feature

Clonony Castle

Schönes Turmhaus aus dem 16. Jahrhundert. Es hat einen gut erhaltenen, befestigten Burghof mit Ringmauer (Bawn). Im 19. Jahrhundert wurde es restauriert.

Clonfert

Am besten zu erreichen über die Strasse von Banagher aus (Taxi). Der Heilige Brendan gründete hier im 6. Jahrhundert eine Klostersiedlung und soll selbst unter einem grossen Grabstein in der Nähe der Kirche begraben sein. Im 12. Jahrhundert wurde Clonfert zum Bischofssitz erhoben. Aus dieser Zeit stammt die Fassade mit ihrem berühmten Eingangstor, einem der prächtigsten Beispiele irisch-romanischer Architektur. Die Kirche wurde verschiedentlich umgebaut. Aus dem 13. Jahrhundert stammt der Chor mit seinem im Übergangsstil gehaltenen Ostfenster. Der mit Engelsfiguren und einer rätselhaften Seejungfrau verzierte Chorbogen wurde im 15. Jahrhundert hinzugefügt. Im 19. Jahrhundert durchgeführte Restaurierungsarbeiten werden stark kritisiert. Anderthalb Kilometer weiter in Richtung Eyrecourt befindet sich in der katholischen Kirche eine aus Holz geschnitzte, aus dem 14. Jahrhun-

The famous doorway at Clonfert Cathedral, one of the finest examples of Irish Romanesque

was retained. The building has been much altered at different times; the chancel is thirteenth century with a transitional east window, and the carved chancel arch, decorated with angels and a strange mermaid-type figure, who seems to be holding a mirror in her hand, was a fifteenth century insertion. A Romanesque south transept is now in ruins and a Gothic north transept has been removed; it was probably added at the same time as the bell tower. Restoration work carried out in the nineteenth century has been much criticised. Nearby is the former bishop's palace and the bishop walked from his cathedral up a fine yew walk which had side walks, creating the impression of a cruciform cathedral; one of the side aisles is now gone but the walk is still impressive. About 1.5 km up the road to Eyrecourt in the RC church there is an interesting wooden statue of the Madonna and Child, said to date back to the fourteenth century. It lay hidden for centuries until it was found locally in a tree and is much venerated today.

The River Suck is currently being made navigable to Ballinasloe with the removal of fords in the river and the construction of a lock and weir at Pollboy. The lock and weir are being constructed to reduce the impact on the fishing and the works including moorings at Ballinasloe are due to be completed in 2000. The river Suck has always been an excellent fishing river with convenient bank mooring in a number of places.

Shannonbridge Most of the bridges along the Shannon were rebuilt by the Shannon Commissioners in the 1840s but this one was considered to be sufficiently sound and just needed some underpinning. This bridge at Raghra, as it was then called, was completed in 1757 at the same time as the early navigation works were commencing. It was found that there was just a fall of 0.3 m to overcome at the shallows here and so a short length of canal was constructed with a flash lock, or single set of gates, on the east side, and the attractive two-storey lockhouse dates from this time. The Grand Canal Company subsequently made a conventional lock here in the early 1800s and the Shannon Commissioners decided to remove the canal and lock and dredge out a channel in the 1840s. Beneath the navigation arch the recesses for the gates of one side of the old lock are visible and the quay wall with the small harbour below the bridge are part of the old canal works.

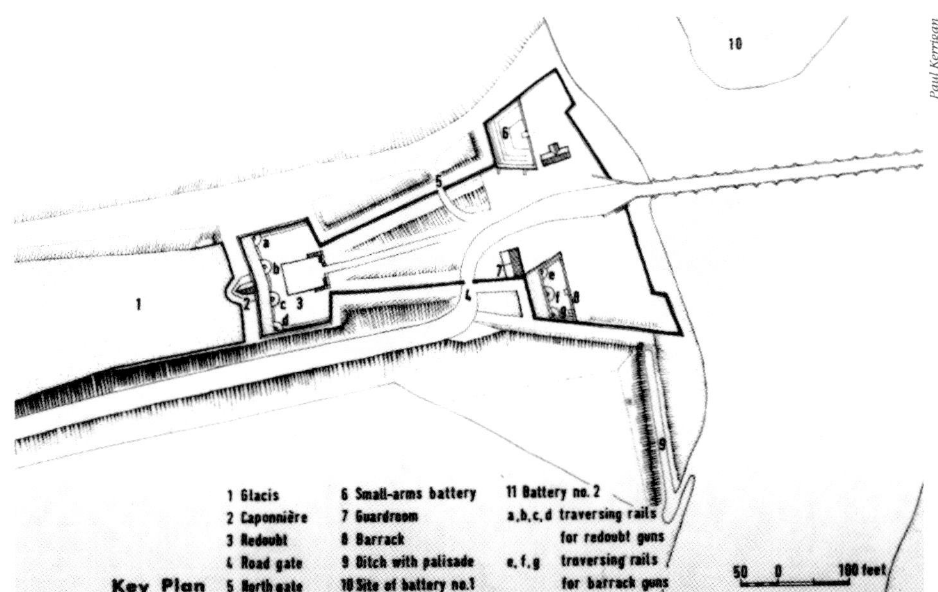

A plan of Shannonbridge fortifications

The nineteenth century anti-Napoleonic defences at Shannonbridge are even more extensive than those at Meelick or Banagher and are considered to be a unique example of artillery fortifications of the Napoleonic period. It is not at first apparent just how extensive they are and the asymmetrical drawing gives an impression of the layout. A glacis (1) or artificial slope, extending some 180 m protected the main redoubt (3) which had four guns on traversing rails with living quarters for the men beneath. A dry moat

dert stammende Madonna mit Kind, die jahrhundertelang verschollen war.

River Suck

Der River Suck ist jetzt fast bis nach Ballinasloe schiffbar. Gemäss Planung sollten die Arbeiten bis zur Stadt noch 1999 beendet sein. Achtung: Die Bord na Mona Eisenbahnbrücke ist sehr niedrig, grössere Schiffe können nicht passieren.

Shannonbridge

Die meisten Brücken entlang des Shannon wurden in den 40er Jahren des 19. Jahrhunderts umgebaut, aber diese erwies sich als weiterhin genügend tragfähig. Sie war 1757 fertiggestellt worden. Damals wurden auch ein kurzer Kanalabschnitt und eine Schleuse mit nur einem Paar Tore auf der Ostseite gebaut. Das schöne zweistöckige Schleusenwärterhaus stammt aus dieser Zeit. Gegen 1840 liess die Shannon Aufsichtsbehörde Kanal und Schleuse entfernen. Unterhalb der Brücke sind die Einbuchtungen für die Schleusentore und die alte Schleuse noch zu sehen. Die anfangs des 19. Jahrhunderts gegen Napoleon errichtete Verteidigungsanlage ist ein einzigartiges Beispiel einer Artilleriefestung aus dieser Epoche. Ein Glacis (1), das heisst ein künstlicher Abhang von etwa 180 m Breite, schützte die Hauptredoute (Schanze, 3). Ein was-

separated the glacis from the redoubt and into it a caponnier (2) projected, from which the defending musket men could pick off anyone who succeeded in gaining access to the moat. High protecting walls surrounded the redoubt and the main road passed through these walls by an arched gateway (4) which was later removed to cater for modern traffic. There was another gateway in the north wall (5) with a small-arms battery (6) protecting the north flank and on the south side, a guardroom (7) and large blockhouse (8). This is the building visible from the river and it was used as a powder magazine and quarters for the soldiers with three guns mounted on the roof. A ditch with a palisade (9) and a battery on the end of Long Island provided additional protection for the bridge. On the east side of the river there was another barracks, now demolished and replaced by the modern garda station, with a further powder magazine set in behind it protected by the high wall. There are indications that there was another earthwork battery on the east side of the river downstream of the bridge. An obvious weakness in these defences was their vulnerability to attack from the east: none of the guns could be trained in this direction. The defences were not completed until 1817 and cost about £30,000. Aware of their existence through their Irish informants, the French had planned to include boats in their invasion force so that the river could be forded elsewhere. These elaborate defences were never put to the test and by the 1860s this type of fortification had been rendered obsolete by the development of rifled artillery.

Exploring inland from the river, in places less than 0.5 km, there is a very different habitat. This is bog or peatland, characteristic of much of the Irish midlands, which began to be formed 3,500 years ago when climatic conditions changed to favour bogforming plants (sphagnum moss in particular). Apparently flat and featureless from a distance, bogs have many interesting plants: heather, cross-leaved heath, bog rosemary, bog cotton, asphodel, cranberry, as well as many species of sphagnum moss and lichens. These bogs provide fuel, traditionally as handcut turf, but since the 1950s mechanical cutting has resulted in large-scale exploitation of these bogs. Shannonbridge power station, visible in the landscape for many miles, is the largest peat-powered electricity generating station in Ireland and commenced operations in 1965.

Shannonbridge to Athlone The river from Shannonbridge to Athlone might be considered by some to be dull and uninteresting, winding its way through the flat central plain, but it is of great ecological interest and is largely unfished because of the few road approaches. On this stretch of river, and particularly well represented at Clonmacnois, is a type of vegetation called callow, which is considered by scientists to be the richest of its kind in Europe. The land is submerged in winter by silt laden floods and dries out sufficiently in summer to allow haycutting and grazing. As the callows have never been drained, ploughed and only recently been artificially fertilised, the vegetation is the same as that used by the monks 1,000 years ago. At the water's edge is an area of reedswamp, behind which is a zone dominated by sedge tussocks. Behind this are the hay meadows made up of grasses and sedges, meadowsweet, ragged robin, meadow bedstraw, the rare marsh pea, purple lousewort and the common buttercup. In drier parts purple moor grass forms dense tussocks. The callows are an important habitat for birds in summer and winter: in summer skylarks, meadow pipits and the now rare corncrake live; in winter, when the river floods and increases in breadth tenfold, the area is teeming with

serloser Graben trennte Glacis und Redoute, in die ein überdachter Wehrgang (Caponnier, 2) hineinführte. Die Redoute war von hohen Mauern umgeben, durch die die Hauptstrasse unterhalb eines Torbogens verlief (4). In der Nordmauer befand sich ein weiteres Tor mit Schiessplatz für Handfeuerwaffen, einer Wachstube (7) und einem grossen Blockhaus (8), das vom Fluss aus zu sehen ist. Die ganze Anlage wurde erst gegen 1817 fertig und kostete 30'000 Pfund. Da die Franzosen von irischen Sympathisanten über diese Festung informiert waren, planten sie, an einer andern Stelle des Flusses zu übersetzen.

Beim Erforschen der näheren Umgebung entdeckt man in unmittelbarer Nähe eine ganz andere Art von Landschaftstyp. Das für grosse Teile der irischen Tiefebene charakteristische Torfmoor hat sich vor etwa 3'500 Jahren gebildet. Es ist reich an interessanten Pflanzen und liefert den auf traditionelle Weise handgestochenen Torf. In den 50er Jahren wurde mit dem maschinellen Torfabbau begonnen, was leider zu einer gefährlichen Übernutzung dieser Moorlandschaft führte. Das Kraftwerk von Shannonbridge ist das grösste Torfkraftwerk Irlands und wurde 1965 in Betrieb genommen.

Von Shannonbridge nach Athlone

Dieser Flussabschnitt ist von grosser ökologischer Bedeutung. Hier wird nur wenig gefischt, und es existiert eine höchst vielfältige Flora. Die im Winter überflutete sumpfige Niederung trocknet im Sommer genügend aus, um Heuernte und das Weiden von Vieh zu gestatten. Die Gegend ist Sommer wie Winter ein Zufluchtsort für Vögel. Sie soll, mit Clonmacnois als Zentrum, wegen ihrer kulturellen und natürlichen Vielfalt als Naturschutzgebiet erhalten und unter staatliche Verwaltung gestellt werden. Westlich von Clonmacnois dehnt sich das Mongan Moor aus. Es bietet ideale Lebensbedingungen für Pflanzen, die wie zum Beispiel Heidekraut, Moose und Flechten säurehaltigen Boden vertragen. Dieses Moor gehört zu den letzten seiner Art in Europa erhaltenen und soll unter Naturschutz gestellt werden. Esker sind gewundene, langgestreckte Geschiebehügel aus der Eiszeit. Sie bildeten sich, als Schmelzwasser unterhalb der Eisdecke grosse Mengen von Sand, Kieselsteinen und Felsbrocken ablagerte.

Es gibt hier noch eine Reihe weiterer Sehenswürdigkeiten wie zum Beispiel die frühchristliche Klostersiedlung von Clonmacnois, den Stein von Clonfinlough, das Blackwatermoor,

ducks, gulls, waders, swans and geese. Most numerous are the widgeon, lapwing, blackheaded gull, golden plover, blacktailed godwit and curlew. The Clonmacnois area has been comprehensively studied and described and because of the richness of its man-made and natural heritage, it is proposed that it be managed and conserved in a coordinated manner as a Heritage Zone.

Raised bog can be seen at Mongan bog, east of Clonmacnois, between two esker ridges. It differs from much of the rest of the Shannon system, encouraging peatland and acid-tolerant species like heathers, mosses and lichen. This is one of the last unworked areas of raised bog in Europe and it is to be preserved as an example of a habitat that once covered a large proportion of the landscape of the midlands of Ireland.

An interesting landscape feature of the river between Portumna and Athlone are the winding ridges of higher ground, known as eskers, which provided early settlers and travellers with dry ground and river crossing points. Eskers cross the river at Banagher, Shannonbridge and Athlone and they can be seen also between Portumna and Banagher and at Clonmacnois from where one esker swings south along the east shore to Shannonbridge, a route still followed by a road today. Eskers were formed at the end of the Ice Age when melted water rivers beneath the ice deposited huge amounts of sand, gravel and boulders. When the ice cover had completely melted a ridge of sand and gravel remained behind. They were once wooded with oak, hazel and elm; now cleared by man most eskers have a species rich grassland. The grasses are predominently fescues, and other plants include dog daisy, milkwort, birds foot trefoil, scabious, yellow wort and clovers.

In addition to the callows and Mongan Bog there are other interesting features in the area. There is of course the monastic

Office of Public Works

Clonmacnois: ORourke's Tower and the Cross of the Scriptures

site at Clonmacnois, the Clonfinlough Stone, the Blackwater Bog to the south, which was cut in the sixties, the limestone quarry at Clorhane, where the Shannon Commissioners obtained some of the stone for their works at Athlone, and Fin Lough, a shallow lake which is rich in fascinating plant and bird life. This lake was deeper at one time and a crannóg (an artificial island, an early lake dwelling) was found at the south-west corner by the Geological Survey in 1884.

Clonmacnois (cluain mhic Nóis—the meadow of the son of Nós) was founded by St Ciarán in about AD 545. He is reputed to have come down the Shannon from his hermit's cell on Hare Island to establish this monastic settlement where the east-west route, the Eiscir Riada, along the esker ridges of central Ireland, met the north-south route of the Shannon. Although St Ciarán died seven months later, Clonmacnois grew into a great monastic city famed throughout Europe. It was subjected to Viking attacks at the end of the eighth and early ninth centuries and again in the tenth century. It was not just the Vikings who attacked, sometimes it was Irish Kings who coveted the wealth of the monastery. From the twelfth century it began to decline in importance and, finally, in 1552, the place was sacked and looted by English soldiers from Athlone. By the end of the sixteenth century the churches were in ruins. It continued to be used as a burial ground and became of interest to antiquarians. The centre has exhibitions and an audio-visual show and there is also a tearoom. The opening hours are: November - mid-March 10.00-17.30; mid-March - mid-May 10.00-18.00; mid-May - early September 09.00-19.00; September - October 10.00-18.00 every day, last admission 45 minutes before closing. Guided tour on request: tel. 0905-74195. There is a small charge. The following are the chief items of interest:

The Cross of the Scriptures at Clonmacnois

Ruth Delany

1. The South Cross dates from the ninth century and has a representation of the Crucifixion on the shaft.

2. Temple Doolin, originally called Temple Hurpain, was built probably some time after 800. The building was restored as a family chantry in 1689 by Edmund Dowling, who inserted a new door.

3. Temple Hurpain, probably added at the same time by Dowling, takes its name from the older church and has also been called MacLaffey's church.

4. Temple Rí, the king's church, or Temple Melaghlin, is late twelfth century.

den Kalksteinbruch in Clorhane und Fin Lough, einen seichten See, der reich an vielen faszinierenden Pflanzen- und Vogelarten ist. An seiner südwestlichen Ecke wurde 1884 ein Crannog, ein Pfahlbau auf einer künstlichen Insel, gefunden.

Clonmacnois

Von St. Ciaran um etwa 548 gegründet. Entwickelte sich zu einer in ganz Europa berühmten Kloster-Universitätsstadt. Gegen Ende des 8., im frühen 9. und wieder im 10. Jahrhundert wurde Clonmacnois von wiederholten Angriffen der Wikinger heimgesucht. Zur Abwechslung raubten auch irische Könige das Kloster aus. 1552 plünderten und zerstörten in Athlone stationierte britische Soldaten den Ort, Ende des Jahrhunderts waren von allen Kirchen nur noch Ruinen vorhanden.

1. Südliches Hochkreuz, 9. Jahrhundert.

2. Tempel Doolin, wahrscheinlich kurz nach 800 gebaut und 1089 renoviert.

3. Tempel Hurpain, vermutlich aus derselben Zeit.

4. Tempel Ri, spätes 12. Jahrhundert. Bemerkenswert sind das Ostfenster im Übergangsstil, ein frühgotisches Spitzbogenfenster, ein spätgotisches Portal und Anzeichen einer hölzernen Empore.

5. Tempel Ciaran, nach der Überlieferung die Grabstätte des heiligen Ciaran. Das Grab soll sich an dem am weitesten vom Eingang entfernten Ende befinden.

6. Tempel Kelly, vermutlich aus dem Jahr 1167.

7. Nördliches Kreuz, ein stark verwittertes Kreuz aus dem 9. Jahrhundert.

8. Kathedrale, ursprünglicher Bau 904. Umbauarbeiten im 11., 14. und 15. Jahrhundert. Die Figuren über dem Portal aus dem 15. Jahrhundert stellen von links nach rechts die Heiligen Dominik, Patrick und Francis dar.

9. Das Hochkreuz der Heiligen Schrift wurde im 9. oder 10. Jahrhundert gestaltet. Es ist eines der prachtvollsten und am besten erhaltenen irischen Hochkreuze.

10. O'Rourke's Turm, oberer Teil erst 1124 vollendet.

11. Tempel O'Connor, erbaut 1010. Im 18. Jahrhundert restauriert, diente als protestantisches Gotteshaus.

12. Tempel Finian, 12. Jahrhundert.

13. Gedenksteine und mit Kreuzen verzierte Steintafeln für die Clonmacnois berühmt ist. Die im 10. Jahrhundert erbaute Nonnenkirche wurde

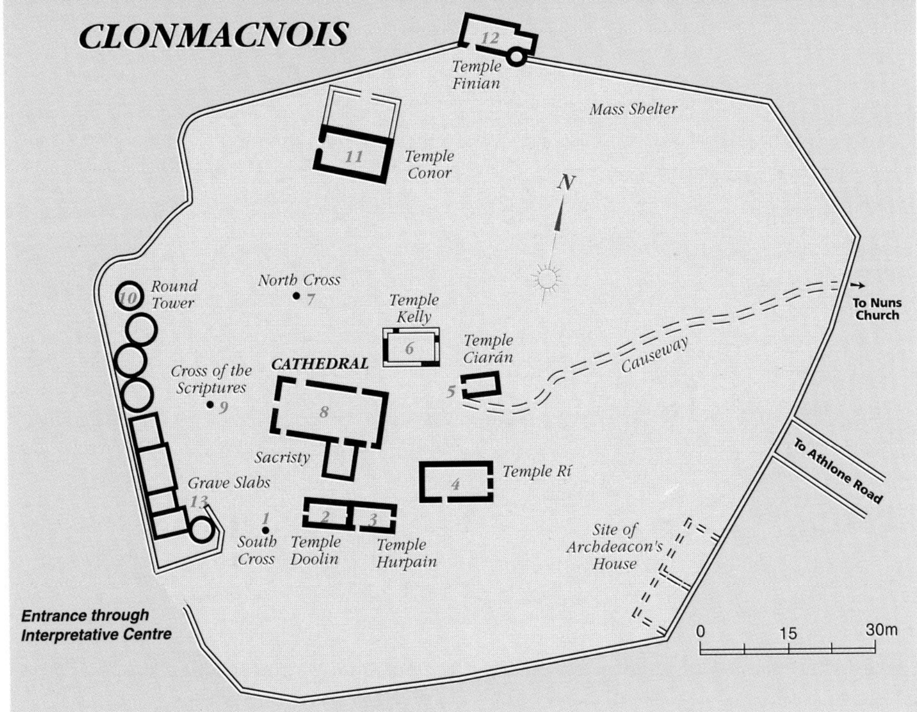

Notable features are the Western Transitional east window with plain moulding, an early Gothic lancet window, a late Gothic doorway and indications of a timber gallery over the west half of the building.

5. Temple Ciarán is traditionally the burial place of the founding saint. The remains of three antae (corner projections) indicate that it could date from about 800 but the building has been altered from time to time. St Ciarán's grave is said to be at the end farthest from the entrance.

6. Temple Kelly is thought to have been erected in 1167 by Conor Kelly on the site of an earlier hospital.

7. The North Cross is a much weathered cross of the ninth century.

8. The Cathedral was originally erected in 904 but little of this early building has survived subsequent rebuilding in the eleventh, fourteenth, and fifteenth centuries. The figures over the fine fifteenth century doorway are, from left to right, St Dominic, St Patrick and St Francis.

9. The Cross of the Scriptures was erected in the ninth or tenth century and is one of the most graceful and best-preserved of the Irish high crosses.

10. O'Rourke's Tower is ascribed to Fergal O'Rourke, King of Connacht, who died in 964, but the upper part was not finished until 1124.

11. Temple Conor was built in 1010 by Cathal O'Conor and was restored in the

1166 wieder aufgebaut. Das Westportal und der freistehende Chorbogen sind herrliche Beispiele des irisch-romanischen Stils. Sie wurden 1865 sorgfältig restauriert. Der Fussweg zur Nonnenkirche ist der Beginn des Pilgerpfads. Der alte Weg verläuft oben auf der Eskerstrasse. Der St. Finnianbrunnen befindet sich nordwestlich vom Tempel Finnian. Der St. Ciaran's Brunnen liegt 400 Meter südwestlich von der Normannenburg.

Die 1214 erbaute Burg wurde vor vielen Jahren durch eine Explosion zerstört.

Der Stein von Clonfinlough

Hinter der Kirche von Clonfinlough steht ein grosser Felsblock, der mit ähnlichen Einkerbungen verziert ist, wie man sie auch in Spanien findet. Sie sollen auf die Bronzezeit zurückgehen.

Athlone

Die Stadt ist der wichtigste Übergangspunkt am mittleren Shannon. 1129 wurden hier wegen der strategisch günstigen Lage eine Festung und eine Brücke aus Holz errichtet. Im 13. Jahrhundert bauten die Normannen die heute noch existierende Burg mit einer Brücke und der Stadtmauer. Im 16. Jahrhundert wurden die Engländer wieder zunehmend mächtiger, nahmen die Burg in Besitz und bauten 1567 eine neue Steinbrücke. Während der Belagerung von 1691 leisteten die Anhänger Jakobs II. tapferen Widerstand. Im Laufe des 18. Jahrhunderts diente die Burg als Kaserne. Sie wurde mehrfach umgestaltet und mit Geschützen ausgestattet, als um 1800 eine französische Invasion drohte. Die runden Türme und Teile des inneren Burgfrieds stammen aus dem 13. Jahrhundert. Im Burgmuseum befindet sich eine Sammlung von Antiquitäten sowie eine Ausstellung über Athlone's

Walter Borner

Clonmacnois

eighteenth century to serve as a C of I church. The west door and the smallest of the south windows are original. On the north side are tombs of the Malone family.

12. Temple Finian is a nave and chancel church of the twelfth century with an interesting small belfry tower attached. It is sometimes called MacCarthy's Church because members of that family were buried here.

13. Commemorative slabs. Some of the finest of the cross-decorated slabs, for which Clonmacnois is renowned, are displayed in the ticket and tourist office by the car park.

The Nun's Church was originally built in the tenth century and was restored in 1166 by Dervorgilla, whose association with Dermot MacMurrough led to the coming of the Normans. The west doorway and chancel arch are beautiful examples of Irish Romanesque architecture and were restored in 1865.

The path leading to the Nun's Church is the start of the Pilgrim's Road, the old route along the ridge of the esker. The crosses erected halfway along the path marked the graves of three thieves who many years earlier were refused burial in the consecrated ground of the graveyard.

St Finian's well is about 180 m to the north-west of Temple Finian and St Ciarán's well is about 500 m south-west of the Norman castle, to the right of the Shannonbridge road. The castle, known as King John's Castle, was erected in 1214 by the English Justiciar, John de Gray. The ruins are of the gatehouse, courtyard and keep which were ripped apart by an explosion many years ago.

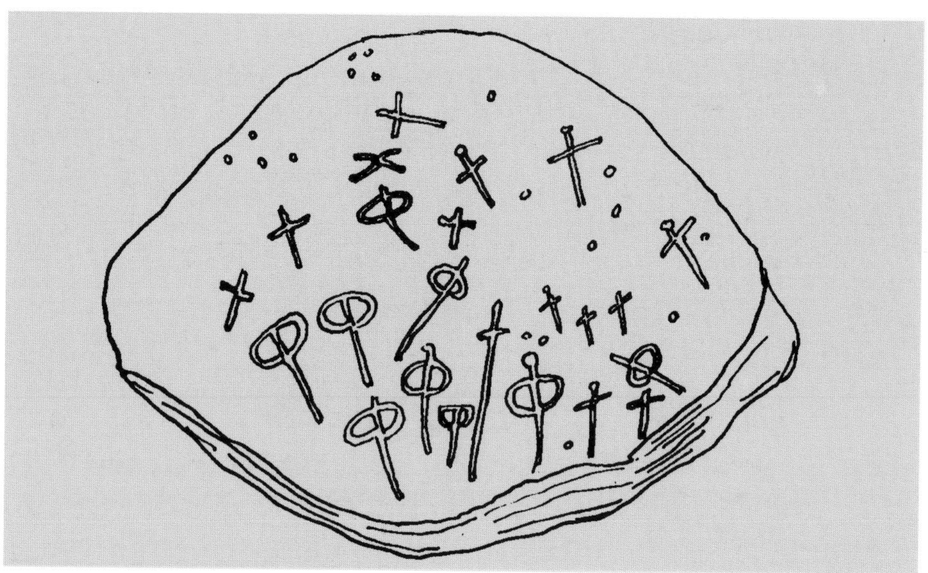

An interpretation of the strange drawings on the Clonfinlough Stone by Harry Rice

The Clonfinlough Stone About 5 km away, a short distance from the road to Athlone, in a field behind Clonfinlough Church, there is a large boulder decorated with markings, similar to rock markings found in Spain which are said to date from the Bronze Age. Some of the markings, which look like little men with arms akimbo, are carved circles with lines through them, but these lines may have been caused by natural erosion.

Athlone (áth Luain—the ford of Luan) owes its existence to its situation on the principal crossing point on the middle Shannon. The earliest evidence of settlement in the locality is a megalithic tomb, dating from c. 2500 BC at Drum on the western edge of the town. Numerous Bronze Age artefacts have been recovered from the river bed. The existence of an Early Christian monastery is suggested by the recent discovery of several early grave slabs now on view in the Castle Museum. Athlone's strategic significance was recognised by 1129 when Toirrdelbach Ua Conchobair, the expansionist king of Connacht, erected a wooden fort and bridge to facilitate his incursions into Meath. The coming of the Normans was followed in the thirteenth century by the erection of the present stone castle on the west bank of the river, with a bridge and a town wall.

berühmten Tenor John McCormack. Für den Stadtrundgang ist im Touristenbüro in der Burg ein guter Führer erhältlich. Die alte, enge Brücke von 1500 wurde 1844-46 durch die noch heute im Gebrauch stehende ersetzt. Die Eisenbahnbrücke wurde 1850 erbaut. 1937 wurde die Peter- und Paulskirche vollendet. Der Innenraum ist mit sehr schönen Buntglasfenstern ausgestattet. Zwischen Kirche und Fluss steht die Bronzebüste des Tenors McCormack. Wer allerdings Athlone näher besichtigen möchte, sollte sich nicht durch den von Paris entlehnten Begriff 'Left bank' (Rive gauche) verwirren lassen. Das linke Ufer liegt nämlich auf der rechten Flussseite.

1950 entbrannte der vorläufig letzte Kampf um die Brücke respektive um alle Brücken am Shannon, die möglichst niedrig über den Fluss geführt werden sollten. Diese Absicht der Behörden führte zur Gründung der Inland Waterways Association of Ireland (I.W.A.I.), die sich erfolgreich für die Offenhaltung des Flusses für die Schiffahrt einsetzte.

There was a Franciscan house from 1240 and, west of the river, the priory of SS Peter and Paul, the sole Cluniac Benedictine foundation in Ireland. The monks owned valuable eel fisheries in the river and benefited in 1290 from an early case of compensation for industrial interference with the environment when they were paid 40 shillings in silver for losses sustained in their fish pools by the erection of the king's mills on the river.

But the settlement declined with the general decay of the Norman colony after 1300. The revival of English authority in Ireland in the sixteenth century was marked at Athlone by the reoccupation of the castle by government forces in 1537, followed thirty years later by the completion in less than twelve months of Sir Henry Sidney's new stone bridge across the Shannon. For the next hundred years the provincial government of Connacht had its headquarters in the castle.

Athlone's revival in the early seventeenth century was marked by considerable building activity. The ruins of Court Devenish House, with its distinctive stone-mullioned Jacobean windows, date from this period. A substantial portion of a new town wall, including two bastions, may be seen at Railway View. The larger of the towers at the nineteenth century C of I church survives from the parish church of 1622. Athlone figured in Confederate and Cromwellian wars and later, in 1690 and 1691, it was the scene of important sieges. In the siege of 1691 over 21,000 cannon-

Walter Borner

Athlone

Coosan Cut

Walter Borner

balls reduced the Connacht town to rubble. The defending Jacobites put up a brave resistance of which the highlight was the defence of the bridge by Sergeant Custume and a small party of soldiers all of whom were killed. Finally the town fell when the Williamites forded the river and stormed the Irish defences.

In the eighteenth century the castle functioned as an extension of the military barracks which was being developed nearby. It was extensively remodelled and equipped with artillery at the time of the French invasion threat around 1800. It is not easy to distinguish between the earlier and later works in the castle: the round towers of the curtain wall facing the river and sections of the central keep are part of thirteenth century works and were reduced in height when heavy guns were mounted on them. At this period, too, very extensive fortifications were erected to the west of the town to protect the bridgehead. In 1967 the military authorities finally handed over the castle to the Board of Works and it its now an interpretative centre. An excellent Tourist Trail is available locally and a copy should be obtained by anyone wishing to explore the town.

The bridge erected in the 1560s was very narrow, only 4.3 m wide, with three mills on it and it was frequently the scene of much confusion. The Shannon Commissioners replaced it in 1844–6 with the present structure a short distance upstream. The location of the old bridge is marked by one of the buttresses on the east side and the street facing it is still called 'Main Street' today. In addition to building the new bridge the commissioners built a new lock and weir and carried out extensive deepening of the river, by-passing the original canal and lock to the west which dated back to the 1750s.

Wineport Restaurant, Inner Lakes

Walter Borner

Part of the old canal is still there but the lock area has been filled in. The new lock and bridge were constructed using coffer dams but a large dam was built above the railway bridge to complete the work on the weir; the water was turned down the old canal and the entire river bed was dried out for two months until the waters could be held in check no longer.

The fine railway bridge, over 163.5 m long, was built in 1850, designed for the Midland Great Western Railway Company by George Hemans, and the line was completed to Galway by 1851. The two stations (the old M&GWR station on the west side has recently been abandoned for the GS&WR one east of the river) are a reminder of the days when the two railway companies were fighting for the territory west of the Shannon.

The church of SS Peter and Paul dominates the skyline on the west shore. It was completed in 1937 and the splendid interior includes windows by the Harry Clarke Studio and Sarah Purser. Between the church and the river is a bronze bust of John McCormack, the famous tenor, who was born in Athlone.

In the 1950s a second battle of Athlone bridge took place when the Inland Waterways Association of Ireland was formed to promote Irish rivers and canals and to fight plans to erect fixed bridges over the Shannon. At that time there was a metal opening span over the navigation at Athlone and resistance to the fixed span was finally withdrawn when the importance of the Shannon as a tourist amenity became recognised and an adequate headroom at all fixed bridges was assured.

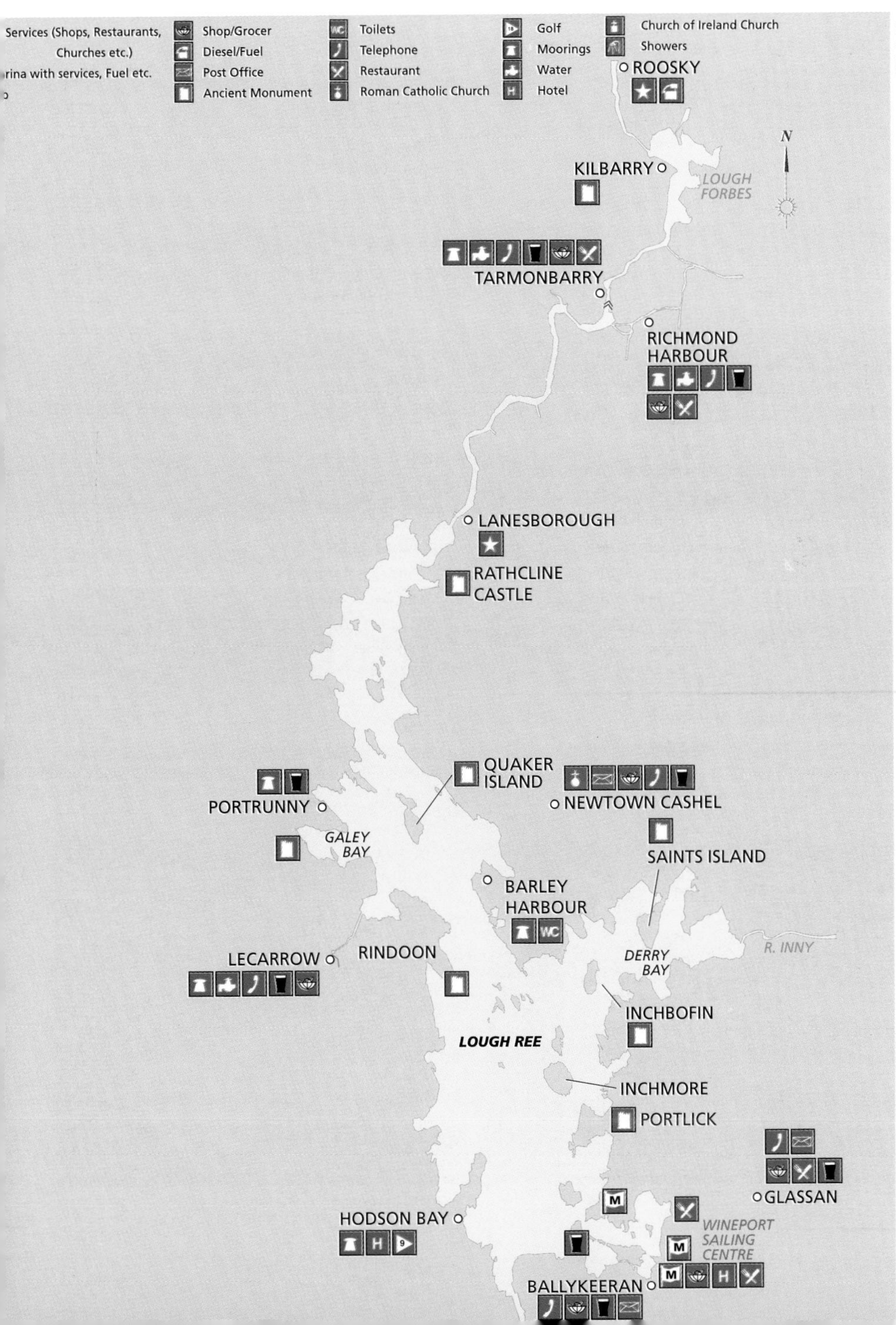

Lough Ree Yacht Club Emerging into Lough Ree, the conspicuous cross on the top of Ballyglass Hill can be seen, one of many erected in Ireland in the Marian Year, 1950. The Lough Ree Yacht Club has its premises here. It lays claim to being the second oldest yacht club in the world although the records of the club do not go back to these early days. There is evidence that there was yacht racing on the lake in the 1730s and the club is said to have dated from 1770. In 1895 the Killinure Yacht Club, which was based in the Inner Lakes nearby, amalgamated with the Athlone Yacht Club and adopted the name Lough Ree Yacht Club, moving to the present premises in 1914. Morgan Giles's Shannon One Design has been raced here since the 1920s and keel boats, which had disappeared from the lake for many years, are now increasing again in numbers. The Hill of Berries (nothing to do with 'berries'—it is in the townland of Barrymore and Barrybeg) opposite Ballyglass Hill is one of the places which people say is the exact centre of Ireland.

Hodson Bay The Hodson family obtained large grants of land in this area in the seventeenth century and their principal house at Hodson Bay is now a hotel. Hodson's Pillar, the stone pillar on the small island close to the shore (not to be confused with the Pinnacle rock in the middle of the bay) is another of the many places that are claimed to be the geographical centre of Ireland and there is yet another to the east of Lough Ree at Kilkenny West, north of Glassan.

Ballybay and Yew Point Ballybay has species-rich reedbeds and marsh while Yew Point has a mainly hazel dominated scrubby woodland where the rare red campion is found.

Slate Rock, a large rock some distance off the point, is so called because a canal boat carrying a cargo of slates struck it and sank many years ago. The Adelaide Rock nearby takes its name from a yacht called *Adelaide*, one of the fleet of yachts on the lake in the 1830s, which must have struck the rock. These local names were adopted by Commander James Wolfe and Lieutenant R.B. Beechey, the naval officers who surveyed the lake in the 1830s. It is said that this end of Lough Ree received particular attention in the survey because Beechey was courting Miss Smyth from Portlick whom he subsequently married. He later became a distinguished amateur painter whose marine paintings are much sought after today.

The Inner Lakes Passing in between Hare Island and Coosan Point, there is a delightful series of three interconnected lakes known as the Inner Lakes. The first lake is Killinure and at the west end of it, just inside the entrance is Quigley's marina. On the Coosan shore, hidden in the trees, is Dunrovin where Colonel Harry Rice lived, the author of *Thanks for the Memory*. In this little house plans to form the Inland Waterways Association of Ireland were made in the early 1950s in an effort to preserve the Shannon Navigation which was threatened with low fixed bridges. At that time there were so few boats on the river that it was difficult to justify retaining the navigation but a small group of people appreciated its potential and managed to win the battle for its survival.

These lakes are a fisherman's paradise and the reedbeds and marshland surrounding them have a rich and interesting flora. The many species of orchids to be found is striking: in early summer the early purple and on drier ground the pyramidal orchid and the bee orchid; in mid-summer the twayblade, the fragrant orchid and the butterfly orchid.The lake bottom here is characteristically covered with a lime-encrusted and branching alga called chara. The scrub and reedbeds provide cover for many species of warbler, including the rare garden warbler and in autumn large flocks of starlings roost in the reeds. Great crested grebe can be frequently seen and large numbers of hand-reared mallard have been released in the past.

Halfway up the outer arm of Killinure Lough the narrow channel into Coosan Lough opens up. Friar's Island is so called because it provided a refuge for some of the friars from Athlone. There is a featureless ruin near the eastern end of the island and there is a tradition that there was a path from the island to the Irishtown area of Athlone along which the friars travelled into the town to say mass for the people.

At the eastern end of Friar's Island there is another narrow channel into Ballykeeran Lough. In Killinure Lough Ballykeeran Marina is at the east end also Chatterton's of Portaneena and Wineport restaurant and sailing centre. Temple Island is so called because it was owned by Robert Temple, the Commodore of the Killinure Yacht Club which used this island as its

Lough Ree

Der an der Einfahrt in den See gelegene Segelclub ist der zweitälteste der Welt. Er wurde 1770 gegründet.

Hodson Bay

Das von der Familie Hodson gebaute Haus ist heute, nach mehreren Umbauten und Erweiterungen, ein bekanntes Hotel. Hodson's Säule soll der geographische Mittelpunkt Irlands sein.

Slate Rock

So benannt, weil vor vielen Jahren ein mit Schieferplatten beladenes Frachtschiff auf den Fels aufgelaufen und gesunken ist. Adelaide Rock ist ebenfalls nach einem Schiff benannt. Diese Namen wurden von zwei Offizieren der britischen Marine, die um 1830 den See vermassen, übernommen.

Inner Lakes

Drei schöne, miteinander verbundene Seen, gut zum Fischen und Ankern. Zwei grosse, gut geführte Restaurants mit eigenen Anlegestellen. Besonders auffällig ist die Vielfalt der hier wachsenden Orchideen.

Friar's Island

Die Mönchsinsel war einst ein Zufluchtsort für Mönche aus Athlone. Am Ostende befindet sich eine Ruine ohne besondere Merkmale.

Temple Island

Die Insel wurde nach ihrem ehemaligen Besitzer Robert Temple benannt, Kommodore des Killinure Yachtklubs in den 30er Jahren des 19. Jahrhunderts. Damals war Temple Island der

Lough Ree Yacht Club

Walter Borner

headquarters in the 1830s. There is a small boat harbour and a ruined building on the island. On the shore below Ladywell there is the small ruined church and graveyard of Bunowen, where some of the graves bear the name of Dillon, the dominant Norman family in this area in the past.

Glassan (glasán—a streamlet) This is an attractive village 2.5 km from the lake. This is Goldsmith country: about 4 km from Glassan, on the Ballymahon road, is the village of Lissoy where Oliver Goldsmith spent much of his childhood. Shortly after Oliver's birth his father, the Rev. Charles Goldsmith, moved to the parsonage at Lissoy, the ruins of which can still be seen, and the writer remained there until his father's death in 1747. This area was to be immortalised as 'sweet Auburn' in 'The Deserted Village'. The 'busy mill' used to be near The Three Jolly Pigeons Pub. This is not the same building but the successor to the one mentioned by Goldsmith in *She Stoops to Conquer;* some would say unkindly that the pub was named after the original in the play!

Hare Island (inis Ainghin—the island of Ainghin) Returning to the lake, it is possible either to circumnavigate Hare Island (watching the chart carefully because the buoyage system here is confusing) or pass back out again through the narrows to the main lake. St Ciarán, who was later to travel downstream to found the monastic settlement at Clonmacnois, is said to have first lived here as a hermit and a small monastic settlement became established here. The island was plundered on many occasions. The largest hoard of Viking gold ever discovered in Western Europe was found here in 1802. The original monastery continued into the twelfth century, probably becoming a house of the Canons Regular of St Augustine some time after 1140. The Romanesque church ruin near the small harbour in the south-east corner of the island probably dates from that time. The

The Three Jolly Pigeons, in Goldsmith country, to the east of Lough Ree, from the Steam Navigation Company's guide book dated 1852

Dillons, who came to dominate the east shore of the lake, are sometimes credited with founding the house and many members of the family are buried here. In modern times the island came into the possession of the Handcocks (lords Castlemaine) who built a lodge and a harbour, known as The Lord's Harbour, and planted the island with trees, shrubs and flowers. The island has magnificent and mature oak trees, and on it and on many of

Standort des Klubs. Heute gehört die Insel zur privaten Marina von Portaneena (keine Anlegestellen).

Glasson

Ein kleines Dorf im Goldsmith Country. Ganz in der Nähe liegt Lissoy, wo der Schriftsteller Oliver Goldsmith einen grossen Teil seiner Jugend verbrachte. Das Dorf wurde in dem Gedicht 'The Deserted Village' unsterblich gemacht. Es ist geplant, eine alte Kanalverbindung zu den Inner Lakes zu restaurieren und den Ort damit wieder an die Wasserwege anzuschliessen. Der Glasson

Walter Borner

Hodson Bay hotel and harbour

the other small islands and wooded points can be found a very rare white-flowered orchid. In April and May the yellow brimstone butterfly is on the wing—it is dependent on buckthorn for food and this is abundant in the area. Hare Island is privately owned. Permission must be sought from Lough Ree Inn, Coosan Point.

Portlick There is a fine Dillon castle here which has one wing dating from the fourteenth century but is largely sixteenth century. A house was built adjoining the castle and the castle was well restored and maintained by the Smyth family who owned it until recent times. The estate is now administered by Coillte (the Forestry Board) and it is best approached by water through the Napper channel from the north at Portlick Bay and not through Rinardo Bay.

Inchmore (inis mór—the big island) is the largest island on Lough Ree. At the south end there is a fine example of a ring fort indicating that this island was inhabited from early times. St Liobán is said to have founded an early Christian monastery here which evolved into a house of Augustinian canons in the twelfth century and there is a featureless ruin of an early church at the north end of the island. The Marquis of Westmeath built a lodge here, Inchmore Lodge, with a walled garden and a road leading up to it from the shore. At the turn of the last century there were some 200 people living on this island and on the neighbouring island of **Inchturk** (inis turc—the island of the boar) but these families gradually moved to the mainland. Inchmore Lodge is now in ruins, the road overgrown and the schoolhouse, built as recently as 1927, is now deserted. Today some people have moved back to the island, establishing holiday homes there. The old quay is on the north east of the island and should be approached by dinghy.

Derry Bay Continuing up the east shore into Derry Bay, the ruined nunnery, Bethlehem House, is down near the shore of Noughaval Bay. It was a house of Poor Clare nuns established in 1631 under the protection of the Dillons but, in the troubled times following the rising of 1641, the convent was destroyed by soldiers from Athlone. The nuns managed to escape and it is said that some of them went to nearby Nun's Island and that some graves there are of these nuns. The name would seem to support this but the ruin on this island is of a much earlier medieval church.

Inny Bay The shores of Inny Bay show many of the characteristic Lough Ree flowering plants. At the head of the bay the River Inny enters the lake, depositing much silt and clay, resulting in rich rush and reedbeds, with wet grassland behind them. This area is remote and is thus important for the breeding and wintering of duck and waders and also the Greenland white-fronted goose. The River Inny is navigable for about 5 km to a low-accommodation bridge.

Golf Club wurde auf dem Gelände eines ehemaligen Herrensitzes eingerichtet. Unterhalb von Ladywell Kirchenruine und Friedhof von Bunowen mit Gräbern der Dillons, einer früher dieses Gebiet beherrschenden Familie.

Hare Island

St. Ciaran, der später das Kloster Clonmacnois gründete, soll hier in einer Einsiedelei gelebt haben. 1802 wurde auf der Insel der grösste Goldschatz der Wikinger gefunden. Ruine einer vermutlich aus dem 12. Jahrhundert stammenden romanischen Kirche in der Nähe des kleinen Hafens. Alte Eichen und eine seltene weissblühende Orchidee sind auf dieser und einigen anderen der kleinen Inseln zu finden. Hare Island ist Privatbesitz, zum Besuch ist eine Erlaubnis nötig. Erhältlich bei Lough Ree Inn, Coosan Point.

Portlick

Schönes Dillon Schloss, zum grossen Teil aus dem 16. Jahrhundert. Das Gut ist Privatbesitz und Naturschutzgebiet.

Inchmore

Grösste Insel auf Lough Ree. Am Südende steht ein schönes Beispiel eines Ringwalls, am Nordende die Reste einer alten Kirche. Das Jagdhaus Inchmore Lodge mit einem von einer Mauer umgebenen Garten ist ebenfalls eine Ruine. Bis ins frühe 20. Jahrhundert lebten um die 200 Leute auf dieser Insel. Inzwischen sind alle aufs Festland gezogen.

Vikings on Lough Ree

Walter Borner

Saint's Island is now linked to the mainland by a causeway. The Priory of All Saints was probably founded about the year 1200 by the Dillons. It became very prosperous and developed a great reputation for learning. Its most famous scholar, Augustine Magraidain, who died in 1465, was one of the compilers of the Annals of All Saints. The priory appears to have survived the dissolution of the monasteries because another famous scholar, John Colgan, records that he consulted manuscripts here and he also visited the nuns at Bethlehem nearby in the 1630s. The principal surviving feature, which is in the north-west corner, is the church which has a fine switch-line traceried window in the east gable, probably fifteenth century in date. There is a dilapidated transept off the south side of the nave and, to the north, traces of the domestic buildings of the priory survive with fragments of the cloisters littered about the site.

Inchbofin (inis bófin—the island of the white cow) The channel out of Derry Bay is around the south of Inchbofin. There was an early Christian settlement founded here by St Rioch in the sixth century. Although the site is at the north end of the island, the best anchorage is at the south-east corner. The monastery was burned and plundered on several occasions by the Vikings: two bronze objects in Hiberno-Norse style were found on the island which confirm these incursions. There are some early Christian grave slabs and two churches: the southerly one is a simple nave and chancel structure with a well preserved but plain chancel arch; the church to the north is known as the monastery. The immediate site is enclosed by a low stone wall, but it is possible to trace the outline of a much larger monastic enclosure in the neighbouring fields. This church consists of a nave with a ruined altar at the east end. Beside the altar in the north wall is an exceptionally fine example of a twelfth century Irish Romanesque window. Opposite this on the south wall is a projecting piscina (a basin with drain hole for washing sacred vessels). To the north of the nave a transept was added to the church with two fine fifteenth century traceried windows: the one in the north gable is complete and is surmounted on the outside by the mitred head of a bishop or abbot. There is also a sacristy, now used as a store for many of the carved stones which were found on the island.

Rindoon (rin dun—the point of the fort) Items found near here suggest that there may have been an Iron Age or early Christian settlement in the vicinity which evolved into a house of Premonstratensian canons in the twelfth century. Rindoon may have been the base of the Viking fleet led by Turgesius but the visible remains are all from the Norman period. It was the site of a very early Norman town, dating from the early thirteenth century. The town was protected by a fortified wall stretching

Irish Architectural Archive

Saint's Island drawn by Daniel Grose

Derry Bay

Am Ufer liegt die Ruine des vom Orden der Armen Clara 1631 gegründeten Nonnenklosters Bethlehem. Es heisst, einige der Nonnen seien auf die nahe gelegene Nonneninsel (Nun's Island) geflüchtet, aber die Ruine auf Nun's Island ist die einer wesentlich älteren mittelalterlichen Kirche.

Inny Bay

An den Ufern sind viele der für Lough Ree charakteristischen blühenden Pflanzen zu finden. Die Gegend ist abgelegen und daher ein Brut- und Überwinterungsplatz für Enten und Sumpfvögel sowie die grönländische Blässgans. Der River Inny kann bis zur Brücke befahren werden.

Saint's Island

Die Insel der Heiligen ist jetzt durch einen Damm mit dem Festland verbunden. Die Abtei aus dem 12. Jahrhundert, wahrscheinlich von den Dillons gegründet, wurde sehr reich. In der Nordwestecke der Insel befindet sich die Kirche.

Inchbofin

Eine frühchristliche Klostersiedlung, im 6. Jahrhundert von St. Rioch gegründet. Obwohl die Siedlung am Nordende der Insel liegt, ist die beste Anlegestelle in der Südostecke. Die Südkirche ist ein einfaches Kirchenschiff mit Chorraum und einem gut erhaltenen, unverzierten Chorbo-

across the point, much of which still survives, including a number of the square towers and the remnants of a gatehouse. Within the town a massive stone castle was erected in 1227 and enlarged in 1233. The remains include the ruined tower, curtain walls and a gatehouse surrounded by a moat. The town included a priory of the medieval hospital order of Fratres Crucifieri, the featureless ruins of whose church stand nearby. Rindoon is in the parish of St John and the order was dedicated to St John of Jerusalem. For these two reasons the area is called by this name but the order was not a military one and had no connection with the Knights Hospitallers of St John. Another building on the site is a circular tower near the point which if it is a medieval windmill, as some people suggest, would make it unique in Ireland.

North Lough Ree Lough Ree is very important ecologically and supports an interesting fauna, particularly two species which are probably relics from the last Ice Age-the freshwater herring or pollan, and the freshwater shrimp. At certain times, during hot summer conditions, the waters can show symptoms of pollution with decreasing water transparency and the presence of 'algae blooms' caused by the increased growth and multiplication of microscopic plants in the favourable conditions. The rocky shores of the islands and lake edge, especially where these are little grazed by livestock, are rich in flowering plants including mint, purple loosestrife, harebell, ladies bedstraw and the water germander, which is almost unique in Ireland to the shores of Lough Ree and Lough Derg.

St John's Wood to the north is of international importance as a large old oak and hazel woodland little influenced by man, with a rich bird population and diverse plant species on the woodland floor. The very rare birds-nest orchid occurs here. The marshland south east of the wood is of interest also. China clay deposits, known as the Lecarrow clay pits, can be found in an area of gorse on the south shore of Blackbrink Bay which supplied the local clay pipe industry of the nineteenth century.

The Lecarrow Canal was constructed in the 1840s to facilitate the transport of stone from a nearby quarry for the navigation works in Athlone.

Galey Bay There is a ruined castle at the head of the bay. This was the venue for some of the early regattas and Commodore Temple's yacht *Louisa* ran aground on the shoal at the entrance, leaving her mark and

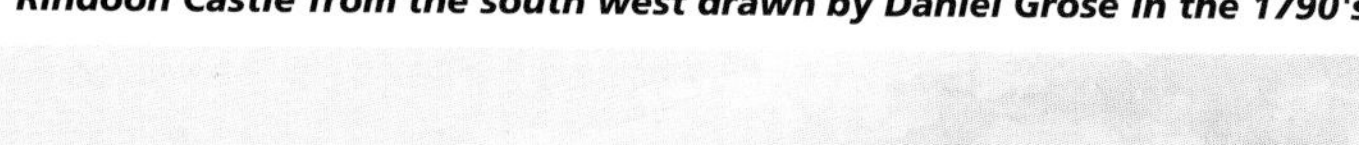

Rindoon Castle from the south west drawn by Daniel Grose in the 1790's

Irish Architectural Archive

gen. Die Nordkirche besteht aus einem Kirchenschiff mit einer Altarruine am Ostende. An der Südwand befindet sich eine Piscina mit Wasserablauf zur Reinigung heiliger Gefässe. Am Nordende des Kirchenschiffes ein Querschiff mit zwei schönen, mit Masswerk versehenen Fenstern aus dem 15. Jahrhundert. Eines davon ist vollständig erhalten.

Rindoon

Möglicher Stützpunkt der Wikingerflotte. Die sichtbaren Überreste sind die einer Normannenstadt aus dem frühen 13. Jahrhundert. 1227 erbaute, massive Burg, die 1233 vergrössert wurde. Ausserdem steht hier ein runder Turm, der eine mittelalterliche Windmühle gewesen sein könnte. In diesem Fall wäre sie die einzige aus dieser Zeit erhaltene in Irland.

Nordende von Lough Ree

Ökologisch sehr wichtig. Hier leben einige interessante Tierarten wie der Süsswasserhering (pollan) und Unmengen von Süsswasserkrabben.

St. John's Wood

Von Menschen unberührt gebliebener Bestand an alten Eichen und Haselbäumen von internationaler Bedeutung. Beherbergt eine Vielzahl von Vogelarten.

Lecarrow Canal

In den 40er Jahren des 19. Jahrhunderts gebaut, um den Transport von Steinen aus einem nahegelegenen Steinbruch zu erleichtern. Nach Befahren unbedingt Kühlwasserfilter reinigen.

Galey Bay

Turmhausruine.

Portrunny

Gutes, vor kurzem neu erstelltes Pier.

Barley Harbour

Mietschiffen ist das Anlaufen von Barley Harbour wegen einiger unter Wasser liegender Felsen nicht gestattet.

Inchcleraun

Auch Quäker-Insel genannt, weil dort vor bald zweihundert Jahren ein Quäker lebte. Der Legende nach soll Königin Maeve von einem vom Ufer von Longford aus geschleuderten Stein getötet worden sein, als sie sich auf der Wiese unterhalb der Clogas-Kapelle sonnte. Das Kloster wurde im 6. Jahrhundert von St. Diarmuid gegründet. Die meisten Ruinen stammen aus dem 12. Jahrhundert. Clogas Kapelle (1) wahrscheinlich aus dieser Zeit. Das Hauptschiff von Tempel Mor (3) hat im Ostgiebel zwei schöne Fenster aus dem 13. Jahrhundert. Daneben Sakristei und Klostergebäude aus dem 15. Jahrhundert. Chor-

The legend of the Quaker

When Mr Fairbrother, the Quaker, was building the present little cottage in which his sons live during the summer seasons he, the tasteless follower of the Cobbler, George Fox, ... had the audacity to pick the beautiful corner stones out of the Clogás and to yoke a horse to carry them to where he intended to build and did build his little cottage; but St Dermot was none of those tame listless saints who would care nothing about the monuments of history or allow such sacrilegious darings to pass unrevenged, for, after the second load, he smote the beast with the bolt of his holy revenge which caused him to run furiously, untameably, terribly, outrageously, irresistibly mad, and the Quaker, fearing for his own safety, was obliged to shoot him. All the beasts on the island (from the cow down to the mouse) also exhibited symptoms of madness but it subsided soon when the Quaker had formed a fixed resolution of touching no other stone of St Dermot's Clogás.

John O'Donovan's *Ordnance Survey Letters*, Co Roscommon, 1837

her name for posterity. In the next bay, **Portrunny Bay**, there is a quay which has recently been constructed suitable for cruisers. There is a strange lake called Funshinagh about 6.5 km from Lough Ree to the west which is a turlough (a disappearing lake). It is connected with the Shannon by an underground river and when the river falls below a certain level this lake empties, leaving its fish floundering on the bottom.

Barley Harbour, which is prohibited to hire craft, is inside Collum Point at the entrance to Elfeet Bay. It is a pleasant walk along a leafy lane to Newtown Cashel almost 5 km away.

Inchcleraun is often called **Quaker Island** because a man of that faith, named Fairbrother, lived there in the early nineteenth century. It was the island of Clothara, the sister of the legendary Queen Maeve, and it is here that the latter is said to have been killed by Forbaid, the son of the Ulster king from whom she stole a bull in the famous Cattle Raid of Cooley. Forbaid, the story goes, killed her with a stone from a sling cast from the Longford shore while she was basking in the sun on the east side of the island in her bower, which was said to be in the field below the Clogás Oratory (1).

The monastic remains here are the

The legend of the slaying of Queen Maeve

Queen Maeve had stolen a bull from the king of Ulster in the famous Cattle Raid of Cooley (but that's another story) and his son Forbaid learnt that she was living with her sister on Inchcleraun. He discovered that she bathed herself each day in a particular spot on the island and so he measured with a thread the distance from the spot to the opposite shore and carried the thread back to Ulster. There he fixed two stakes in the ground at both ends of the thread and on top of one of the stakes he placed an apple. He then took his sling and standing at the other stake practised shooting at the apple until he became so expert as to strike it at every shot. Returning south he perceived Queen Maeve bathing herself and there upon he fixed a stone in his sling and making a shot towards her aimed directly at her forehead and killed her on the spot.

John O'Donovan's *Ordnance Survey Letters*, Co Roscommon, 1837

kapelle (4), Totenkapelle (5) aus dem 12., Frauenkapelle (6) wahrscheinlich 13. Jahrhundert. Oberhalb der Gruppe von Kirchen stehen das verlassene Haus der Farrells (7), dahinter dasjenige des Quäkers, im Norden die Ruine des Hauses der Familie Walsh. Zum Besuch der Insel mit dem Beiboot ankert man am besten auf der Ostseite.

Inchenagh

1898 lebten hier 35 Personen in sechs Häusern. Die Familien zogen nach und nach auf das Festland.

Rathcline Castle

Traditionelles Turmhaus, im 17. Jahrhundert durch Anbau erweitert.

Lanesborough

Das Nadelöhr bei Schlechtwetter auf Lough Ree. Thermisches Kraftwerk, das mit maschinell abgebautem Torf aus der Umgebung beheizt wird. In Lanesborough war 1706 eine Steinbrücke gebaut worden, die um 1840 ersetzt wurde. Früher lief ein kurzer Kanal mit einer eintorigen Schleuse westlich des Flusses. Das Schleusenwärterhaus steht über dem Kanal. 1820 Bau des kleinen Hafens. Es ist geplant, wegen des zunehmenden Schiffsverkehrs einen neuen Hafen in der Bucht zu erstellen.

Von Lanesborough nach Termonbarry

Seichte Flussstrecke, die kürzlich ausgebaggert wurde. Bei Niedrigwasser mit reduzierter Geschwindigkeit fahren.

Lecarrow Cut with the barge Snark

Walter Borner

Ruth Delany

The Clogás, Inchcleraun

most important on the lake. The monastery was founded by St Diarmuid in the sixth century but the only relics of this time are some grave slabs, the cashel (or bank) surrounding the site and, possibly, the diminutive Temple Diarmuid (2). In the twelfth century a house of canons of St Augustine was established here and most of the remains date from this period onwards. On the highest point of the island is the Clogás Oratory (1) which is probably twelfth century, with a later square tower added to it. A stone staircase in the wall may have led to a loft or gallery.

The nave of the largest church in the group down near the shore, Temple Mór (3), is lit by two fine thirteenth century windows in the east gable. It is adjoined by a sacristy and monastic buildings which appear to date from the fifteenth century. An upper room was lit by an attractive window with a charming stone seat running round its interior. A portion of the cloister arcade still stands and the foundations of the walks can be traced on two sides. Other buildings were the Chancel Church (4) and the Church of the Dead (5). Both have finely cut plain round-headed windows and may date from the twelfth century. A poorly restored church just south of the enclosure is known as the Women's Church (6); some thirteenth century carving on its altar suggests its date. Above the group of churches there is the deserted cottage of the Farrells (9) and behind it is the house of the Quaker (7). To the north, close to the isthmus connecting the island to Muckinish, are the ruins of the Walshes' cottage (8). The last of the Farrells lived on the island until the late 1950s. There is a good landing place for dinghies near the main site of the churches and a convenient IWAI mooring buoy close by.

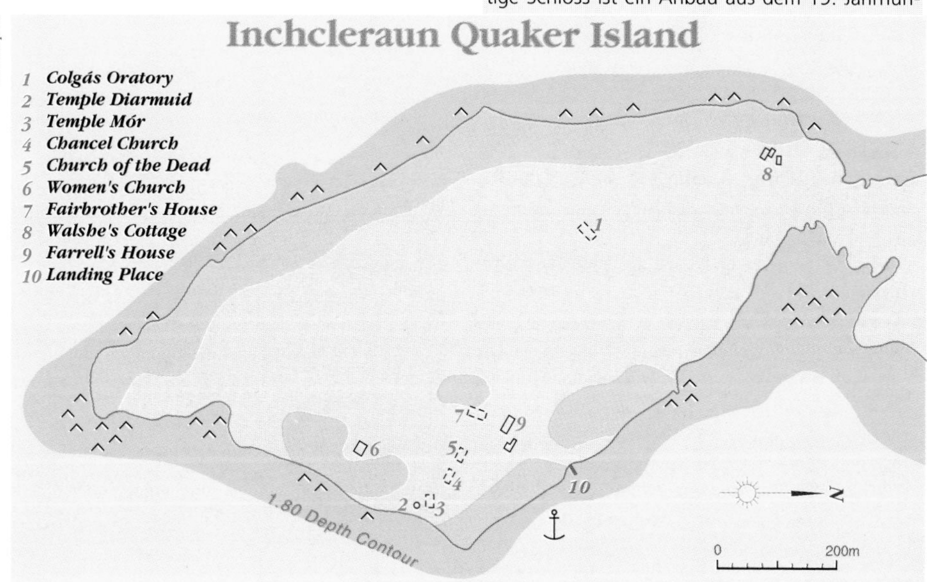

ERA-Maptec

Termonbarry

Die alte Schiffahrtsroute führte durch den Camlin River an Termonbarry vorbei. Der alte Kanal kann wieder benützt werden, es ist möglich, in den Richmond Harbour hinaufzuschleusen.

Richmond Harbour

1817 wurde der Royal Canal von Dublin her vollendet. Er konnte nicht mit dem Grand Canal konkurrieren. Der Verkehr ging ständig zurück. 1961 wurde der Kanal stillgelegt. Vor einigen Jahren wurde mit der Restaurierung begonnen, die nahezu vollendet ist. Richmond Harbour besitzt in reichem Mass die Atmosphäre der alten Kanalzeit mit seiner Reihe von Häusern aus dem 18. Jahrhundert, dem Trockendock und dem für den Royal Canal typischen Schleusenwärterhaus mit seinen Nischenfenstern. Origineller Pub.

Clondara

Neben der katholischen Kirche die Überreste einer Kirche mit uraltem Friedhof. Interessante Grabsteine. Anfangs des 19. Jahrhunderts war hier eine sehr produktive Whiskeybrennerei.

Lough Forbes

See und Landgut von Schloss Forbes sind von ökologischer Bedeutung wegen ihrer Wald- und Sumpfgebiete und der dort beheimateten Vögel. Das graue Eichhörnchen, das 1913 aus den USA hierher gebracht wurde, hat sich im ganzen Land verbreitet. Westlich des Sees sehenswerte Torfmoorlandschaft.

Schloss Forbes

1641 von Sir Arthur Forbes gebaut. Das heutige Schloss ist ein Anbau aus dem 19. Jahrhun-

Inchenagh (inis an dambh—the island of the one ox). There is a small group of ruined cottages on the high ground surrounded by trees. In 1313 six cottages were occupied with a total of 35 occupants but the families gradually moved to the mainland. The northern end of the lake is much shallower than the south end and is therefore very good fishing ground. Because most of it is so remote and inaccessible from roads it is a favourite habitat of wildfowl and mammals, including the otter.

Rathcline Castle at the head of the bay bounded on the north by Curreen Point, was a tower house of the traditional type which was later enlarged and embellished with a walled enclosure and a fine classical gateway by George Lane, the first viscount Lanesborough in the seventeenth century. Plans of Rathcline, which survive from the Caroline period show that it was intended to construct a canal from the castle to the lake but this does not seem to have been carried out. The castle was attacked and damaged by Cromwell's forces and later the repaired castle was gutted by fire.

Lanesborough owes its name to George Lane who received extensive grants of land here in the seventeenth century. For many years it remained a small town but today it is a much busier place because of the increase in boating on the river and the ESB power station and Bord na Mona activities on the adjacent bogs. There are many miles of narrow gauge railway feeding turf to the power station and a railway bridge was erected upstream of the town in 1957. Some of the turf is cut into sods but most of it is milled to a fine powder. The power station can consume 300,000 tons of milled peat and 110,00 tons of sod turf per year.

Ruth Delany

Lanesborough Bridge

A many-arched stone bridge was erected at Lanesborough in 1706, similar to the Elizabethan bridge in Athlone. It was replaced by the Shannon Commissioners when the extensive navigation works were being carried out in the 1840s. There is little evidence now of the earlier navigation works. At that time a short canal ran along the west side of the river with a single set of gates to overcome the 0.5 m fall in the river here. A lock-keeper's house, similar to the houses at Shannonbridge and Clondara, straddled the canal just below the bridge. A harbour was added in 1820 and this was incorporated into the new works in the 1840s when the canal was removed; the river was dredged out to permit navigation and new quay walls constructed. The old harbour has now been refurbished and is in use today.

Lanesborough to Tarmonbarry This stretch of river is very shallow and there are few signs of habitation. The bog stretches away to the west towards the hills.

Tarmonbarry (tearmann Bearaigh—the churchlands of Barry) Emerging from Lodge Cut the navigation enters a small lake and passes the entrance to the River Camlin and the Royal Canal before

Tarmonbarry

Walter Borner

swinging across to the west shore to Tarmonbarry lock. The original navigation by-passed the river here, following the route up through a lock and short canal into the Camlin River and along this river to rejoin the Shannon south of Lough Forbes. In 1968 this was opened up again as an alternative route. The original eighteenth century lockhouse still stands at the bridge over the canal leading up to the harbour.

Richmond Harbour, Clondara The Royal Canal was finally completed from Dublin in 1817. It had taken 28 years to complete, about half the time it had taken to complete the Grand Canal but the cost was £15,000 per mile whereas the cost of the Grand had only been about £6,000 per mile. Many investors in the Royal Canal Company were ruined in the early years and eventually the government had to take it over and complete the last 30 miles. Richmond Harbour was named after the Lord Lieutenant of the day who officially opened the harbour. The canal never managed to compete successfully with the Grand Canal and the whole concern was purchased in 1845 by the Midland & Great Western Railway Company. Traffic steadily declined and the canal was officially closed to navigation in 1961. Richmond Harbour was restored by O.P.W in 1968 marking the first step in reopening the waterway. In recent years there has been an active campaign for its restoration and a considerable amount of work has been carried out at the eastern end but a number of culvert bridges make restoration of the western end more difficult. It is possible to walk back along the towpath to the 45th lock. There is a great atmosphere of the past about Richmond Harbour with its row of eighteenth century houses, dry dock and typical Royal Canal lockhouse with recessed windows.

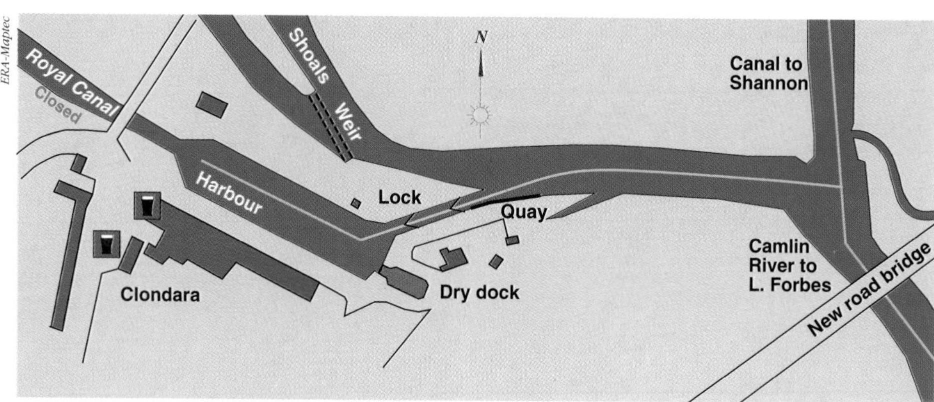

Richmond Harbour and Approaches

Clondara (Cluain dá rath—meadow of two ring forts) Beside the RC church at Clondara are the ruins of a church and an ancient graveyard with some interesting grave slabs. This was the site of an early monastery and hospice. In the 1830s the distillery here was a busy one, producing about 70,000 gallons of whiskey each year with a workforce of 70 people. It subsequently became a corn mill.

Lough Forbes The channel cut out by the Shannon Commissioners from Tarmonbarry follows the west shore before entering Lough Forbes. Ecologically Lough Forbes and the Castle Forbes demesne are of national importance for their woodland, marshland habitats and the birds which these habitats support. The area is second in importance in Ireland as a wintering site for the Greenland white-fronted goose and is important too for other wildfowl. The grey squirrel was first introduced here in 1913 from the United States via Britain and

Richmond Harbour

Walter Borner

Roosky pubs are known for traditional music sessions

the species has subsequently spread throughout much of the country. West of the lake is a considerable area of bog and this is worth a visit. The raised bog south of the Feorish river is the site of the original introduction from Canada of the insectiverous pitcher plant and it has naturalised here and in other midland bogs where it has been planted.

Castle Forbes In 1619 Sir Arthur Forbes was granted the lands on the east side of the lake by James I and he built a castle here in 1641. His widow managed to resist an attack by the parliamentary forces and the family was eventually rewarded with an earldom. The present house, an addition to the old castle, is a nineteenth century building.

Kilbarry (cill Bearaigh—the church of Barry) It was on some high ground in the boggy terrain west of Lough Forbes that St Barry chose to found his monastery. His churchlands extended from here to include Tarmonbarry. This place was always known as The Seven Churches of Kilbarry. The remains of at least two churches survive and the site preserves some stones of a round tower which formerly stood there. The square headed doorway denotes the antiquity of the ruined church and there is a local legend that a night spent within its walls will cure the mentally ill. Along the lane, nearer the lake, is St Barry's holy well. There is a legend that when St Barry was searching for a place to found his settlement he arrived at the edge of the river on the east shore and, failing to find a boat, used a large boulder to make the crossing. A large stone in the grounds of Whitehall church nearby is said to be the one used by him.

A new marina is being developed at Cloonart Bridge up the River Rinn and about 3 km from here l.5 km off the main Sligo road, there is an ancient church at **Cloonmorris** built about 1200 with attractive east and south lancet windows. The moulding on the outside of the east window ends with two upturned heads. The north doorway was inserted in the fifteenth century. There is a stone in the graveyard with the ogham inscription 'Qenuven', probably the name of the person commemorated; the rest of the letters have been defaced.

dert an das alte Gebäude.

Kilbarry

Der heilige Barry gründete hier sein Kloster. Die Überreste von zwei Kirchen bestehen noch. Im Volksmund der Gegend heisst es, eine Nacht in den Mauern der Klosterruine genüge, um einen Geisteskranken zu heilen. Nach der Legende überquerte der heilige Barry den Fluss mit Hilfe eines grossen Felsens. Ein solcher Felsen auf dem Kirchengelände von Whitehall in der Nähe soll derjenige des Heiligen gewesen sein.

Cloonmorris

Um 1200 erbaute Kirche mit schönen östlich und südlich gerichteten Spitzbogenfenstern. Nordportal aus dem 15. Jahrhundert. Auf dem Friedhof ein Stein mit Ogham-Inschrift.

Roosky

Walter Borner

Gazetteer - Roosky to Lough Key

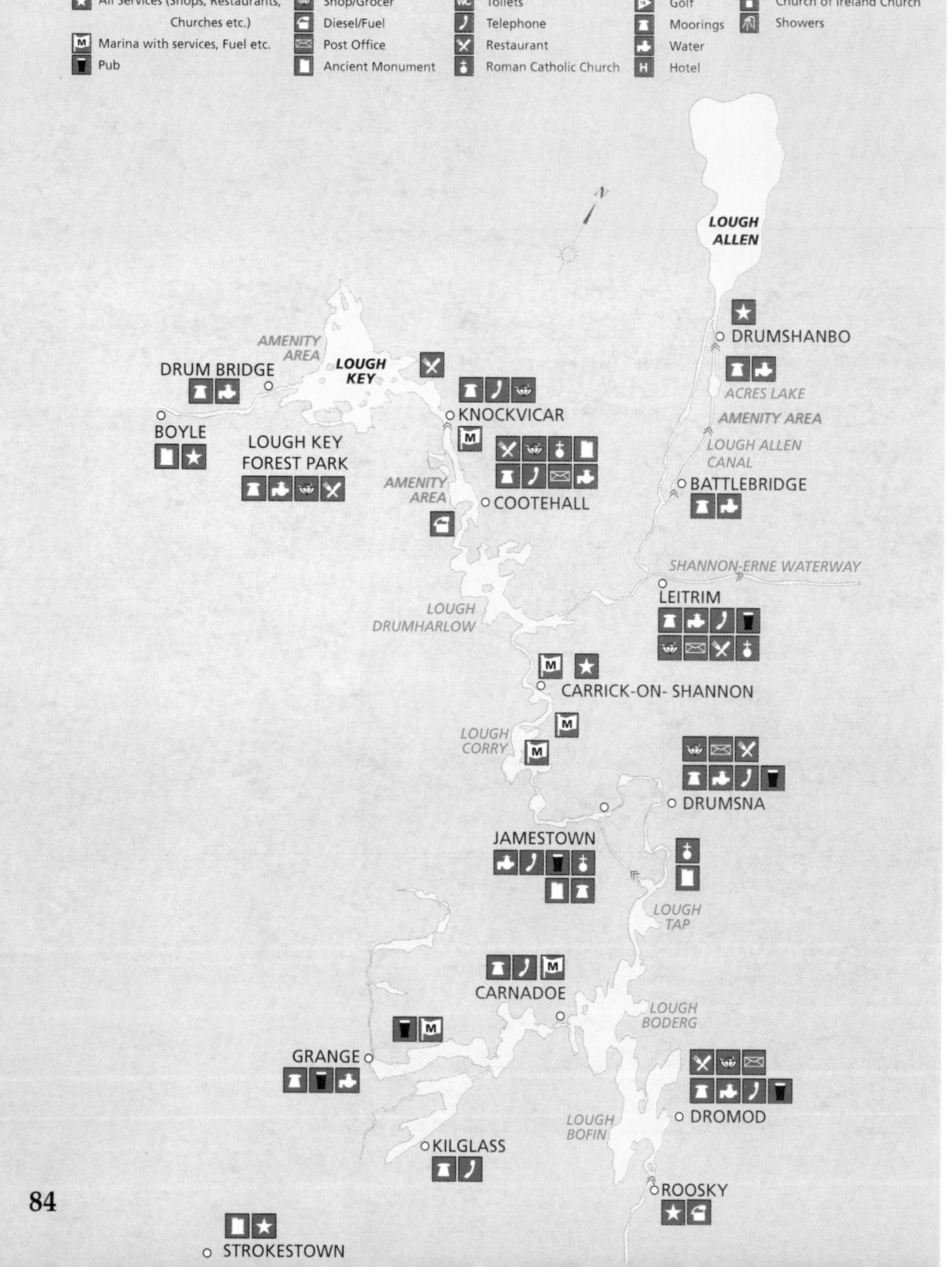

Roosky (rúscaigh—the marshy place) There are many attractive mooring places between the lock and the road bridge at Roosky, sufficiently removed from the noise of the main Dublin to Sligo road which skirts the village. Roosky is a popular stop-over for those in search of pubs where there is traditional music and singing to be heard. The early navigation passed down a canal and through a lock to the west of the river. This canal and lock were built in the 1760s and, unlike all the other early locks, this one was never rebuilt or altered. The stonework is in surprisingly good repair and the only obvious difference in construction was the use of smaller and more irregular sized stones. The early lockhouse, which was sited along the canal nearer the village, was removed. The canal re-entered the river at the back of the small island a short distance upstream of the bridge. The present lock, the weir and the road bridge were all built by the Shannon Commissioners in the 1840s but the original opening span had to be replaced in recent years by a lifting bridge.

Dromod Harbour (dromod—a ridge) makes a pleasant stopping place on Lough Bofin with the village of Dromod a short distance away. Dromod is on the main Dublin to Sligo road and is also a stop on the main railway line to Sligo. The old harbour was built by the Directors General of Inland Navigation in 1829 at a cost of £139. The little house here was formerly a store and the outline of the doors can be seen in the gable wall as well as the stone supports for the crane for lifting goods. The Board of Works lowered the walls of the old harbour to accommodate modern cruisers and a new harbour has now been constructed here to cater for the increasing traffic.

Walter Borner

Dromod

The Lough Scannel area has a very rich lake, marsh and woodland flora, largely unaffected by agricultural activities and it is important too for wintering wildfowl including the Greenland white-fronted goose.

Derrycarne Narrows (derraigh carn—the wood of the cairn) separate Lough Bofin from Lough Boderg. This was an important fording place in the past and there were eel weirs here so the navigation channel is narrow. A battle took place here between the Williamite forces and Sarsfield's army; Sarsfield's dead were buried in a communal grave, known as 'James's heap' but it's not clear whether this is the cairn of the name. The Nesbitt family built a fine house here but eventually the estate was bought by the state and turned into a Forest Park; the house was demolished and the site turned into a car park. It is not possible to come alongside at either of the old quays. The best place to anchor off is in the little bay to the east before passing through the narrows. The park contains some interesting mixed woodland in which most native trees can be found including, oak, ash, hazel, birch, alder and willow. The rarer helleborine is locally frequent here. Marshland north of Derrycarne has a very rich flora: here occurs an unusual but unobtrusive chickweed and bedstraw, a diverse range of sedges and the bulrush, among many other interesting plants.

Roosky

Beliebter Ort für Leute auf der Suche nach traditioneller irischer Musik. Hier gibt es eine Reihe von Pubs mit Volksmusik. Früher wurde die Schiffahrt über einen Kanal mit Schleuse im Westen des Flusses vorbeigeführt. Die jetzige Schleuse, das Wehr und die Brücke wurden in den 40er Jahren des 19. Jahrhunderts gebaut. Die ursprüngliche Brücke musste vor einiger Zeit durch eine Hubbrücke ersetzt werden.

Dromod

Ein schöner Liegeplatz auf Lough Bofin. Der alte Hafen wurde 1829 gebaut. Lough Scannel hat eine sehr reiche See-, Marsch- und Waldlandflora, da die Gegend noch weitgehend von der Landwirtschaft verschont geblieben ist. Daher ist sie auch ein wichtiger Überwinterungsort für Vögel.

Derrycarne

Wichtige Furt. Hier fand die Schlacht zwischen den Williamiten und der Armee Sarsfields statt. Die Gefallenen wurden in einem Gemeinschaftsgrab, das 'James Heap' genannt wurde, bestattet. Das ehemalige Landgut der Nesbitts ist jetzt ein Naturpark. Das Marschland nördlich von Derrycarne ist reich an seltenen Pflanzen. Bei der Anfahrt von Norden muss unbedingt die westlichste der schwarzen Bojen beachtet werden.

Carnadoe Bridge with Schollevaar made famous in the TV series 'Waterways'

Walter Borner

Strokestown Park House

The Carnadoe Waters open off the River Shannon in the south-west corner of Lough Boderg. These are waters for the naturalist rather than the antiquarian. Perhaps they are best summed up in a quotation from Harry Rice's classic book about the Shannon, *Thanks for the Memory*: 'It has a fascination all of its own. It is a place for quiet contemplation and so the wireless should be turned off before entering, for its sound seems rude and vulgar in the great solitude that encompasses the traveller on every side'. There is a marina upstream of Carnadoe Bridge and a new development under construction in Grange lake.

Carnadoe, Kilglass and Grange These are three lakes connected by narrow winding channels with many small islands which are a refuge for birds. Botanically, this area has not been thoroughly explored: the lakes themselves are largely fringed with rushes and reeds backed by a species rich marsh flora. The white water lily is locally frequent here. There is an interesting aquatic insect fauna because the area acts as a collecting point for three rivers which drain a large and diverse area. The Mountain River, which feeds into Kilglass Lough, is navigable for less than 1 km and then shallows quickly. It is a good location for observing the kingfisher.

On the high ground at Muckinagh, on the ridge between Kilglass and Grange loughs, there is a large ring fort, indicating that there was a very early farmstead here. Grange Quay was formerly quite a busy station for goods arriving by water for nearby Strokestown.

Strokestown is a walk of just over 5km from Grange quay. The town was constructed in the latter half of the eighteenth century by the local landlords,

Kilglass Lough

Walter Borner

Carnadoe Waters

Ein Gebiet, in dem sich langsames Fahren lohnt, ein Schilfgebiet von ausserordentlicher Schönheit. Carnadoe, Kilglass und Grange sind drei ineinander übergehende Seen mit vielen kleinen Inseln. Die Seeufer sind reich bewachsen mit Schilf und Binsen, vermischt mit einer abwechslungsreichen Marschlandflora. Auf der Höhe von Muckinagh steht ein grosses Ringfort. Grange war früher ein wichtiger Anlege- und Umschlagplatz.

Strokestown

Marktflecken mit einem Herrenhaus der Zeit James' I. Es kann besichtigt werden.

Lough Tap

Die Eisenbahnstrecke Dublin-Sligo überquert den Fluss oberhalb des Sees. Dort teilt sich der Shannon. Schiffe nach Carrick benützen den Jamestown Cut. Der eigentliche Fluss ist bis zur Brücke von Drumsna schiffbar.

Drumsna

Sehr schöner Flussabschnitt. Protestantische Kirche von Annaduff aus dem 19. Jahrhundert mit Friedhof und Ruinen einer älteren Kirche, deren Bausteine von der Abtei von Annaduff aus dem 8. Jahrhundert stammen sollen. Die alte Brücke von Drumsna wurde von der Shannon Aufsichtsbehörde nicht ersetzt. Der Hafen wurde 1817 erbaut. Zwischen Hafen und Brücke wird der Fluss rasch seicht und ist nicht mehr schiffbar.

the Mahon family. Its unusually wide streets once accommodated a thriving weekly market. The Gothic entrance gate at the eastern end of the town leads to Strokestown Park House, an imposing Palladian mansion which is now open to the public. It is now owned by the Westward Group, a local company which is responsible for its restoration and development. The house has good examples of eighteenth and nineteenth century interiors complete with original contents. Of particular note is the elaborate vaulted stable and the galleried kitchen. Each day the menus were dropped to the cook from the gallery so that the lady of the house did not have to contend with the kitchen commotion! The stable yard has now been converted into Ireland's only museum devoted to the Great Famine of the 1840s. Approximately 2.5 million people, one quarter of the population, either died or emigrated when blight devasted the potato crop, the staple diet of the poor. The Strokestown landlord, Major Denis Mahon, was assassinated on the estate during the Famine having attempted to clear approximately 8,000 of his impoverished tenants through assisted-emigration and eviction. The museum used the extensive estate archives to explain the significance of the Famine nationally and to reflect critically on the ongoing spectacle of contemporary world hunger and poverty. The 2.2 hectares pleasure garden at Strokestown Park is also being restored. Its main features include the longest herbaceous border in these islands, a pergola, a rose garden and a pond. The house and garden are open from 1 June to mid-September and the Famine Museum from 1 May to mid-October. Meals and snacks are served during opening hours and taxi service to and from Grange quay can be arranged (tel. 078-33013 fax 078-33712).

Lough Tap to Carrick-on-Shannon

The characteristic riverside vegetation of the north Shannon, which includes marsh marigold, flag iris, mint, bogbean, purple and yellow loosestrife and water plantain, can be commonly seen in this section. Look out as well for the more unusual great spearwort, water hemlock and the floating leaved frogbit.

Lough Tap Leaving Lough Boderg, the navigation passes through a short stretch of river and into Lough Tap. The Dublin to Sligo railway runs along the east side of the lake and then crosses the river upstream of the lake. From here to Carrick-on-Shannon the railway follows the river closely and at night the roar of an occasional goods train can be heard shattering the otherwise peaceful scene. The river divides upstream of the railway bridge: the navigation enters the Jamestown Canal, while the river bends off to the right, commencing a great loop, which is only navigable as far as Drumsna.

Drumsna (drum snámha—the ridge of the swimming place) It is an attractive stretch of river up to Drumsna. The nineteenth century C of I church of Annaduff is set in a backdrop of trees on the east bank. In the graveyard there are some ruins of an earlier church and the stones of this are thought to have been from some of the eighth century Annaduff Abbey buildings which were on this site. The bridge at Drumsna, unlike most of the other Shannon bridges, was not replaced by the Shannon Commissioners. The old harbour, constructed in 1817, was lowered by the Board of Works, who have also built a fine new quay extending downstream. The river shallows rapidly between the harbour and the bridge. It is a lovely stretch of river to explore by dinghy up to the weir at Jamestown but when the sluices are open at the weir, there is a strong flow through the bridge.

Despite its position on the busy main road, Drumsna has retained its old-

The lockkeeper at Albert Lock, Mr Bourke has time for a chat while the large lock is filling

Ruth Delany

Jamestown Cut

Erbaut um 1770, um die grosse Flussschleife zu umgehen. Der ursprüngliche Kanal beschrieb zwei Biegungen, war wesentlich enger, und die Schleuse befand sich in einiger Entfernung kanalaufwärts. Die Shannon Aufsichtsbehörde begradigte und verbreiterte ihn und verlegte die neue, grössere Schleuse an das untere Ende. Spuren des alten Kanals kann man noch unterhalb des Kais und der Brücke am oberen Kanalende sehen.

Das Dún

Erdwall-Ringfort, in vorgeschichtlicher Zeit gebaut. Eine grosse Erdaufschüttung von 4,8 m Höhe, deren Basis 30,5 m breit war. Teile des Dún können von der Nähe der Corlara Brücke aus gesehen werden.

Jamestown

Befestigte Stadt von strategischer Bedeutung. James I. gewährte ihr den königlichen Freibrief. Sie war von einer 6 m hohen und 1,8 m

Ruth Delany

The archway at Jamestown before the upper part was removed

fashioned air. It was here that Anthony Trollope was stationed for a time and drew on the nearby ruined Headford House for his first novel, *The Macdermotts of Ballycloran*.

The Jamestown Canal was first constructed back in the 1770s to by-pass the great loop and its shallows. The early engineers encountered hard rock; there were originally two bends on this canal, it was considerably narrower than now and the lock was sited some distance up the canal. The Shannon Commissioners straightened out and widened the canal and built a new large lock at the downstream end. But it is still possible to find traces of the early canal where it curved around. The best place to see this is on the west side, in the field just below the quay and bridge at the upper end of the canal.

The Dún In very early days the loop of the Shannon offered a good strategic site protected on three sides by the fast flowing river. An earthwork rampart, known today as the 'Dún' was constructed to defend the landward approach. This was a great bank 5 m high and 30 m wide at the base which extended from the high ground by Jamestown bridge right across to meet the river again at the bend just downstream of Drumsna. Parts of the Dún can still be traced: the best place to see it is on the road from Corlara Bridge to the main road which passes through the line of the Dún itself.

Jamestown Bridge, the upstream limit of navigation of the loop

Walter Borner

dicken Mauer umgeben. Davon existiert nur noch das quer über der Hauptstrasse stehende Tor, dessen oberer Teil aber entfernt werden musste.

Carrick-on-Shannon

Seit Jahrhunderten wichtige Übergangsstelle. 1718 wurde eine Brücke mit 17 Bogen gebaut, die vor rund 150 Jahren durch die jetzige ersetzt wurde. Gerichtsgebäude aus dem 18. Jahrhundert. In der Stadtmitte steht die zweitkleinste Kapelle der Welt, die Costello Gedächtniskapelle. Sie ist nur 4,8 x 3,6 Meter gross und 9 Meter hoch. Erbaut wurde sie 1877.

Von Carrick nach Leitrim

Etwa drei Kilometer oberhalb von Carrick fliesst der River Boyle von Westen her in den Shannon. Die Hartley Brücke aus den 30er Jahren ist die erste Brücke Irlands aus armiertem Beton. Der Fluss wird sehr schmal. Im Osten erhebt sich der Berg von Knocknasheen mit seinem prähistorischen Hügelgrab. In Port war früher eine Klostersiedlung mit einer Furt, die von einer Festung geschützt wurde. Nach der nächsten Biegung teilt sich die Fahrrinne, rechts geht es nach Leitrim und zum Shannon Erne Waterway, links nach Battlebridge.

Leitrim

Obwohl das Dorf der Grafschaft seinen Namen gibt, ist es nicht mehr als ein kleiner, aber gemütlicher Flecken. Hier fand O'Sullivan Beare nach seinem langen Marsch Zuflucht.

Jamestown was later recognised as an important strategic site for a fortified town. James I granted it a royal charter and it was surrounded with a wall 6 m high and 1.8 m thick. A castle was erected here but despite these fortifications it changed hands several times and finally the defences were thrown down by Sarsfield's forces. Little remains of the castle by the river but there are some ruins of a Franciscan convent which was founded here in the mid-seventeenth century. A chapel lay inside the walled area but the old graveyard and the ruined church were outside the walls. All that remained of the wall was one of the gateways to which crenellations were added at the end of the eighteenth century by a local proprietor. It spanned the main road but the upper part had to be dismantled to cater for the large modern lorries. It is still hoped that one day the village will be by-passed and the gateway can be restored.

Carrick-on-Shannon (cora droma rúisce—the weir of the marshy ridge) has been an important river crossing down through history. The tolls of the bridge were granted to the local landlord Sir George St George, in 1684 and in return he contracted to keep it in repair. A new bridge with 17 arches was erected in 1718 and the Shannon Commissioners replaced it by the present bridge in the 1840s. Up to this time the navigation works had not been extended north of Carrick but there does appear to have been some trade in small boats upstream to Cootehall on the Boyle River. The town retains some of its old world character with its narrow streets; the old jail complex was removed to make way for the new marina but the eighteenth century courthouse remains. Beside the crossroads, in the centre of the town there is what is reputed to be the second smallest chapel in the world. The Costello Memorial Chapel is only 4.8 m x 3.6 m x 9 m high and it was built in 1877 of stone imported from Bath to house the coffins of Edward Costello and his wife which lie sunk in the floor covered by glass. On the altar there is a motif of two hearts intertwined. There is a marina on the east shore of Lough Corry and another, Carrick marina, a short distance downstream of Carrick-on-Shannon. Emerald Star and Carrick Craft have bases upstream of Carrick bridge.

Walter Borner

Carrick-on-Shannon

Battlebridge

Ende des schiffbaren Teil des Shannons. Durch die Schleuse fährt man in den Lough Allen Kanal.

Lough Allen

Der Kanal wurde für den Transport der im Bergwerk bei Arigna abgebauten Kohle erstellt. Lough Allen wird heute als Reservoir für das Kraftwerk bei Ardnacrusha benutzt. Seit 1978 ist der Kanal wieder bis Acres Lake und seit 1994

Walter Borner

Leitrim

Carrick-on-Shannon to Leitrim About 3 km upstream of Carrick the Shannon is joined from the west by the Boyle Water and continuing up the river the navigation passes awkwardly under Hartley Bridge which was built between 1912-15, one of the first bridges in Ireland to be built using reinforced concrete. The river now assumes a different character and becomes narrow and fast flowing as one approaches the mountains which encircle Lough Allen and its source on Cuilcagh Mountain. The prominent hill of Knocknasheen with its cairn can be seen to the east. There is a paricularly strong flow at Port where in early days there was a ford; there was a small monastic settlement here and the crossing place was later guarded by a fort. Around the next bend the navigation again divides: the righthand channel leads to Leitrim and the Shannon-Erne Waterway, while the river continues on upstream to Battlebridge and the entrance to the Lough Allen Canal.

Leitrim (liath iomaire—the grey ridge) Although it gives its name to the county, this is a small village but is a pleasant place to moor and a visit to the site of Leitrim Castle by the bridge will evoke that day long ago when O'Sullivan Beare sought refuge after his long march. A plaque bearing the O'Sullivan arms recounts:

Here on January 14th 1603 Brian Óg O'Rourke welcomed Donal O'Sullivan Beare and his followers after their epic march from Glengarriff in 14 days. Though one thousand started with him only thirty-five then remained, sixteen armed men, eighteen non-combatants and one woman, the wife of the chief's uncle, Dermot O'Sullivan.

Peter Somerville Large in *From Bantry Bay to Leitrim* describes how he traced the route in the 1970s from a diary kept by the twelve-year-old Philip O'Sullivan, who survived the march. The indefatigable broadcaster Donncha O'Dulaing also followed in the same footsteps in January 1987 and his effort is also commemorated.

Ruth Delany

Lough Allen sluices at Ballintra

Battlebridge Here the river shallows and the navigation enters the Lough Allen Canal. There is a fine old stone bridge which pre-dates the Shannon Commissioners' works. The name infers a battle at some time in the past and there were skirmishes here and further upstream when the French forces led by General Humbert pushed east after their victory at Castlebar in 1798.

The Lough Allen Canal was constructed in 1819-20 to enable coal mined in the Arigna area to be carried down via the Shannon Navigation to the Royal Canal, which had just been completed, and thence to Dublin. But the anticipated coal trade did not materialise because Arigna coal could not compete with coal from across the water either in quality or price. The completion of a railway with a tramway extension to the mining area further diminished trade and when the hydro-electric works were carried out in the 1920's, traffic on the canal had virtually ceased and so it was decided to use Lough Allen as a reservoir with sluices

bis Lough Allen geöffnet. Durch den Bau einer Zweiweg-Schleuse konnte das Problem des unterschiedlichen Wasserstandes zwischen Lough Allen und dem Kanal eliminiert werden. Der See ist 11,2 km lang und 8 km breit. Er kann sehr stürmisch sein, wegen der Berge muss unbedingt auf Fallböen geachtet werden. Von den beiden Anlegestellen aus kann das Land nur mit dem Beiboot erreicht werden. Der Slieve Anierin am Ostufer, der Eisenberg, ist 587 m hoch. Früher wurden hier Eisenerz und Kohle abgebaut. Das Städtchen Drumshanbo kann zu Fuss entweder von der Schleuse oder von der Anlegestelle im Acres Lake erreicht werden. In der Nähe der Ortschaft Dowra am Nordufer findet man die sagenumwobene Feldschanze 'The Black Pig's Race', die angeblich von einem riesigen schwarzen Wildschwein gebaut wurde.

Das Seengebiet von Boyle

Auf der ganzen Strecke ist dies einer der schönsten Abschnitte. Es handelt sich um eine Reihe miteinander verbundener Seen. Die Fahrrinne wurde an einigen Stellen vertieft und eine Schleuse gebaut, um das Gebiet bis in das Lough Key schiffbar zu machen.

Tumna Narrows

Kirchenruine, daneben prähistorische Grabkammer. Vor vielen Jahren seien hier sieben hühnereigrosse Goldkugeln ausgegraben worden.

to control it at Ballantra. This resulted in great fluctuations in levels making it impossible to continue to use the canal; the last boat passed through in 1932. The canal was re-opened to Acres Lake in 1978 but could not be extended into Lough Allen because of these fluctuations. Power from the Shannon scheme now forms a very small part of the national grid and so the ESB agreed to keep Lough Allen at a more constant level and the canal was re-opened into Lough Allen in 1996. Because the level of the lake will vary a two-way lock had to be constructed where the canal joins the lake.

Acres Lake The canal passed through this small lake before reaching Lough Allen and there are good moorings here at a local amenity area. Much of Acres Lake is surrounded by grassland subjected to fluctuating water levels. Here small trees of alder and willow are common with rushes, horsetails, meadowsweet, flag iris and marsh ragweed dominant. The canal is fringed for much of its length by ash, hawthorn, alder and blackthorn with wild roses, honeysuckle and other woodland plants.

Drumshanbo can be approached either from the moorings in Acres Lake or from the new lock. It is a busy town and was formerly an important centre for iron smelting.

Lough Allen Lough Allen is 11.2km long and 8km wide at its widest point. It is surrounded by hills and as you would expect it is a very deep lake. On the east side Slieve Anierin, the iron mountain, rises to 587m. As its name denotes deposits of ironstone were found here and were worked initially using charcoal. Supplies of timber eventually ran out and the iron workings ceased in the 1760's but were restarted in 1788 when three brothers called O'Reilly began to use local coal for smelting. The hills on the west shore are carboniferous and contain some horizontal seams of a semi-bitumous type of coal. Mining fluctuated in the nineteenth century but it was developed in the 1940's when over 1000 tons per week were being railed from Arigna. In the early 1970's a small power station was built on the shores of the lake but despite this mining has now ceased and the government is subsidising other means of providing employment in the area.

The configuration of the hills can produce sudden squalls. There is good mooring above Drumshanbo lock. The canal enters through a small bay at the southern end and there are two mooring places on the lake: one on the east shore at Cleighran Mor and the other at Spencer Harbour on the west shore behind Corry Island.

When the hydro electric works were being constructed and the level of the lake dropped evidence of an ancient bridge out to O'Reilly's Island, near the south east

Lough Drumharlow

Einige der Buchten weisen Riffs auf. Am Südufer steht Woodbrook House, das in dem berühmten Roman 'Woodbrook' von David Thompson unsterblich gemacht wurde.

Cootehall

Cootehall Castle, nahe der Brücke, war ursprünglich ein stattlicher vierseitiger Bau, umgeben von hohen Mauern mit vier Ecktürmen. Während des Aufstands von 1798 wurde es von Rebellen angegriffen und niedergebrannt. Um 1840 wurde die neue Brücke mit acht Bogen gebaut. Östlich der Bucht von Cootehall steht ein Ringfort.

Oakport Lake

Keine Anlegestelle für Schiffe.

Clarendon Lock, Knockvicar

Der alte Baumbestand macht diesen Abschnitt besonders schön.

Walter Borner

Drumshanbo Lock

corner were found. There was also evidence of crannogs, or lake dwellings, in this vicinity and bronze swords and dugout canoes were also exposed along the shores. On Inismagrath in the north east corner of the lake are the remains of a church ascribed to St Beog. There are two other ruined churches on promontories on the west shore at Tarmon and Conagh, all that remains of religous houses. Tarmon was occupied by nuns until they were expelled by Cromwell's soldiers. The village of Dowra lies on the Shannon a few miles upstream of where it enters the lake. From Dowra there is a three-mile stretch of an ancient frontier earthwork running roughly south west from the village to the lake. This is known as the Worm Ditch or the Black Pig's Race because of the legend that it was made by a great serpent or a monstrous black pig.

The Boyle Water This stretch of water from the junction with the Shannon up to Lough Key is one of the most attractive on the entire navigation. It is a series of lakes connected by short stretches of river. It was

Ruth Delany

Knockvicar Bridge

Above Clarendon Lock, Knockvicar

Ruth Delany

Lough Key Forest Park, Rockingham

Für den Naturschutzpark gibt es im Kiosk einen ausgezeichneten Führer mit Angaben aller Sehenswürdigkeiten und der Naturpfade, die ideal zum Spazieren sind. Rockingham ist ein typischer Herrensitz des 19. Jahrhunderts. Im 12. Jahrhundert bauten die McDermots eine Burg auf der Insel, die damals 'The Rock' hiess und heute Castle Island genannt wird. Später errichteten sie noch ein Schloss auf dem Festland. Sir John King baute etwa 1670 das erste Rockingham Haus an der Stelle, wo die Burg gestanden hatte. Nach einem Brand wurde 1810 ein neues Herrenhaus gebaut, das 1957 ausbrannte. An seiner Stelle steht jetzt der viel kritisierte Moylurg Turm. Falls er nicht abgeschlossen ist, bietet er eine wunderbare Sicht über die Gegend. Die Kellerräume und die unterirdischen Gänge sind erhalten, sie wurden von Dienstboten benutzt. Interessant sind die Gutskirche, die Wirtschaftsgebäude, das Eishaus, der Wishing Chair, der demjenigen, der auf ihm sitzt, alle Wünsche erfüllt, der kleine Tempel am Ufer, zwei Kanäle mit ornamentalen Brücken und vieles mehr. Die heutige Ruine auf Castle Island war ein Lustschlösschen aus dem 19. Jahrhundert, das aus den Überresten der alten Burg erbaut und ebenfalls vom Feuer zerstört wurde. Innerhalb des Landguts gibt es fünf Ringforts.

used from early times by small trading boats until the Shannon Commissioners deepened the channel in a few places and constructed one lock to make it fully navigable into Lough Key and up the Boyle River to within a short distance of Boyle.

Tumna Narrows The ruined church of Tumna is on the south shore at the narrows and nearby is St Eidin's Grave, a prehistoric chamber tomb. Samuel Lewis in his *Topographical Dictionary*, published in 1837, records that seven gold balls, the size of eggs, were dug up here.

Lough Drumharlow Some of the bays of this lake are rocky but it is possible to pass either side of Inishatirra. It is a fine expanse of water and it was here in the 1890s that yacht racing under the burgee of the North Shannon Yacht Club first started and later moved downstream to Lough Boderg and then Lough Bofin. On the south shore at the upper end of the lake is Woodbrook House, which was immortalised in David Thomson's classic, *Woodbrook*, in which he describes the years he spent here in the 1930s as tutor to Major Kirkwood's daughter, Phoebe.

Cootehall has also a literary connection: it was here that the novelist John McGahern spent his youth and he used the police station here as the setting for his novel *The Barracks*. The Coote family had been granted extensive lands in this area in the seventeenth century and Sir Charles Coote, and later his son, were greatly feared and hated landlords. Cootehall Castle, near the bridge, was originally a large quadrilateral enclosure with high walls and towers at each corner. It was attacked and burned by insurgents in 1798. Parts of some of the towers remain today and some of the castle buildings which were later converted into a farmhouse. The Shannon Commissioners replaced the former eight-arch bridge here in the 1840s. There is a ring fort in the field to the east of Cootehall Bay.

Oakport Lake There is an amenity area in the south-west corner of the lake but no mooring for cruisers. Oakport House and the wooded demesne make a pretty setting. The navigation winds up the

Walter Borner

Drumman's Island, Lough Key

Trinity Island
Frühchristliches Kloster. Die Ruine einer Abtei aus dem 13. Jahrhundert ist einen Besuch wert (nur mit dem Beiboot möglich).

Walter Borner

Lough Key Forest Park

Rockingham House in the early 1900s

National Library of Ireland

narrowing river passing Tara Marina to Knockvicar Bridge which replaced an older eight-arch structure.

Clarendon Lock, Knockvicar Trees line the river on both sides upstream of the Bridge before the river opens out at the lock and weir, making this a very beautiful stretch.

Lough Key The many wooded islands of Lough Key make this one of the most attractive lakes on the navigation. "The Moorings" restaurant and marina is on the north shore near the entrance to the lake.

Lough Key Forest Park, Rockingham The park is now administered by Coillte (the Forestry Board) and there is an excellent guide book available at the shop, pointing out all the interesting landscape features, the flora and fauna to be seen and the nature trails to be followed. This place is characteristic of a nineteenth century estate with its ornamental buildings and tree-planting of non-native species, its gardens and walkways and it is rich in history and legend.

In the twelfth century the MacDermots built a castle on the island off the shore, known at that time as The Rock and now called Castle Island and later built another castle on the mainland. Sir John King was granted the estate in the seventeenth century and his grandson, Robert, built the first Rockingham House on the site of the MacDermot castle in the 1670s. This house was destroyed by fire and a new mansion was built in 1810. It was designed by John Nash as a two-storey house with a dome but Lord Lorton, great-great-grandson of the first Sir Robert, removed the dome and added another storey because he thought that Nash's design was not as imposing as other great houses of the time. This fine house was gutted by fire in 1957 and two years later Sir Stafford King Harman sold the estate to the state. The much criticised Moylurg Tower now stands on the site of the house and affords a fine view out over the lake and parklands; there are plans to build a hotel on this site. The basement apartments and subterranean passages remain: the latter were used to convey turf

Rockingham House the original design by John Nash

Walter Borner

Lough Key : Rockingham House in 1969

Drum Bridge

Heute noch das Ende der schiffbaren Strecke. An der Öffnung des Flusses bis Boyle wird gearbeitet.

Boyle

Etwa 3,2 km von Drum Bridge entfernt. Sehenswert sind die Ruine der Abtei von Boyle, einer Zisterziensergründung von 1161. Schöne Kirche im Übergangsstil vom Romanischen ins Gotische. Reste der Wirtschaftsgebäude umgeben den früheren Kreuzgang. 1235 Plünderung durch die Anglo-Normannen. Später wurde die Anlage von den Soldaten Cromwells heimgesucht, die viel Schaden anrichteten. In letzter Zeit wurden das zweistöckige Eingangstor sowie das Pförtnerhaus wieder instand gestellt. Besucht werden kann auch das Haus der Kings, das anfangs des 18. Jahrhunderts gebaut wurde.

and supplies to the house without impinging on the view of those living 'upstairs'.

Other interesting features are the estate church, the farm buildings, an ice house, a wishing chair and 'The Temple', a gazebo down on the lakeshore. There are two canals spanned by ornamental bridges, a bog garden and, away to the north-east, another canal with a lock which was used to bring down turf from the neighbouring bog. The castle on the island is a nineteenth century folly built from the remains of the old castle: damaged by fire it is now in a dangerous condition. There are five ring forts within the estate, one with a souterrain or underground passage.

Trinity Island is said to have been the site of an early Christian monastery and in the thirteenth century a house of Premonstratensian canons was established here and the ruined abbey is worth visiting. Church Island and Hermit Island also have featureless ruins.

Boyle Canal The limit of navigation used to be at Drum Bridge on the Boyle River but because of road works a new canal has been constructed leading up to a harbour which is nearing completion.

Lough Key : Castle Island

Walter Borner

Boyle It is a short walk from the new harbour into Boyle. The ruins of Boyle Abbey are well worth a visit. It was established by the Cistercians in 1161 and retains the classic lay-out of a Cistercian monastery, but with some concessions to decoration of which St Bernard of Clairvaux would scarcely have approved. The fine church took many years to build and displays a changing architectural style: Romanesque evolving into Gothic, spanning the first 60 years or so of the monastery's existence. Fragments of the domestic buildings surround what was once the cloister. The abbey was one of the largest and wealthiest in Connacht and had many adventures in medieval times. It took a leading role on the Irish side when a split developed in the Cistercian order in Ireland in the early thirteenth century in opposition to the growing determination of the Anglo-Normans and it was plundered by the latter in 1235. The abbey was finally dissolved in the general suppression in the mid-sixteenth century. The abbey buildings were subsequently used in 1659 by Cromwellian soldiers who showed scant respect and did much damage. In recent conservation works, the two-storey entrance gateway with porter's lodge has been restored and houses the plan of a Cistercian monastery on an upper floor. Boyle was an important coaching stage and is an attractive town. Boyle Barracks, looking out on the river, was the mansion of the King family and is worthy of note. It was built about 1722 almost certainly to the design of the leading Irish exponent of Palladianism, Sir Edward Lovett Pearce.

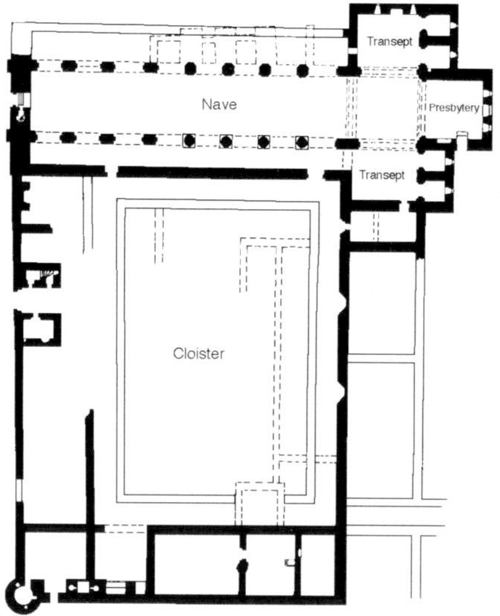

Gill and Macmillan

Boyle Abbey plan

Walter Borner

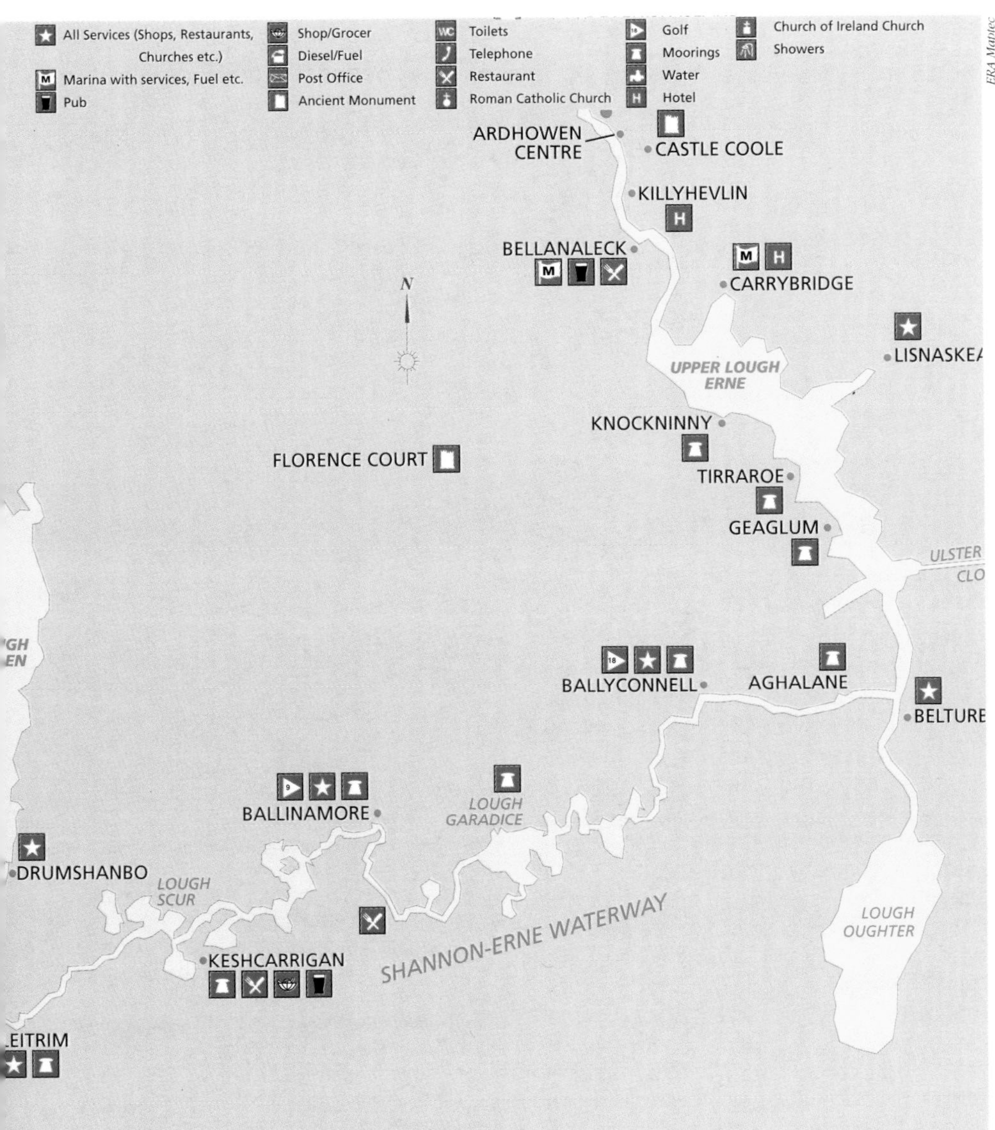

When you leave the River Shannon and move up to **Leitrim** quay you have entered the Shannon-Erne Waterway. This waterway is 61km long and links the Shannon and Erne systems. It is however much more than just a link canal, it is a delightful waterway in its own right passing through rolling drumlin countryside with the higher hills of the Cuilcaghs to the north. It takes 13 hours to make the trip from Leitrim to the Erne. Six new public moorings have been installed at strategic points along the waterway, each fully equipped with a slipway and hard standing for trailer-boats, car park, telephone, toilets, showers, fresh water. . . and what is politely termed 'a pumping-out facility'.

All navigation markers take the form of 'perches', fixed stakes with a distinctive top-mark. For 20 per cent of the route, from the Shannon at Leitrim to the Summit, the top-marks follow the conventions of the Shannon navigation system; but they change near Keshcarrigan to the Erne system for the final stretch to the Erne.

Locks are numbered from 1 to 16, starting from the Erne.

The first of a series of 6 mooring places is sited just above the bridge at **Leitrim.** This sleepy little hamlet, with its old stone quayside and bridge, has new public moorings of the floating-dock type. Close by is the last remaining wall of **O'Rourke's Castle,** goal of an epic exploit. Following the crushing defeat of the Irish and Spanish forces at the Battle of Kinsale in 1601, Donal O'Sullivan Beare was determined to continue the war against the English. In 1602, in the depths of winter, he led 1,000 of his remaining kinsfolk from Bantry Bay in the far south-western corner of Ireland on a fighting march to the north. He planned

to join forces with Brian of the Battleaxes, Leitrim's hereditary O'Rourke chieftain and one of the few remalning Irish leaders still holding out against the common enemy. O'Sullivan arrived here 14 days later with only 35 of his people; all the rest were dead or fallen by the wayside.

As with the 15 locks that follow, the cut-stone chamber is fitted with steel gates, activated electrically from a push-button console on the bank. The instructions are conveyed by diagrams to avoid language difficulties.

The first 10.45km of the waterway is canal rising up 24m through 8 locks to the summit level where the waterway passes through a spectacular stretch of rock-cutting before entering **Lough Scur.** Here the waterway enters Summit Reach, a level stretch of water at the highest part of navigation, crossing the watershed between the Erne and Shannon catchments. There was a bardic school near here in former times. Today, the solitary lake is off the beaten track but it was evidently a popular place to live in prehistoric times. A dolmen at the south-western end was set up by Stone Age farmers some 4,500 years ago. Almost certainly, the builders lived in the extensive lake-dwellings discovered here. Excavations revealed that they fished in the lough, hunted in the forests with flint-tipped arrows, and tended their crops and livestock along the shore. The National Museum in Dublin has some interesting finds from the lake, most notably a dugout canoe carved from a tree-trunk and several wooden shields.

The ruin on Prison Island has a gruesome history. It was built in Elizabethan times by John Reynolds, a formidable gentleman who deserted his fellow countrymen to become High Sheriff of the county under the English Crown. He was feared far and wide as Séan na gCeann, or 'John of the Heads', because of his partiality for decapitating people! He built the prison in around 1570 to hold his rebellious neighbours. It's a miniature Alcatraz, standing on a rock jutting into the lake, its massive walls loop-holed to defend it against attack from without. Many a poor wretch died here in torment. Reynolds also built Castle John, the ruined fortified mansion on the north shore. He invited a company of local chieftains to a banquet here one night; after they had handed up their swords and sat down to wine, their genial host ordered his henchmen to fall on them. They were all massacred. Keeping to the south shore of this attractive lake to the exit point in the south east corner, the navigation passes close to the village of **Keshcarrigan** Where the second mooring area is located. The peace of this tiny lakeland village has not been seriously disturbed for 200 years. The last time was in 1798 when General Humbert, commanding a revolutionary

Walter Borner

Loch Scur

Der Shannon-Erne-Wasserweg verbindet Leitrim mit dem Upper Lough Erne. Er führt über eine Distanz von 61 km durch eine reizvolle Landschaft mit vielen kleinen Hügeln und den Cuilgaghs-Bergen im Norden, wo der Shannon entspringt. Sechzehn nach modernstem Standard konstruierte Schleusen sind bis zum Lough Erne zu passieren, je acht auf der Berg- und acht auf der Talfahrt. Schleusenwärter gibt es hier nicht, die Besatzung muss also die Schleusen selber bedienen. Als reine Fahrzeit für die ganze Strecke von Leitrim bis zum Upper Lough Erne sollte man rund dreizehn Stunden rechnen. Offizielle Anlegestellen befinden sich in Leitrim, Keshcarrigan, Ballinamore, Houghton's Shore, Ballyconnell und Aghalane, jede hat Telefon, Toiletten, Duschen, Frischwasser und zum Teil sogar Waschmaschinen, die mit der gleichen Karte wie die Schleusen bedient werden.

Obschon der offizielle Name Ballinamore-Ballyconnell-Kanal lautet; handelt es sich nur bei ungefähr einem Sechstel um Kanalfahrt. Der Rest sind Seen und Flüsse. Von Leitrim kommend ist man nach etwa elf Kilometern auf dem Scheitelpunkt bei Lough Scur angelangt, von wo aus die Talfahrt an Keshcarrigan vorbeiführt und durch

Ruth Borner

Operating the Control Panel

expedition to Ireland, marched through it at the head of a mixed army of French regulars and Irish insurgents on his way south to the fateful Battle of Ballinamuck. History has put down deep roots here. A local find, the Keshcarrigan Bowl, now features in the National Museum's fabulous collection of prehistoric gold objects. During the season you can take a tour on "The Gertie" tour boat, telephone 078 - 42252.

Keshcarrigan, sits at the foot of Sheebeg, junior partner of Sheemore, the other fairy mountain nearby. The two hills, abodes of the Sidhe - the Little People - inspired the intricate melody, Sheemore, Sheebeg, which is a sort of local national anthem. A favourite with traditional musicians all over Ireland, it is doubly valued because it was composed by blind Turlough O'Carolan (1670-1738), the last Irish bard, who lived not far away near Mohill. History does not record if O'Carolan borrowed the tune from the Little People. All his life, the great harper and poet travelled the land with his music, equally welcome in the mansions of the gentry and the cottages of the poor. It would be a strange thing indeed if the Little People neglected to invite him to play for them in their secret palaces under the hills! Sheebeg is well worth the climb for the view. Fionn Mac Cumhal (or Finn McCool), the hero of a voluminous folklore, is supposed to be buried on the hill. The summit is crowned by a passage-mound, precision-built by the Stone Age farming community for observing the annual cycle of the sun and predicting the seasons of the year. It is important to follow the marked channel on this stretch because some of the surrounding area had to be flooded to obtain navigation depths in the channel.

From here the waterway is river navigation with further passages through a number of lakes. This means that at each of the descending locks there is also a weir. The first of these locks is at Castlefore. 2.4km downstream the navigation enters **St John's Lough** and two futher small lakes before reaching the second descending lock at **Ballyduff**. From here it's on to the town of **Ballinamore**, where the third mooring area is provided near the weir, a short distance above the town, at the head of a large artifical island, now

Control Panel

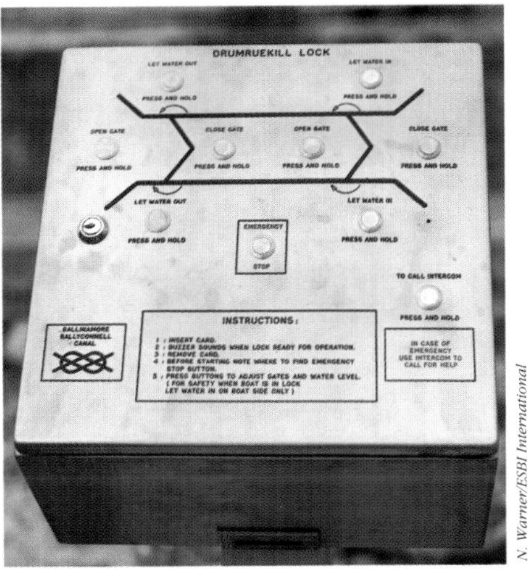

N. Warner/ESBI International

St. Johns und Lough Garadice den Woodford River erreicht. Die Markierungen, auf dem Shannon rot und schwarz, wechseln bei Keshcarrigan auf das Erne-System mit der weiss-roten Bezeichnung der Fahrrinne. Speziell im oberen Teil des Wasserweges sind sowohl die Seen als auch der Fluss zum Teil sehr seicht, man muss sich unbedingt an die Markierungen halten.

Direkt nach der Brücke in Leitrim, einem ruhigen, kleinen Dorf, befinden sich die ersten Anlegeplätze. In der Nähe liegt die Ruine von O'Rourke's Castle. Nach der Niederlage der irischen und spanischen Truppen in der Schlacht von Kinsale im Jahre 1601 versuchte im folgenden Winter eine Hilfstruppe, von Bantry Bay aus zu den in Leitrim ausharrenden Iren zu gelangen. Nach zwei Wochen erreichten von den ursprünglich tausend Mann nur noch deren 35 das Ziel.

Wie schon erwähnt, führen die ersten elf Kilometer mit einem Höhenunterschied von 24 Metern, zu deren Ueberwindung acht Schleusen gebaut wurden, zur Wasserscheide und durch einen bemerkenswerten, in Felsen gehauenen Kanal zum Lough Scur. Ganz in der Nähe befand sich früher eine Schule für Barden. Heute liegt der See abseits des Verkehrs, Ausgrabungen haben aber gezeigt, dass in der Steinzeit, so etwa vor 4500 Jahren, die Gegend besiedelt war. Die Fundstücke sind heute im National-Museum in Dublin ausgestellt.

Die Ruine von Prison Island hat eine grausame Geschichte. Erbaut wurde das Gefängnis um 1570 von einem gewissen John Reynolds, der sein Land verriet, um High Sheriff unter der englischen Krone zu werden. Weit und breit war er unter dem Namen 'Séan na gCeann' oder 'John von den Köpfen' gefürchtet wegen seiner Vorliebe für das Enthaupten der Gegner. Der Bau gleicht einem kleinen Alcatraz. Einmal lud er die lokalen Häuptlinge zu einem Nachtessen ein. Nachdem sie ihre Waffen abgegeben hatten, fielen seine Anhänger über die Gäste her und brachten alle um.

Verlassen wir die blutrünstige Geschichte und wenden wir uns Keshcarrigan zu, dem zweiten Anlegeplatz auf unserer Fahrt zum Erne. Während der letzten 200 Jahre wurde der Friede hier nicht sonderlich gestört. Das letzte Mal war das 1798, als General Humbert mit einer aus Iren und Franzosen zusammengesetzten Armee zur verhängnisvollen Schlacht von Ballinamuck marschierte.

Keshcarrigan liegt am Fuss des Berges Shee-

Walter Borner

Lock on Shannon-Erne Waterway

attractively landscaped. The river proper flows down around it on the town side, under a three-arch stone bridge carrying the road to Carrick-on-Shannon. The navigation negotiates the other side of the island along a steep cutting. It passes through Lock No.6 (Ballinamore Lock) and under a separate road bridge to rejoin the river below the town. Before continuing downstream, a turn to the left here will bring you to another mooring place by the town bridge.

Ballinamore's pubs can be relied on for well-drawn pints and lively conversation. It's a good town for shops, too. Potato bread ('boxty') is a local speciality that should on no account be missed, though it could take some time to sample the many varieties on offer! An interesting Heritage Centre, which is also the headquarters for genealogical research for the county, is housed in the restored County Library. The town also has a 9 hole golf course.

If you have a taste for poetic justice, take a second look at the arcade along the river wall near the town bridge. It was built to carry the Cavan and Leitrim Railway, which helped seal the fate of the original waterway in 1866-67 by spanning it with obstructively low - and quite unlawful - bridges in several places. In a final gesture of contempt, the railway company commandeered the waterway's cut-stone wharf as the site for its workshops. The track has long since been uprooted, the offending iron bridges sold for scrap and the railway workshop buildings converted to other uses so the waterway has the last laugh in the end.

Three more locks lead down to the beautiful **Lough Garadice**. This is undoubtedly the jewel of this waterway, a most attractive winding lake with a number of wooded islands which is well known for its fishing. The fourth mooring area is at **Haughton's Shore** at the exit from Garadice. Four small lakes, **Ballymagauran**, **Derrycassan, Coologe** and **Woodford** follow and from here the navigation is in the Woodford River for the remaining 20.8km to the Upper Erne. Three more locks have to be negotiated to the Erne the middle one is at the town of **Ballyconnell** where the fifth mooring area is located.

beg, der kleineren Ausgabe des nahegelegenen Sheemore. Der letzte irische Barde, der blinde Turlough O'Carolan (1670-1738), wurde von diesen beiden Hügeln zur Komposition der Melodie 'Sheemore, Sheebeg' inspiriert, einer noch heute in Irland gern gespielten Weise. Es ist zwar nicht erwiesen, ob er die Melodie nicht vom Kleinen Volk erhalten hat. Sein ganzes Leben wanderte der Harfenspieler und Poet nämlich durch das Land, spielte in den Häusern der Reichen und der Armen, und es wäre ein Wunder, hätte er nicht auch das Kleine Volk besucht, das unter den Bergen wohnt.

Von hier aus fährt man flussabwärts durch mehrere Seen. Um genügend Tiefe für die Schifffahrt zu erhalten, musste zum Teil das Land auf beiden Seiten des Flusses unter Wasser gesetzt werden. Es ist deshalb sehr wichtig, sich hier genau an die Fahrrinne zu halten.

Kurz nach der Castlefore-Schleuse werden St. Johns Lough und zwei weitere kleine Seen erreicht, bevor die Schleuse von Ballyduff passiert werden kann. Die nächste Anlegestelle befindet sich in Ballinamore nahe dem Wehr, nur einige Minuten oberhalb des Städtchens an einer künstlichen Insel. Der Fluss läuft an der Stadtseite unter der alten Steinbrücke mit der Strasse nach Carrick-on-Shannon durch, die Schiffsroute folgt der andern Seite der Insel, führt durch die Schleuse und nach dem Passieren einer Brücke in den Fluss zurück.

Ballinamore ist ein angenehmer Rastplatz. Die Pubs sind bekannt für ihre Pints, die Einheimischen offen für Gespräche an der Theke. Einkaufsmöglichkeiten hat es mehr als genug, und wer gerne Kartoffelbrot (boxty) isst, darf sich die Gelegenheit zum Probieren dieser lokalen Spezialität nicht entgehen lassen.

Wer Sinn für ausgleichende Gerechtigkeit hat, sollte sich die Arkade in der Nähe der Stadtbrücke ansehen. Sie wurde für die Cavan and Leitrim Railway gebaut, jener Eisenbahn, welche vor über hundert Jahren das Schicksal des Kanals durch ihre niederen und gegen das Gesetz verstossenden Brückenbauten besiegelte. Wer zuletzt lacht, lacht am besten, denn der Kanal ist mittlerweile auferstanden, während die Bahn längst verschrottet ist.

Drei weitere Schleusen, die erste noch mitten in Ballinamore, führen zum schönen Lough Garadice, dem unbestreitbaren Juwel dieses Wasserwegs. Garadice ist ein attraktives Gewäs-

Walter Borner

Ballinamore Harbour

This little community at the foot of Slieve Russell mountain (406m), earned the remarkable distinction of winning the National Tidy Towns Award on two occasions. It is a popular fishing centre and also boasts a luxurious country club and championship golf course at the Slieve Russell Hotel. Ballyconnell's pubs offer lots of music, traditional and modern, and there is a good selection of provision shops. The local Church of Ireland, built in the troubled 17th century, is surrounded by earthen fortifications. Two diamond-shaped redoubts date from the bitter war between James II and William of Orange for the throne of England, 1689-90.

The town is named after the legendary warrior, Conal Cearnach (Conal the Victorious), a central figure in Táin Bó Cuailnge (the Reeving of Cooley) and other epic tales from the pagan Celtic Iron Age. He was killed here - possibly around the first century BC in a river-ford near the town bridge - fighting the men of Connacht who had come to avenge the death of their king. A tangible survivor from that period, the Killycluggin Stone, stands some 5km from the town along the road to Ballinamore. It is carved in graceful La Têne patterns and may have been the stone at which the kings of the territory were inaugurated.

Magh Sleacht, the Plain of Slaughter, is 6km outside Ballyconnell. According to early Christian legend, this was an important pagan cult-centre where human sacrifices were offered to placate a

ser mit vielen bewaldeten Inseln. Die vierte Anlegestelle ist Haughton's Shore am Ausgang des Sees. Dann folgen vier kleinere Seen, Ballymagauran, Derrycassan, Coologe und Woodford. Für die verbleibenden gut zwanzig Kilometer folgt der Wasserweg dem Lauf des Woodford-Rivers zum Upper Erne. Bis dorthin müssen noch drei weitere Schleusen passiert werden, wobei die mittlere im Städtchen Ballyconnell liegt.

Dieser kleine Ort am Fuss des Slieve Russel Berges (406m) ist ein bekanntes Zentrum für Sportfischer und verfügt ebenso über einen luxuriösen Golf-Club. Seine Pubs sind berühmt für traditionelle und moderne irische Volksmusik, seine Läden eignen sich ausgezeichnet zum Füllen des Bordkühlschranks. Die mit Erdwällen befestigte Kirche stammt aus dem 17. Jahrhundert.

Der Name des Städtchens geht auf den legendären Krieger Conal Cearnach (Conal der Siegreiche) zurück, eine zentrale Figur in 'Tain Bo Cuailnge' und andern Erzählungen aus der keltischen Eisenzeit. Er wurde hier im Kampf gegen die Männer aus Connacht getötet, die gekommen waren, den Tod ihres Königs zu rächen. Etwa fünf Kilometer entfernt, an der Strasse nach Ballinamore, steht der Killycluggin-Stein. Er weist Muster aus der keltischen La Têne-Zeit auf und war möglicherweise die Krönungsstätte der regionalen Könige.

Magh Sleacht, die Blutige Ebene, liegt etwa sechs Kilometer ausserhalb der Stadt. Nach einer Legende handelt es sich um einen Platz, auf dem in vorchristlicher Zeit für einen hölzernen Gott Menschenopfer dargebracht wurden. Im Jahre

Ballinamore Lock

Ruth Borner

bloodthirsty wooden idol called Crom Cruaic, the Hunched One of the Mound. In AD 432, during the first months of his mission, Saint Patrick is said to have come here, in defiance of the prohibitions of the druids and the High King of Ireland, to confront the gold-bedecked monster and its twelve satellite idols. By tumbling them to the ground without being struck down himself in retribution, he demonstrated that his God was the more powerful. It was a crucial turning point in his campaign to win credibility for Christianity.

The bridge at Aghalane, the last of 31 bridges spanning the waterway, was a handsome three-arch affair built in 1849 at an early stage of the original construction. The bridge was demolished during the recent troubled years and will have to be replaced to restore this cross border route. The spanking new public moorings nearby are very much a modern product. This one is a floating dock, allowing you to step comfortably ashore whatever the water level.

On the right, a short distance before entering the Erne, is Lough Tee-more, from which a cutting leads to the market town of Belturbet in County Cavan.

The waterway's exit into Upper Lough Erne is directly across the lake from romantic Crom Castle, seat of the Earl of Erne. Its 1350 acres of woodland, wetland and parkland on the County Fermanagh shore (open to the public) are among Northern Ireland's most important conservation areas. The last 10km of the waterway actually form the boundary between Northern Ireland and the Republic as it wends its way along the course of the Woodford River.

The Reconstruction

The project to re-open this navigation commenced in 1990 and was completed in 1994. It was a joint undertaking funded by the Irish and British governments, the E.C. Structural Funds, the International Fund for Ireland and the ESB at an estimated cost of £30 million. The project was managed by ESB International, a subsidiary of ESB and is now administered by the Waterways Service and the Department of Agriculture, Northern Ireland.

The restoration has been a major undertaking involving the enlarging of the channel throughout, the rebuilding of banks, repairing eight of the locks and completely rebuilding the remaining locks on the eastern end of the waterway together with new weirs required at each of these locks. Four bridges had to be completely replaced and extensive work carried out on the thirty other bridges. In both the lock and bridge reconstruction the attractive cutstone facing was restored The locks are operated by an automatic system which the crews of the boats work themselves.

A detailed environmental impact study was carried out before work began and an important element of the scheme was the preservation of the wildlife habitats and attractive natural features along the waterway. This was achieved by endeavouring to leave one bank intact

Walter Borner

Haughton's Shore

432 gelang dem heiligen Patrick der Beweis, dass sein Gott stärker war als das angebetete Stück Holz. Das war ein wichtiger Schritt auf dem Weg zur Christianisierung des Landes.

Die Brücke von Aghalane, die letzte von total 31, wurde 1849 erbaut. Im Zuge der Wirren wurde sie demoliert und muss nun, um die Strasse über die Grenze wieder zu öffnen, neu gebaut werden. Auf der rechten Seite, vor der Einfahrt in den Erne, liegt Lough Teemore. Die direkte Durchfahrt zum Marktflecken Belturbet wurde ausgebaggert und ist gut markiert.

Der eigentliche Wasserweg mündet hier in das Upper Lough Erne. Auf der Gegenseite liegt Crom Castle, Sitz des Grafen von Erne. Seine 1350 acres (1 acre = 36 Aren) Wald, Moor und Parklandschaft, die dem Publikum offen stehen, gehören zu Nordirlands wichtigsten Reservaten. Die letzten zehn Kilometer des Wasserwegs bildet der Woodford-River die Grenze zwischen der Republik und Nordirland.

Wiederaufbau

Die Rekonstruktion dieses in der Mitte des letzten Jahrhunderts entstandenen Wasserwegs begann 1990 als Gemeinschaftswerk der irischen und der britischen Regierung sowie weiteren Institutionen. Die Kosten betrugen rund 30 Millionen Pfund. Acht Schleusen konnten restauriert werden, weitere acht wurden neu erstellt. Vier Brücken mussten ersetzt werden, bei den übrigen waren grosse Unterhaltsarbeiten erforderlich. Im Gegensatz zum Shannon werden im

wherever possible. Access routes and a towpath for walkers were also provided.

History.

This canal was constructed to provide the final link in a waterway system from Belfast to Limerick in 1853-60. By this time there was less demand for such a route and the work was never completed to the full specifications and attracted virtually no traffic. It operated from 1860-69 and only 8 boats paid tolls amounting to £18, a poor return on the investment of a quarter of a million pounds. The canal was closed and quickly deteriorated and a railway was later built along much of its route in 1887. Periodic flooding drew attention to the waterway and the Inland Waterways Association of Ireland suggested a full survey should be commissioned. The Office of Public Works carried out surveys and studies on the waterway from 1971 and produced a feasibility report in 1986. Eventually the Irish and British governments decided to carry out the restoration as a flagship project. It was considered that not only would it link these two great waterways providing a navigation unrivalled in Europe but it would be a scheme of immense importance in forging crossborder links and bring back prosperity to this area on both sides of the Border which had suffered so much from the years of conflict.

Fishing

The Shannon-Erne Waterway is a great fishery with excellent bream, roach and pike fishing. Lough Scur is a great water for bream and other species. Church shore, Connolly's shore and Haughton's shore on Garadice Lake hold good roach and bream and Little Garadice is also a favourite place for bream and roach. Coologue Lake is rich with quality bream and the connecting link with Derrycassin Lake is also good for roach and bream. The river sections down to Lough Erne all have good roach, bream, roach and bream hybrids, pike, perch and eels.

The lock and weir at Ardrum near Ballinamore under construction

N. Warner/ESBI International

neuen Kanal die Schleusen von den Benützern selbst bedient. Die offizielle Eröffnung des Wasserwegs erfolgte 1994, gegen 200 Privatboote nahmen daran mit einem zehntägigen Rally teil.

Bei den im Gelände und den Ufern notwendigen Arbeiten wurde strikte auf eine naturnahe Verbauung geachtet. Das Resultat darf sich sehen lassen, und bereits in wenigen Jahren wird nichts mehr an die dreijährige Bauzeit erinnern. Wegen der Erosion der Ufer muss unbedingt starker Wellenschlag vermieden werden, deshalb ist die Geschwindigkeit begrenzt.

Geschichte

Der Ballinamore-Ballyconnell-Kanal wurde zwischen 1853 und 1860 gebaut und sollte als wichtige Verbindung zwischen den Städten Belfast und Limerick dienen. Wie die übrigen Kanäle in Irland war er aber schon bei der Fertigstellung von der Entwicklung überholt und nur neun Jahre in Betrieb. Den Baukosten von rund 200'000 Pfund standen Betriebseinnahmen von total 18 Pfund gegenüber. Im Jahre 1887 wurde entlang dem Kanal eine Eisenbahn gebaut, der Wasserweg verfiel. Erste Studien zur Wiedereröffnung wurden von der irischen Regierung bereits 1971 aufgenommen, und es ist zu hoffen, dass durch die Inbetriebnahme dieses in Europa einmaligen Wasserwegs, der zwei bisher getrennte Reviere verbindet, auch die Zukunft dieser Region beidseits der Grenzen neu beginnen kann.

Fischen

Der Shannon-Erne-Wasserweg eignet sich ausgezeichnet zum Fischen von Brassen, Plötzen und Hechten. Aufzuzählen, wo die besten Plätze liegen, macht wenig Sinn. Erstens merkt ein richtiger Sportfischer selbst, wo die Fische stehen, und zweitens sollte auch ein wenig Spannung bleiben. Egli und Hechte hat es vor allem im unteren Teil des Wasserweges.

Gazetteer - Erne Navigation

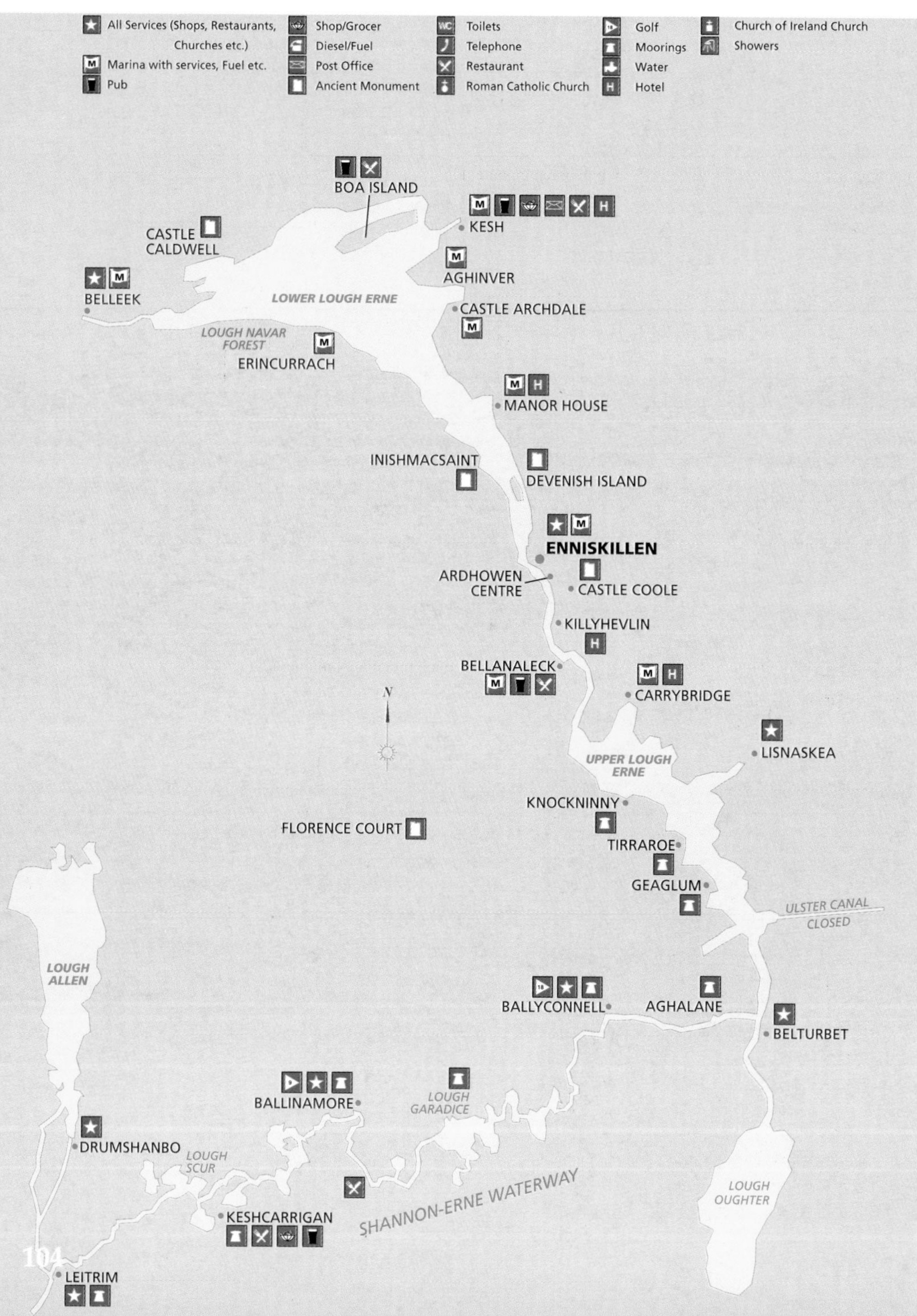

Emerging from the Shannon-Erne Waterway into Upper Lough Erne a maze of channels present themselves. The navigation is marked with an extremely simple and efficient system which makes moving among the islands and bays very easy and foolproof. The Erne catchment lies in drumlin country and the drumlins or mounds of glacial drift create a series of islands which break the lake up into what appears to be a series of small lakes. Roughly one fifth of the area of the Upper Lough is made up of islands and the total shore line is over 100 miles long.

Belturbet lies upstream and can be approached either through Foalies Cut or by taking a much longer route around Inisfendra. A glance at the map will show that you have been cruising along the line of the Border for much of the time and that Belturbet lies in the Republic. It is a good centre with two marinas, an Emerald Star hire boat base and a town with all facilities where you can enjoy pubs with traditional Irish music, with good mooring places convenient to the town. This is the limit of navigation but there are plans to put a lock here which would extend the navigation into Lough Oughter, a similar drumlin country lake with many islands and the attractive Killykeen Forest Park.

Heading downstream again, a different route can be followed into the delightful **Quivvy Waters** up to Wattle Bridge. This is the limit of navigation and before returning downstream it is worth mooring to the bank to inspect the 26th lock on the Ulster Canal which is just short of the bridge on the port hand looking towards the bridge. The Ulster Canal is now derelict but if it were to be restored it would link the Shannon Erne systems with the waterways of the north east through Lough Neagh. Because of its strategic importance the feasibility of restoration is under consideration by both governments.

Walter Borner

Gad Island

There is good bank mooring in this area and a number of good mooring jetties including a jetty at **Lanesborough Lodge**. This was formerly the home of the Butler family which was burnt during the troubled years in the early 1920s. At one time, up to the 1914-18 War, this part of the Erne was the scene of many boating and sailing parties with the Butlers joining with the Crichtons of Crom Castle, the Saundersons of Castle Saunderson and other society families to race in Crom Bay. Yet another channel passing under Galloon Bridge swings back again to Crom Bay.

There is a mooring near the old **Crom Castle** where a visitor centre has been established in the former farm buildings. This centre provides a very good introduction to the Erne Navigation over the centuries, including the period when all the big houses in the area were occupied and there was much social activity, together with information about the flora and fauna (National Trust, tel. 013657-38174). The old Crom Castle dates back to the early seventeenth century and it came into the possession of the Crichton family in the mid 1660s, who later took the title of Earls of Erne. Because of its strategic postion on the lakeshore commanding the main navigation, it played a role in the Williamite wars. The castle was badly damaged by an accidental fire in 1764 but the new castle was not built until the 1830s and was constructed in the neo-Gothic style. While this house is not open to the public, it is possible to visit the old castle and enjoy walks around the estate. Another small castle lies on the tiny **Gad Island** which is a nineteenth century folly.

One of the attractions of the Upper Lough are the quiet mooring places and there is one of these at **Geaglum**. A short distance to the north **Trasna Island** almost

Wer vom Shannon-Erne-Wasserweg in das Upper Lough Erne einläuft, findet sich in einem Labyrinth von Inseln und Durchfahrten. Aber die Navigation ist sehr gut mit einem einfachen System markiert, welches das Fahren und sich Zurechtfinden einfach und narrensicher macht. Wichtig ist, sich immer genau nach den Markierungsnummern über die gegenwärtige Position klar zu sein und sich beim Einlaufen wegen der Untiefen genau an die Markierungen zu halten. Die Erne-Seen liegen in einem Feld von Drumlins aus der letzten Eiszeit, die den See in eine - wie es scheint - Vielzahl von kleinen Seen unterteilen. Ungefähr ein Fünftel des Gebiets vom Upper Lough Erne besteht aus Inseln, die Uferlinie wird dadurch über hundert Meilen lang.

Belturbet liegt am oberen Ende und kann entweder direkt durch den Foalies Cut oder auch auf dem längeren Weg rund um Inisfendra erreicht werden. Ein Blick auf die Karte zeigt, dass das Schiff längere Zeit auf der Grenze fuhr und die Besatzung steuerbord sich in der Republik, diejenige backbord aber in Nordirland aufhielt. Belturbet wiederum gehört zur Republik und ist ein gutes Zentrum mit zwei Marinas, einer Emerald Star-Basis und direkt beim Ort gelegenen Anlegeplätzen. Heute ist hier noch das Ende der Schiffahrt, aber es bestehen Pläne für den Bau einer Schleuse, welche die Fahrt bis Lough Oughter ermöglichen würde, einem ähnlichen See mit Inseln und dem attraktiven Killykee-Wald. Im Ort selbst hat es eine Anzahl guter Pubs mit und ohne irische Volksmusik.

Stromabwärts kann man einer neuen Route folgen, welche direkt in die Quivvy Waters bis hinauf zur Wattle Bridge führt. Hier lohnt es sich, kurz anzulegen und die 26. Schleuse des Ulster-Kanals zu besichtigen. Dieser Kanal ist nicht in Betrieb, bei einer allfälligen Restaurierung würde er aber das Shannon-Erne-System mit dem in der Nähe von Belfast gelegenen Lough Neagh verbinden. Wegen seiner Bedeutung für den Tourismus wird die Instandstellung zur Zeit von beiden Regierungen geprüft.

In dieser Gegend hat es nebst den Jetties auch an den Ufern viele gute Anlegestellen. Lanesborough Lodge war früher der Sitz der Butler Familie, bevor es in den Wirren der 2Oer-Jahre niederbrannte. Ein guter Anlegeplatz befindet sich ebenfalls nahe dem alten Crom Castle, wo in einem früheren Bauernhaus ein Besucherzen-

forms a bridge across the lake, there were ferries here from early times and now the Lady Craigavon and Lady Brooke bridges span the channels. South of the bridge at **Derryad** on the east shore is the Lisnaskea Water Ski and Motor Boat Club. There are good places to eat in **Lisnaskea** and they will provide a taxi service to the lakeside on request. You may even encounter a Viking longship in these waters which is attached to the nearby Share Holiday Village.

Ahead lies a maze of islands and channels to follow with a quiet mooring at **Tirraroe** which is a good example of the Erne Navigation saying: "More space, less pace". At **Knockninny** Carrick Craft have their Erne base and it is well worth climbing the little hill here from which it is possible to see the lake spread out and the complexity of its islands and channels are unravelled.

There is a choice of channels once again at the northern end of the lake: one takes you through **Carrybridge** where there is a marina and a hotel, which is a popular stopping place for cruisers, and from here the east channel is the main navigation. The other channel to the west of **Inishmore** is narrower and has a restricted headroom of 4.5m. The Sheelin restaurant at **Bellanaleck, The Moorings** and the **Killyhevlin Hotel** are further places where you can tie up and have a meal ashore before reaching Enniskillen. There is also a large public jetty at the **Ardhowen Arts Centre** where there is a theatre, exhibition area and restaurant; it is worth calling in to check the programme which is very varied. This is a good place from which to visit **Castle Coole House**, seat of the Earl of Belmore. Built at the end of the eighteenth century it is one of the finest neo-Classical mansions in the country. The house with its fascinating

Crom Castle

N.I. Tourist Board

trum eingerichtet wurde. Dort erhält man ausgezeichnete Informationen sowohl über die Erne-Navigation wie auch über die vergangenen Zeiten, als die grossen Herrensitze der Umgebung noch bewohnt waren.

Das alte Schloss wurde anfangs des 17. Jahrhunderts erbaut und gehörte seit 1660 der Crichton Familie, die später den Titel der Grafen von Erne erhielten. Wegen seiner strategisch günstigen Lage spielte es eine grosse Rolle in den Williaminschen Kriegen. 1764 wurde es durch ein Feuer zerstört, der Neubau des neuen Schlosses im neugotischen Stil erfolgte allerdings erst 1830. Im Gegensatz zum neuen können das alte Schloss und das Grundstück besichtigt werden. Ein anderer, im 19. Jahrhundert erbauter Turm steht auf Gad Island und empfängt die Richtung Enniskillen fahrenden Schiffe.

Einer der vielen schönen Anlegeplätze des Upper Lough Erne ist Geaglum. Die nördlich gelegene Insel Trasna Island bildet fast eine Brücke über den See. In früheren Zeiten verkehrte hier ein Fährschiff, heute überspannen die Lady Craigavon und die Lady Brooke-Brücken das Wasser. Südlich der Brücke, in Derryad am Ostufer, liegt der Lisnaskea Wasserski- und Motorboot-Club. Der Ort hat ausgezeichnete Restaurants, die auch einen Taxidienst zum See betreiben. Manchmal begegnet man hier sogar einem Langschiff der Wikinger, das zum nahegelegenen Share Holiday Village gehört.

Voraus liegt ein Irrgarten von Inseln und Durchfahrten, in Knockninny die neue Erne-Basis von Carrick Craft. Ein Spaziergang auf den kleinen Hügel lohnt sich wegen der Rundsicht über den See mit seinen Inseln und schmalen Passagen. Eine Auswahl von Durchfahrten steht am Nordende des Sees zur Verfügung. Man kann entweder über Carrybridge mit seiner Marina und dem Hotel, einem beliebten Anlegeplatz der Besatzungen, fahren oder diejenige von Inishmore nehmen. Von hier aus wird meistens die Ostpassage benützt. Die andere, westlich von Inishmore ist schmäler und hat bei der Brücke eine auf 4,5 Meter begrenzte Durchfahrtshöhe. Das Sheelin Restaurant in Bellanaleck, The Moorings und das Killyhevlin Hotel sind weitere Möglichkeiten, der Bordküche zu entfliehen, bevor Enniskillen erreicht wird. Eine weitere grosse Jetty befindet sich beim Ardhowen Arts Centre mit seinem Theater, seinen Ausstellungsräumen und

interiors and furnishings is open to the public (National Trust, tel. 01365-322690).

Enniskillen is built on an island and it was the principal place to cross the Erne from early times. There is good mooring at the Lakeland Forum jetty which is convenient to the main street shopping area. **Enniskillen Castle** was first erected in the fifteenth century by the Maguires to guard this important crossing place. The castle had to be largely rebuilt in the early seventeenth century and at this time the two distinctive turrets, known today as the **Watergate**, were added which dominate the river approach. Originally a drawbridge crossed the river from the gate but the lowering of the water levels in the Upper Lough make it difficult to envisage this today. The castle houses the Fermanagh County Museum, the Watergate History and Heritage Centre with dioramas and audio visual displays and the Regimental Museum of the Royal Inniskillings Fusiliers (open daily and afternoons on Saturday and Sunday tel.01365-325000 for opening hours). **St Macartan's Church of Ireland Cathedral** was built in 1840 but incorporates a seventeenth century tower and north porch. There is also a fine early nineteenth century **Townhall** with a decorated clocktower. The restored **Buttermarket** is well worth a visit. It was built in the mid nineteenth century and now houses craft workshops and craft exhibitions with street entertainment and traditional music performances (open daily Monday to Saturday). You can also climb the 108 steps to the top of the Cole Monument for a spectacular view of the town (open daily, afternoons only on Saturday and Sunday).

Castle Coole House

NI Tourist Board

Restaurant. Von hier aus kann das Castle Coole House besucht werden, Sitz des Grafen von Belmore. Das im 18. Jahrhundert erbaute Haus ist offen für Besichtigungen.

Enniskillen ist auf einer Insel erbaut. Die beste Anlegestelle befindet sich am Anfang der Stadt auf der rechten Seite. Das Zentrum liegt ganz in der Nähe. Enniskillen Castle wurde im 15. Jahrhundert durch die Maguires erstellt, um diesen wichtigen Flussübergang zu schützen. Im 17. Jahrhundert wurden die beiden Türme, die heute als Watergate bekannt sind und die Anfahrt dominieren, angefügt. Ursprünglich führte eine Zugbrücke über das Wasser, aber wegen der Regulierung des Flusses lässt sich das heute kaum mehr erkennen. Wer Zeit hat, sollte unbedingt eines der Museen besuchen oder die 108 Stufen zum Cole Monument hinaufsteigen. Der Lohn ist eine ausgezeichnete Sicht über die Stadt. Empfohlene Ausflüge sind die Marble Arch Caves mit ihren Wasserfällen oder Florence Court, Sitz der Grafen von Enniskillen. Die Höhlen liegen etwa zwölf Meilen südwestlich der Stadt und sind leicht mit einem Taxi erreichbar. Wer gerne genaues Kartenmaterial von den Seen haben möchte, kann in jeder Buchhandlung die Ordnance Survey of Northern Ireland, Ausgaben Upper und Lower Lough Erne, kaufen.

Die Weiterfahrt in das Lower Lough Erne führt durch die Schleuse bei Portora Barrage. Sie dient der Regulierung des oberen Sees und steht meist offen. Kurz nachher erreicht man Devenish Island, eine der wichtigsten Klosterinseln in Irland. Die Abtei wurde im 6. Jahrhundert von St. Molaise gegründet. Allerdings stammen die ältesten vorhandenen Bauten aus dem 12. Jahrhundert, die St. Molaise-Kirche geht auf anfang des 13. Jahrhunderts zurück. Der gut erhaltene Rundturm ist 81 Fuss hoch.

Die ersten paar Meilen des Sees gleichen dem Upper Lough Erne mit seinen vielen bewaldeten Inseln. Die Jetty bei Carrickreagh erlaubt den Zugang zu einem weiteren Aussichtspunkt. In der Nähe liegen der Castle Hume Golfplatz und das bewaldete Ely Island mit seinen Ferienhäusern. Gegenüber Carrickreagh sieht man Goblusk Bay mit dem Lough Erne Yacht Club, der auf dem Gelände einer RAF-Basis aus dem Zweiten Weltkrieg liegt. Manor House Hotel verfügt über eine gute Anlegestelle, von hier aus kann der Killadeas Friedhof besucht werden.

It is worth taking time to visit **Marble Arch caves**, 12 miles to the south west of Enniskillen off the Swanlinbar road. These present a fascinating underworld of river and waterfalls. You can pass along spectacular walkways and wind your way through passages and chambers in electrically powered boats (open daily from 10.30 am mid March to September, tel. 01365-348855). Nearby is **Florence Court**, the seat of the Earls of Enniskillen, built in the 1740s with its flamboyant Rococo plasterwork and fine furnishings, its walled garden and excellent walks through the forest park (National Trust tel. 01365-348249).

Before heading downstream to the Lower Lough you may have to negotiate a lock at the **Portora Barrage**; in any event you must pass through the lock. This lock and weir were added when the hydro electric scheme was introduced at Ballyshannon to the north where the River Erne emerges from the lake at **Belleek** and plunges down about 150 ft, in 3 miles to enter the sea. At times it is necessary to hold the Upper Lough, which is very shallow, at a higher level and then the lock comes into use. **Portora** was an important fording place and the Maguires built a castle here which was subsequently rebuilt by the planter, William Cole, in the fifteenth century. Portora Royal School was established by James 1 in 1608, one of five Royal Free schools in Ulster, and the school moved to Portora Hill in 1777 when the present buildings were erected. Over the years it, has had many distinguished pupils including Oscar Wilde and Samuel Beckett.

Devenish Island is one of the most important monastic sites in Ireland. It was founded by St Molaise in the 6th century but the earliest surviving buildings are a small 12th century oratory known as St Molaise's House. There is an exceptionally fine round tower which stands 81ft high and has a Romanesque cornice carved with 4 human heads. The foundations of a second round tower lie beside the first. St Molaise's Church dates back to the early 13th century and there is a late medieval residential annexe to the north and a Maguire Chapel to the south with 17th century heraldic slabs and a two-sided bullaun which was used for grinding. It is said that the base of a sarcophagus inside the west end of the church known as St Molaise's Bed was associated with a cure for back ache. St Mary's Priory was built in the mid-15th and early 16th century. There is an interesting graveyard with a superb 15th century High Cross. The unobtrusive thatched site museum contains many interesting items. Access to the round tower is possible and a ferry service operates from April to September from Trory Point and there are also Erne Tours from the Round O Jetty in **Enniskillen**.

Am Westufer, nördlich von Carrickreagh, liegt Inishmacsaint Island. Hier gründete im 6. Jahrhundert St. Ninnidh eine Abtei. Uebrig geblieben sind die Ruine einer Kirche sowie ein grosses Hochkreuz, von dem die Legende sagt, dass es sich am Ostersonntag bei Sonnenaufgang dreimal dreht.

Der See öffnet sich jetzt und kann bei Sturm oder schlechter Sicht ähnlich wie Lough Ree oder Lough Derg Probleme bereiten. Ein anderer aus der Kriegszeit stammender Flugplatz, Castle Archdale, hat gut geschützte Anlegestellen und ist Ausgangspunkt für viele Spaziergänge durch den Park. Wer gerne für kurze Zeit das Schiff mit einem Pferd tauschen möchte, hat hier Gelegenheit dazu. Auf diesem Platz stand früher eine Burg, die 1689 zerstört wurde. Uebriggeblieben sind die Ställe, in denen jetzt eine Ausstellung mit alten Landwirtschaftsmaschinen und Ueberbleibseln des Zweiten Weltkriegs gezeigt werden. Eine Fähre führt zum nahe gelegenen White Island (Juni-September). Hier steht die Ruine einer Kirche mit einem romanischen Tor. Verschiedene Steine mit Reliefs wurden von den Kirchenbauern im 12. Jahrhundert in die Nordmauer integriert, es wird vermutet, dass die Köpfe möglicherweise St. Patrick oder St. Columba;

The Watergate at Enniskillen

Walter Borner

The first few miles of the lake are rather similar to the Upper Lough with many attractive wooded islands. The jetty at **Carrickreagh** provides access to another spectacular viewing point. Nearby is the Castle Hume Golf Course and the wooded **Ely Island** with its holiday homes.From Carrickreagh you can look across to **Goblusk Bay**, the home of the Lough Erne Yacht Club, occupying the site of a wartime RAF base and **Manor House Hotel** where there is a marina for mooring and from here you can get to **Killadeas** graveyard nearby where there is an Early Christian carved stone known as the "Bishop's Stone". The Necarne Castle Equestrian Centre is a short distance to the east near **Irvinestown**.

On the west shore to the north of Carrickreagh is **Inishmacsaint** Island where St Ninnidh founded a monastery in the 6th century. Here there is a later ruined church

N.I. Tourist Board

Devenish Island

Ardhowen Arts Centre

N.I. Tourist Board

König Leary und seinen Sohn Enna darstellen.

Die Route führt weiter den Kesh River aufwärts zum Dorfe Kesh mit einem Kai sowie Hotel und Restaurant. Auf der Fahrt westwärts entlang dem Nordufer kann man an den Inseln Lusty More oder Lusty Beg anlegen. Auf der letzteren steht sogar ein Restaurant. Von hier aus fährt ein Fährschiff nach Boa Island. Dies ist der beste Weg, die alte Begräbnisstätte von Caldragh zu besuchen und sich die vermutlich aus vorchristlicher Zeit stammenden Janus-Figuren anzusehen.

Am Westufer liegt bei Tully Castle eine weitere Anlegestelle. Das Schloss wurde von Sir John Hume anfangs des 17. Jahrhunderts erbaut und am Weihnachtstag 1641 erobert, zerstört und danach fast die ganze Besatzung hingemetzelt.

Das Westufer steigt steil an, und es ist möglich, an der Magho Jetty anzulegen und zu Fuss zum Aussichtspunkt Lough Navar Forest hinaufzusteigen. Von hier aus hat man eine unvergleichliche Aussicht auf den See, die allerdings hart verdient werden musste.

Der Nordarm von Lower Lough Erne führt zur Castlecaldwell Jetty. Eine in Stein gehauene Fiedel am Tor erinnert an Denis McCabe, einen Schiffer, der sein Leben 1770 auf dem See verlor. Die Umstände, welche zu diesem sicher traurigen

N.I. Tourist Board

A view from Carrickreagh

and a tall undecorated High Cross; legend says that this cross rotates three times to the rising sun on Easter Sunday morning.

The lake now widens out considerably and can present problems for cruisers in windy weather when rough seas develop. **Castle Archdale**, another wartime air base, has good sheltered berthing facilities in the marina and many lovely walks through the Country Park with nature trails and pony trekking. There was yet another Plantation castle here which was destroyed in 1689. The ruins of the T-shaped building and bawn are in the demesne. The former Palladian house here has been demolished and all that remains are the fine stable buildings in which there is an Exhibition Centre with old farm machinery on display and some relics of the war years and naturalist displays. There is a ferry from here to nearby **White Island** (June to September) which has ruins of a church with a Romanesque south door and a carved head and six stone carved figures have been built into the north wall originally used by 12th century church builders. Much has been written about these stones and Mary Rogers whose book "Prospect of Erne" is strongly recommended, identifies three of them as possibly St Patrick or St Columba, King Leary and his son Enna. One of the other

The famous stone figures on White Island

Ruth Delany

Unfall führten, gehen unzweideutig aus der Inschrift hervor: 'Auf festem Land nur übe deine Fertigkeit, dort kannst du spielen und dich sicher füllen.' Oder in ebenso unmissverständlicher deutscher Sprache: 'dich sicher vollaufen lassen.' Anstelle der Fiedel hätte der Steinmetz als Motiv auch eine Flasche wählen können. Das 1612 erbaute Schloss ist heute eine Ruine, der Park ein Reservat für Vögel und Hirsche.

Ein aussergewöhnlich schönes Stück vom Lower Lough Erne führt am Südende zum Fluss und nach Belleek. Ein schöner, geschützter Hafen liegt kurz vor der Ortschaft. Hier ist die schiffbare Strecke zu Ende, der Fluss fällt ziemlich steil zum Meer ab, seine Kraft wird für die Erzeugung von Elektrizität genutzt. Lohnenswert ist ein Besuch der weltberühmten Töpferei, die das ganze Jahr an Werktagen besichtigt werden kann. Ganz in der Nähe liegt das ExplorErne Center, das sehr informativ die gesamte Geschichte der Seen und ihres Hinterlandes erzählt.

figures is a female probably an abbess and the small cross legged figure has been called a sheela-na-gig, a female fertility figure.

The navigation extends up the Kesh River to the village of **Kesh**. where there is a quay and hotel and restaurant. Passing along the north shore there are quays providing access to **Lusty More** and **Lusty Beg**, with a restaurant at the latter. From here there is a ferry to **Boa Island** and this is the best way to approach the ancient burial ground of **Caldragh** where you can find the famous Janus figures. The larger stone has carved cross armed figures placed back to back and the smaller one brought here from Lusty More is very weathered but a similar figure can be distinguished; it is thought that these stones may be pre-Christian.

On the west shore there is another mooring place at **Tully Castle**. This was a fortified house and bawn built by Sir John Hume in the early seventeenth century which was destroyed on Christmas Day 1641 when most of the garrison were slaughtered. Considerable work has been carried out in restoring the seventeenth century garden.

Fine craftsmanship at Belleek

N.I. Tourist Board

The west shore of this stretch of lake rises steeply and it is possible to moor at **Magho Jetty** and climb the steep path to the viewing point of **Lough Navar Forest** from which there is a magnificent view of the lake below. You can also drive to the viewing point, the entrance is off the Enniskillen to Garrison road.

The northern arm of the lake leads up to **Castlecaldwell** jetty.A stone fiddle carved on a stone at the entrance gate to the old estate commemorates Denis McCabe, a boatman who lost his life on the lake in 1770 in circumstances which are obvious from the inscription: "On firm land only exercise your skill, there you may play and safely drink your fill". The castle built in 1612 is now a ruin but the park is a sanctuary for wildbirds and deer.

Returning to follow the south arm of the lake, a short stretch of river leads up to **Belleek**. This is the limit of navigation because from here the river falls steeply down to the sea. A visit to the world famous pottery established here in 1857 is recommended where you can see craftsmen at work carrying on skills learnt from earlier generations (open weekdays throughout the year but not on Saturdays and Sundays in winter, tel. 013656-58501). Nearby is the new interpretive centre ExplorErne which tells the complete story of the lakes and their hinterland using the latest technology (tel. 013656-58866).

The brochures enjoin you to "Discover the Erne before everyone else does" and this sums up the secret of this waterway: It is hard to understand why these enchanted lakes are so uncrowded.

Ruth Delany

One of the strange stone figures on Boa Island

Für die Besichtigung der verschiedenen Sehenswürdigkeiten geben folgende Telefonnummern Auskunft:

- Crom Castle 013657-38174
- Castle Coole House 01365-322690
- Museen Enniskillen 01365-325000
- Marble Arch caves 01365-348855
- Florence Court House 01365-348249
- Töpferei Belleek 013656-58501
- ExplorErne 013656-58866

Appendix - Limerick to Killaloe

NAVIGATION NOTES

Navigation between Limerick and Killaloe is currently suspended pending the completion of a major navigation and drainage scheme which is due for completion in late summer 2000.

The Shannon Estuary: It is advisable to obtain a set of Admiralty charts and the Irish Coast Pilot. These waters are very open to the Atlantic and exposed in windy weather. Commercial traffic is usually concentrated around high water but most pleasure craft have sufficient water at all states of tide if they keep to the channel and avoid the sandbanks.

Limerick City to Ardnacrusha From the 1920s, when the hydro electric scheme was constructed, until 1999 the first stretch of the navigation from Limerick to Ardnacrusha was tidal and passed up the Abbey River to the Tail Race of the power station. This was an extremely difficult stretch to navigate because it involved working out the tides to provide sufficient headroom and draft under the bridges which could only be achieved during a very restricted tidal window. In addition there were strong flows in the Abbey River on the ebb tide and, if the power station happened to be discharging on an ebbing tide, the flow increased greatly.

In 1999 a combined navigation and main drainage scheme was commenced involving the construction of a new weir joining Curragour Point to Sarsfield Lock, the deepening of the Abbey River and the insertion of lock gates into Sarsfield tidal lock. This scheme is due for completion in late summer 2000. The following notes are based on information available while work is in progress and may be subject to correction when the scheme is completed.

It is anticipated that it will make safe non-tidal navigation possible in the Abbey River for about 9.5 hours per tidal cycle on neap tides and 6 hours on springs. In future navigation will be through Sarsfield tidal lock, which will be completely refurbished,

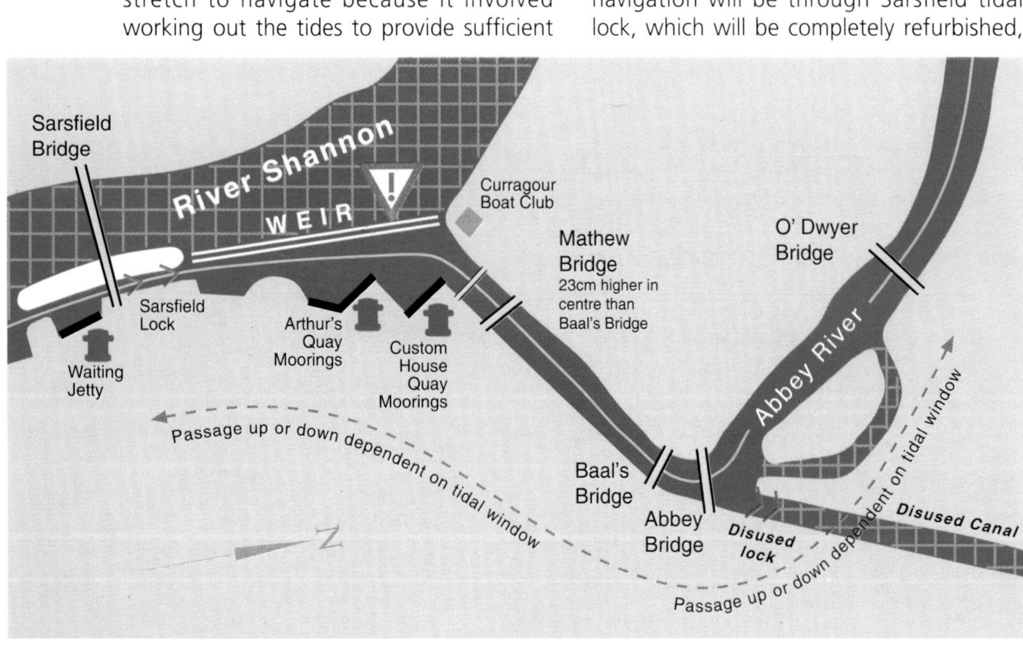

Passing through Limerick

but there will still be some restriction for a period on either side of high water because the tide will overtop the new weir, raising the level in the Abbey River and limiting headroom under the bridges. There will no longer be a current caused by the ebbing tide and it is not anticipated, therefore, that the flow in the Abbey River will present a problem when the power station is discharging. The headroom under the two lowest bridges in the Abbey River, Baal's Bridge and Mathew Bridge, during the navigable tidal window will be 4.8m, allowing for the curved arch of the bridges, and the draft will at all times exceed 1.7m, bringing the navigation in line with the headroom at the bridges across the headrace and the guillotine gate at Parteen which have a minimum clearance of 5m.

Boats entering the navigation from the Shannon Estuary during the high water period will be able to wait for the tidal window at the lay-by at the entrance to Sarsfield Lock where there will be floating jetties and there will also be floating jetties above the lock at Arthur's Quay and at Custom House Quay. A waiting jetty will also be provided for boats proceeding downstream but the location of this jetty has not yet been decided.

Ardnacrusha: The lock is double chamber with a rise and fall of 30.5m. The chambers are 32m x 6m. It is advisable to alert the ESB in advance when you wish to pass through the lock; there is no one in attendance at weekends except by prior request. The approach is though a short length of cutting. There can be considerable turbulence in the Tail Race below this cutting when the Power Station is discharging and eddies at the entrance to the cutting. The lower chamber is entered through a guillotine gate. As there is such a large rise it is not practical to pass warps up to the cope level, instead use loops of rope on the handles provided. There is a jetty above the lock.

Head Race to Parteen Villa: There is a fish trap in the Head Race where the navigation channel is on the east bank and one shoal patch marked by two black buoys. There is ample clearance at all the road bridges, minimum 5.4m. At the Parteen end of the Head Race there is a Ship's Pass with guillotine gate with 5.2m headroom. This gate is usually kept open but coming downstream it is advisable to telephone in advance to Ardnacrusha. At Parteen the gates of the weir controlling the flow down the Head Race only project a few centimetres above the water and the superstructure is quite high. Going downstream, care should be taken not to mistake any opening in this weir for the ship's pass.

Parteen Villa to Killaloe: There are unmarked hazards in the flooded area above the weir. Keep to the sailing course. Use the navigation span at Killaloe, headroom 3.4m. When there is a strong flow in the river it is possible to pass up the old canal at Killaloe instead of using the river.

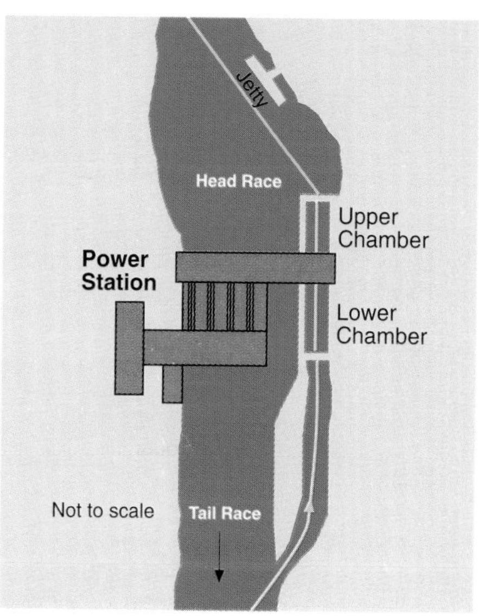

Ardnacrusha Lock

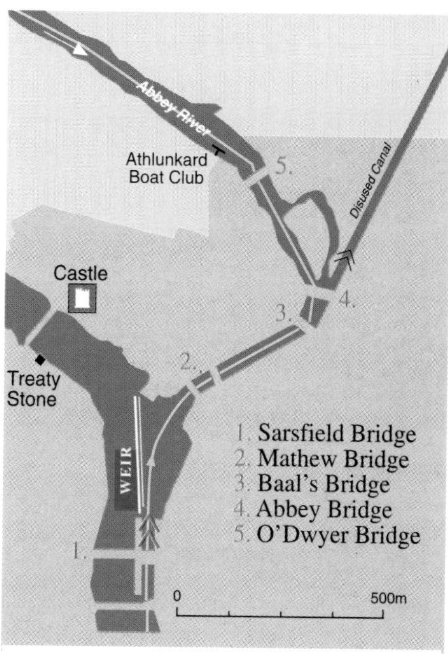

Limerick bridges

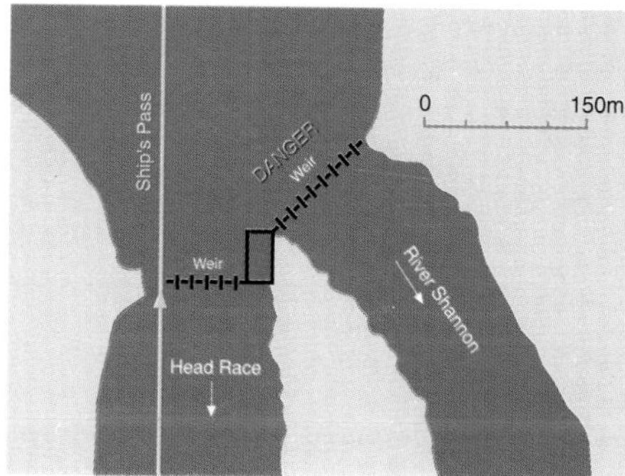

Parteen weirs

Appendix - Fishing Notes

The margins of the lake which are often weedy and shallow hold coarse fish in summer months. Eels are also common. In the places marked "Dinghy only" or "By foot", cruisers should be moored at the nearest convenient mooring on the navigation channel.
Fishing on the larger lakes is usually done from open lake boats of not less than 5.5m. The smaller dinghies supplied with most hired craft are not suitable.

Hinweise für Angler
In den Sommermonaten sind die seichten, verschilften Ufer voll von Fischen. Hier stehen die Hechte, die in der kälteren Jahreszeit ins tiefe Wasser ziehen. Aale sind häufig anzutreffen. An mit 'Dinghy only' oder 'By foot' bezeichneten Stellen sollten die Kabinenkreuzer am nächsten Anlegeplatz bleiben.

LOCATION	**SPECIES**	**NOTES**
Lough Derg	brown trout	Trolling or fly fishing March to September. Dapping with mayfly in May/June.
Parker's Point & Scilly Island	rudd, perch, pike	Found in the deeper water at the lower end of the lake.
Scarriff River	bream, rudd, perch, pike	
Mountshannon Bay	bream, rudd, perch, pike	By dinghy
Around Hare Island	bream, rudd,	By dinghy
Ryan's Point & Corrikeen Islands	hybrids, perch, pike	
Youghal Bay	pike, perch	By dinghy along reedline
Williamstown Bay	tench, rudd, bream	By dinghy May June
Rinharra Point	bream, rudd,	By dinghy
Coose Bay	tench, pike, perch	
Rossmore Bay & Woodford River	all species, good for rudd	By dinghy
Terryglass Bay	perch, pike	By dinghy
Portumna Bridge	bream, rudd	
In slack water behind the islands between Portumna & Meelick	pike, perch bream, rudd hybrids	By dinghy-the back channels of the islands are silted up.
The black-water of Ballymacegan Island	perch bream, rudd	By dinghy
The mouth of Little Brosna, Meelick	rudd, perch, hybrids, pike	By dinghy

LOCATION	**SPECIES**	**NOTES**
Below Meelick weir	rudd, perch, hybrids, pike	On foot
Meelick to Banagher	bream greatly increasing, roach increasing but not fully established, rudd hybrids, perch, pike	
Banagher Bridge vicinity	bream, rudd, perch, pike	On foot
Back-water of Bullock Island	all species	By dinghy
River Brosna	rudd, perch, pike	By dinghy
Grand Canal	perch, bream, rudd	On foot
Back-water of Lehinch Island	all species	By dinghy
At Shannonbridge power station outlet	specimen rudd, hybrids, tench, roach increasing	On foot
River Suck confluence	rudd, bream, hybrids, perch, pike, roach	
River Suck, particularly at Correen Ford & Culliagh Island	bream, rudd, hybrids, tench, occasional trout roach increasing	
Shannonbridge vicinity	rudd, bream tench, hybrids	On foot
Back-water of Long Island	bream, rudd, perch, tench, hybrids, pike	By dinghy
Shannonbridge to Athlone	bream, rudd, roach, hybrids, pike, perch	
Wren Island vicinity	bream, rudd, pike	By dinghy
Wren Island to Athlone	bream, rudd, pike, roach	
Old Canal mouth	rudd, perch	
Below Athlone weir	perch, bream, rudd, roach, hybrids, occasional trout	On foot
Athlone Bridge to Lough Ree	bream, rudd, pike, eels, perch,roach	By dinghy
Charlie's Island	specimen rudd, hybrid, roach, perch	By dinghy
Inner Lakes: Around Coosan & Kilinure Point	all species especially rudd	
South shore of Killinure Lough	rudd, tench, perch	

LOCATION	SPECIES	NOTES
Deeper water of Killinure Lough	bream, pike, perch, rudd hybrids	
Small bay to east of Stramore Island	bream, rudd	
Ladywell shore & north west bay	rudd, bream, tench, hybrids	
Thatch Island, Coosan Lough	bream, tench, rudd, perch, hybrids	
Gibraltar Island, Coosan Lough	tench, bream, rudd, perch, hybrids	
Friar's Island	rudd, tench, perch, pike	
Ballykeeran Lough	bream, rudd, tench	
Ballykeeran River mouth	bream, perch, rudd	
Derry & Inny Bay	specimen bream, rudd	In shallow bays
River Inny	specimen hybrids, roach	By dinghy
Inchcleraun vicinity	perch, pike	
Cruit & Galey Bay	large pike, perch, rudd, bream	
Ballyclare Cut to Lanesborough	roach, specimen bream, hybrids, perch, rudd	
Below Lanesborough power station	roach, specimen bream, rudd, tench, perch, hybrids	On foot
Bord na Mona bridge	roach, bream, tench, pike, hybrids, perch, rudd	On foot
Mouth of Feorish River	bream, trench, roach, hybrids, perch	
Entrance to Camlin Canal	roach, pike, perch, bream	
Camlin River	roach, pike, perch, rudd, tench, occasional trout	
Below Tarmonbarry weir	roach, perch, hybrids pike, specimen bream, occasional trout	On foot
Lough Forbes	roach, bream, rudd, hybrids, pike, perch	
River Rinn	roach, bream, perch, rudd	By dinghy
Roosky Bridge to Lough Bofin	roach, bream, perch, pike	On foot
Loughs Bofin & Boderg	roach, pike, bream, perch	
Lough Scannel	roach, pike, perch, bream	By dinghy

LOCATION	SPECIES	NOTES
Carnadoe Lough	rudd, tench, pike perch, roach	
Kilglass Lough	specimen rudd, perch, pike	
Grange Lough	specimen rudd, bream, tench, perch, pike	
Grange River	roach, rudd, perch, pike	On foot
Lough Tap to Albert lock	roach, bream, rudd, perch, pike	
Lough Tap to Drumsna	roach, bream, rudd, hybrids, perch, pike	
Upstream of Drumsna Quay	roach, rudd, hybrids, perch, pike	On foot
Jamestown Bridge	roach, rudd, hybrids	On foot
Below Jamestown weir	roach, perch, hybrids	On foot
Lough Corry	roach, bream, pike, perch	By dinghy in bays
Carrick vicinity	roach, bream, perch	Fishing stands
Leitrim River	roach, bream perch, pike	By dinghy
Leitrim River to Battlebridge	roach, perch, pike	
Upstream of Battlebridge lock	roach, bream, perch, occasional trout	On foot
Lough Allen Canal	roach, small bream, tench	On foot
Lough Allen	roach, bream, specimen pike, trout	
Lough Drumharlow	roach, bream, perch, pike, rudd	
Oakport Lough	roach, bream, perch, rudd, pike	
Cootehall vicinity	roach, bream,	Fishing stands
Below Clarendon weir,Knockvicar	roach, bream, perch, pike	On foot
Lough Key	roach, bream perch, pike brown trout	By dinghy off navigation channel around islands and reeded shores
Boyle River	roach, bream, perch, occasional trout	On foot or by dinghy upstream of Drum Bridge

Appendix - Flora of the River

The notes which follow are brief and limited to the most identifiable features. Notes on distribution refer to the Shannon system. Bear in mind also that the plants described may not be restricted to the habitats described; some plants can be found in more than one habitat.

The key to the abbreviations used is as follows:
A = abundant C = common F = frequent
O = occasional R = rare

AQUATIC PLANTS

Algae

Many species of microscopic plants float in water or live attached to mud, rocks and navigation marks especially in nutrient rich areas. Some form into floating green mats known as 'blanket weed'. In favourable nutrient-rich warm conditions 'algal blooms' occur near the surface of the water, appearing as bluish green scum, and this can lower the oxygen level of this layer of water to the detriment of some plant and animal life.

Floating rootless plants

Common duckweed *(Lemna minor)*—C Plant single green disc, 3–4 mm, with single root. Rarely flowers. Widespread, floating in sheltered shallow bays. ditches and reedbeds.

Ivy-leaved duckweed *(Lemna trisulca)*—O Plant transparent green disc, 8–12 mm, grouped together. Floating in sheltered shallow waters.

Frogbit *(Hydrocharis morsus-ranae)*—O Floating round, long stalked leaves in tufts, 30 mm. 1–3 flowers, white with 3 petals. July–August. Floating in sheltered bays, reedbeds and ditches.

Plants of deeper water with floating leaves

Yellow water lily *(Nuphar lutea)*—A Large floating oval leaves, submerged leaves bright green. Single yellow flower raised above the water surface. June–July. Sheltered areas with muddy bottoms. Widespread.

White water lily *(Nymphaea alba)*—O Large floating oval leaves. White, many petalled, floating flowers, June–July. Found in 'colonies' in sheltered or slow flowing waters e.g. Carnadoe Waters, Inner Lakes and Meelick canal.

Pondweed *(Potamogeton)*—A A very variable and difficult group of plants to identify. Those with floating leaves include P. natans, P. polygonifolius, most commonly. Submerged leaves translucent. Widespread.

Amphibious bistort *(Poygonum amphibium)*—F Floating oblong leaves, 10 cm, more rounded in land form. Flowers pink in dense spikes, July–September. Widespread water edge or in sheltered slow-moving waters.

Bur-reed *(Sparganium minimum)*—O Stems and leaves floating, thin and ribbon-like. Flowers in spiky globular heads, July–August. In sheltered waters with peat/silt rich bottom.

Water-starwort *(Callitriche)*—F Leaves 10mm in floating rosettes: others submerged. Flowers minute and inconspicuous, May–September. Margins of muddy lakes, slow water and ditches, a difficult group to identify.

Plants of shallow water, leaves submerged

Canadian pondweed *(Elodea canadensis)*—C Leaves I0 mm, dark translucent in whorls of 3. Widespread on soft bottoms. Introduced to Ireland to Lough Neagh in 1836 and has spread widely.

Water milfoil *(Myriophllum)*—C Small, branched, hair-like leaves in whorls of 3–5. Flowers small, inconspicuous on emergent spike, June–August. Three different species may be found throughout the system in slow water with soft bottom.

Stonewort *(Chara)*—C Strong, green, jointed plants encrusted with lime. Algae, particularly common in clear still water with marl bottom especially Inner Lakes

Bladderwort *(Urticularia)*—F Rootless, colourless/green hair-like leaves; bladders to trap aquatic animals on leaves. Flowers yellow (7–30 mm) above water surface, June–July. Three different species found throughout system in shallow lake margins and ditches rich in peaty mud.

Water crowfoot *(Ranunculus)*—O Aquatic: white-flowered members of buttercup family difficult to identify as leaves vary with depth of water and speed of flow. **R. circinatus**, **R. trichophyllus** and **R. peltatus** *(rivers)* most widespread.

Plants of shallow water, dominant leaves emergent

Arrowhead *(Sagittaria sagittifolia)*—O Leaves broad, 7 cm, arrow-shaped on stalks above water surface. Numerous 3-petalled white flowers with purple centres, July–August. Still shallow bays, canals and harbours. Intolerant of pollution.

Lesser water plantain *(Baldellia ranunculoides)*—O Leaves long, lance-like and stalked. Flowers pale mauve in whorl on top of stem, 15–40 cm above water surface, June–July. Still shallow bays, canals and ditches throughout system.

Water plantain *(Alisma plantago-aquatica)*—F Leaves oval, pointed on long stalks. Stems 30–80 cm above water with many whorls of pale mauve flowers, July–August. Still shallow bays, canals and ditches throughout system.

Mare's tail *(Hippuris vulgaris)*—F Linear leaves, 25 mm, in whorls of about 10 on unbranched stem projecting above water surface, June–July. Flowers insignificant. Widespread in slow waters and shallow lake margins.

Flowering rush *(Butomus umbellatus)*—R Long erect, narrow, 3-angled leaves. Stem 125 cm bearing many 3-petalled pink flowers, umbrella-like at top, June–August. A beautiful plant rarely encountered. Can be found near Kilgarvan Quay, Lough Derg.

REEDBED PLANTS

Club-rush or Bulrush *(Scirpus lacustris)*—A Dark green cylindrical stems, up to 2 m high, dying down in winter. Widespread throughout system, lake margins and river edges, preferring deeper water than other reedbed plants.

Common reed *(Phragmites australis)*—A Stout leafy stem, up to 3 m high. Flowers purple feathery, July–August. Widespread lake margins and river edge in shallower water than club-rush.

Reedmace *(Typha latifolia)*—O Stem 1–2 m high with dense, persistent, dark brown flower-spike at top, July—August. Occurs in pockets throughout system in shallow waters. Intolerant of pollution.

Great fen-sedge *(Cladium mariscus)*—O Stout hollow stems, 2 m. Leaves angular, pointed with rough serrated edges. Pale brown flowers in clusters, July. Inner edge of reedbeds and fen in pockets throughout system.

Bur-reed *(Sparganium erectum)*—F Leaves green angled. Flower heads spiky globular in groups on end of stem, 1 m high, June–July. Slow waters and shallow reedbeds, throughout system.

Horsetails *(Equisetum)*—F Many species occur all with hollow green stems with longitudinal ridges, conspicuously jointed. 30–100 cm. Shallow edges of reedbeds and in fens.

Purple loosestrife *(Lythrum salicaria)*—F Stems up to 1 m high. Leaves opposite. Flowers bright purple in dense spikes, July–August. Widespread and conspicuous in reedbeds, marshes and lakeshores.

Yellow loosestrife *(Lysimachia vulgaris)*—F Downy leafy stems up to 1 m high. Leaves opposite. Yellow flowers, 5-petalled in loose terminal pyramid, July. Reedbeds, fens and river edges, often in shady places, throughout system.

Hemp agrimony *(Eupatorium cannabinum)*—F Stems up to 1 m high. Leaves opposite, slightly hairy. Many pink flower heads, July–August. Reedbeds, river margins and lakeshores throughout system.

Greater spearwort *(Ranunculus lingua)*—F Stems up to 1 m high. Leaves without stalks. Large buttercup yellow flowers, June–July. Reedbeds, fens, marshes and river edges. A characteristic Shannon species found especially in north and central Shannon.

FEN AND MARSH PLANTS

Sedges *(Carex)* Characteristic vegetation of fens, intermediate in habit between grasses and rushes; stem 3-angled; flowers brown in spikelets of varying form. Often form tussocks. Many rare and interesting sedges can be found throughout the system among the very numerous sedge species occurring.

Black bog rush *(Schoenus nigricans)*—C Narrow bristle-like leaves in tufts, 50 cm high. Black dense heads of flowers on wiry stem, June. Widespread in fens, marshes and lake edges.

Purple moor grass *(Molinia caerulea)*—F Stems and leaves form large tussocks up to 100 cm high. Flowers in long purple spikelet, July–August. Widespread throughout system in marshes, fens and boggy places.

Flag iris *(Iris pseudacorus)*—A Pale green strap-like leaves. 2–3 yellow flowers, similar to garden irises, June–July. Widespread in marshes, fens, ditches and riversides.

Bog bean *(Menyanthes trifoliata)*—C Three oval leaflets, 5 cm, on long stalk. Flowering stems 50 cm high with pale pink funnel-shaped flowers fringed with white hairs, May–June. Widespread throughout system in wetter marshes, fens and lake margins.

Mint *(Mentha aquatica)*—A Aromatic stems and leaves up to 90 cm high, hairy with bluish-mauve flowers, July–September. Widespread in all wet habitats.

Grass of Parnassus *(Parnassia palustris)*—C Long, stalked heart-shaped leaves. Stem 30 cm with single white petalled flower, petals veined, July–August. Common in marshes and fens throughout Shannon system, rare elsewhere in Ireland.

Marsh pennywort *(Hyrdocotyle vulgaris)*—C Leaves round 25 mm across. Flowers small green in compact heads, May–July. Widespread throughout in fens and marshes.

Early purple orchid *(Orchis mascula)*—F Stem 30 cm, leaves oblong, often spotted. Flowers reddish purple April–May. Widespread in fields, marshes and scrubby areas.

Marsh orchid *(Dactylorrhiza incarnata)*—F Leaves narrow on stout hollow stem, 50cm high. Flowers pink, red, white or purple cylindrical spikes inJune. Widespread in marshes and fens.

Water forget-me-not (Myosotis scorpoides)—F Blue flowers, June–August. Widespread in muddy places.

Butterfly orchid *(Platanthera bifolia)*—F Leaves opposite, large at base, oval. White, fragrant flowers in spread out spike June–July. Petals and spur pointed and long. 30 cm high. Central Shannon especially in fens and marshes, rare elsewhere in Ireland

Marsh helleborine *(Epipactis palustris)*—F Stem leafy, 60 cm high. Leaves lance-shaped. Flowers pink and white in spread-out spike, June–July. Marshes and fens especially in central Shannon, rare elsewhere.

Marsh pea *(Lathyrus palustris)*—R Straggling stem, leaves ending in tendril, leaflets 2–4. Flowers purple. 15 mm, in groups of 3–8, resembling garden sweet-pea in shape, July. Fen and marshes mainly in central Shannon, very rare elsewhere.

Ragged robin *(Lychnis flos-cuculi)*—O Stems 100 cm, slightly hairy, leaves linear. Flowers pink, 5 petals each divided into 4 lobes, June–July. Widespread through system.

Meadow sweet *(Filipendula ulmaria)*—A Stem 120 cm high with large leaves white beneath. Flowers small and numerous, creamy white and scented, June–August. Widespread throughout system.

LAKE SHORE PLANTS

Long-leaved helleborine *(Cephalanthera longifolia)*—R Slender stems 60 cm high with numerous linear strap-shaped leaves. White flowers in spike, May–June. Found on islands and wooded shores south east Lough Ree, very rare elsewhere.

Shore weed *(Littorella uniflora)*—F Bright green tufted grass-like leaves, l0 cm. Forms carpet between stones at lake edges. Throughout Shannon, rare elsewhere in Ireland.

Purple loosestrife *(Lythrum salicaria)* See under Reedbed plants.

Water germander *(Teucrium scordium)*—A Stems branched and hairy, 20 cm. Leaves oblong, toothed. Flowers pinkish mauve, July–August. Abundant on shores of Lough Ree and Lough Derg, very rare elsewhere .

Grass of Parnassus *(Parnassia palustris)*—F see under Fen and Marsh plants.

Sneezewort *(Achillea ptarmica)*—F Stem 80 cm high with linear toothed leaves. Flowers white on outside, grey green in centre, in flower-head, July–August. Frequent at lakes and river edge, rarer elsewhere in Ireland.

Bedstraw *(Galium boreale)*—F Stem 50 cm high. Leaves linear 3 veined in whorls of 4. White numerous flowers, June–August. Frequent on shores of Lough Ree and Lough Derg, rarer elsewhere.

Ladies bedstraw *(Galium verum)*—C Stem 60 cm high. Leaves linear in whorls of 8 or more. Flowers numerous bright yellow, July–August. Common in rocky, sandy shores throughout system.

Carline thistle *(Carlina vulgaris)*—F Stem and leaves hairy and very prickly, 40 cm high. Flower heads single or 2–4, outer leafy, prickly bracts with purple centre, July–September. In central Shannon in dry pasture and lake edges, rare elsewhere.

Irish fleabane *(Inula salicina)*—R Stems 50 cm high with lance-shaped, toothed leaves. Flower heads 35 mm across, yellow, July–August. On some rocky shores and islands of Lough Derg, unknown elsewhere in British Isles.

Blue-eyed grass *(Sisyrinchium angustifolium)*—R Stem 30 cm high, leaves grass-like; flowers blue, shortlived in groups of 2–4, June–July. In marshy ground, at edge of Lough Derg, elsewhere rare.

CHARACTERISTIC SCRUB AND WOODY PLANTS

Buckthorn *(Rhamnus catharticus)*—O Shrub, spiny. Leaves broadly oval. Fruit black. Lake shores in rocky places, very rare elsewhere in Ireland.

Dogwood *(Cornus sanguinea)*—R Shrub with reddish twigs. Many white flowers in compact heads, June–July. Fruit black. Lake shores and rocky places.

Guelder rose *(Viburnum opulus)*—F Shrub with toothed leaves. Flat flower heads, white, outer flowers larger and sterile, inner flowers smaller, June–July. Fruit Crimson berries. Lake shores, hedges and scrub.

Spindle tree *(Euonymus europaeus)*—F Shrub with smooth grey bark and 4-angled green twigs. Leaves oval with short stalks. Flowers small green, May–June. Fruit scarlet, heart-shaped. Lake shore, scrub, hedges and rocky places, rarer elsewhere in Ireland.

Irish whitebeam *(Sorbus hibernica)*—O Shrub with simple oval leaves, blue grey above, pale beneath. Flowers in white flower heads, May–June, Fruit red. Rocky places and lake shores, central Shannon.

Appendix - Fauna of the River

The key to the abbreviations used is as follows: W = widespread R = rare C = common O = occasional V = vagrant

AMPHIBIANS, REPTILES AND MAMMALS

Common newt *(Triturus vulgaris)*—W Olive brown on top and silver grey beneath, reaching 10 cm in length, can be found in shallow areas rich in aquatic plants and under stones in winter.

Frog *(Rana temporaria)*—W Found abundantly in marshy meadows.

Common lizard *(Lacerta vivipara)*—W Rarely seen, preferring warm sandy areas and dry stone walls.

Hedgehog *(Erinaceus europaeus)*—W Can be found by searching after dark with a torch, especially in moist grassy areas.

Pygmy shrew *(Sorex minutus)*—W Not commonly encountered but present in all habitats with plenty of cover.

Lesser horseshoe bat *(Rhinolophus hipposideros)*—R Confined to limestone areas of western Ireland.

Whiskered bat *(Myotis mystacinus)*—R Only recorded once in Ireland since 1950.

Natterer's bat *(Myotis nattereri)*—W Poorly recorded.

Daubenton's bat *(Myotis daubentoni)*—W Poorly recorded.

Leisler's bat *(Nyctalus leisleri)*—W Poorly recorded.

Pipistrelle bat *(Pipistrellus pipistrellus)*—W Frequently recorded and often seen feeding over water at dusk.

Long eared bat *(Plecotus auritus)*—W Frequently recorded .

Rabbit *(Oryctolagus cuniculus)*—W Distribution patchy due to recurrent outbreaks of myxomatosis, prefers short grazed grassland adjacent to refuges/warrens, boulders or scrub.

Brown hare *(Lepus capensis)*—R Introduced in northern counties, distinguished from Irish hare by yellow brown colour, black tail and longer ears.

Irish hare *(Lepus timidus)*—W Moves around mostly at dawn and dusk, prefers open grassland.

Red squirrel *(Sciurus vulgaris)*—O Probably absent from mid-Shannon region, being displaced by grey squirrel, prefers large stands of coniferous woodland.

Grey squirrel *(Sciurus carolinensis)*—C Can be commonly seen in mid-Shannon region in mixed woodland particularly. Introduced to Ireland at Castle Forbes, near Roosky, in 1913.

Bank vole *(Clethrionomys alarrdus)*—R Introduced to south east Ireland about 1950 and has spread along west bank of Shannon to Killaloe.

Field mouse *(Apodemus sylvaticus)*—W Distinguished from house mouse by lighter, even sandy colour and long, less scaly tail.

House mouse *(Mus musculus)*—W Found in buildings, hedgerows and open fields.

Brown rat *(Rattus norvegicus)*—W Ubiquitous, preferring areas with dense ground cover near water and buildings.

Fox *(Vulpes vulpes)*—W Common throughout the Shannon seen mostly a dawn and dusk.

Pine marten *(Martes martes)*—O Rarely seen, prefers deciduous or mixed woodland, especially west shore of Lough Derg.

Stoat *(Mustela erminea)*—W Only seen occasionally, active both day and night.

American mink *(Mustela vison)*—W A recent escape from farms, now spread throughout the whole length of the Shannon, smaller, with a distinct tail and less streamlined than the otter, appears fearless of man.

Badger *(Meles meles)*—W Nocturnal, emerging from sett around dusk, favours light soils adjacent to open areas and water.

Otter *(Lutra lutra)*—W Usually nocturnal and very elusive, presence often only determined by droppings left in conspicuous places.

Fallow deer *(Dama dama)*—R Can be seen in Lough Key Forest Park and Portumna Forest Park.

Sika deer *(Cervus nippon)*—V Unlikely to be encountered.

BUTTERFLIES

Speckled wood *(Pararge aegeria)*—W Common in woodland and along hedgerows, brown with orange markings.

Wall brown *(Lasiommata megera)*—C Orange-yellow with black lattice markings, conspicuous as it likes basking on stones in sunshine.

Meadow brown *(Maniola jurtina)*—W Abundant in grassland, dark brown with conspicuous 'eye' on upper wing.

Small heath *(Coenonympha pamphilus)*—W Common in grassy places, yellow-buff with narrow grey borders, inconspicuous 'eye' on wing.

Large heath *(Coenonympha tullia)*—R Found in wet boggy areas, dingy grey brown with dark margin, inconspicuous 'eye' on wing.

Ringlet *(Aphantopus hyperantus)*—W Abundant throughout region in damp grassy places and light woodland, almost black, females with conspicuous 3 and 5 'eyes' on wings.

Dark green fritillary *(Argynnis aglaja)*—R Large butterfly, underwings yellow-buff with green markings, strong flier and difficult to catch.

Silver washed fritillary *(Argynnis paphia)*—C Found in woodland and along hedgerows, similar to above with silver outer margin to wings.

Marsh fritillary *(Euphydryas aurinia)*—R Marshy ground in May–June, yellow with orange/brown bands and black markings.

Small tortoiseshell *(Aglais urticae)*—W Widely known as it hibernates in houses.

Peacock *(Inachis io)*—W Chocolate brown with obvious peacock 'eye', common throughout the region.

Small blue *(Cupido minimus)*—R May be found rarely in grassland on eskers.

Common blue *(Polyommatus icarus)*—W Commonly found in grassland in June–July.

Holly blue *(Celastrina argiolus)*—R Found in woodland which has holly in April–May and July–August.

Small copper *(Lycaena phlaeas)*—W Reddish gold with black markings, common in grassland through summer.

Green hairstreak *(Callophrys rubi)*—O Upper wings dull brown/grey, underwing green, found in rough grassland in May–June.

Wood white *(Leptidea sinapis)*—W Common in light woodland, distinctive by its feeble ability to fly.

Large white *(Pieris brassicae)*—W The well-known large white butterfly of gardens and areas rich in plants related to the cabbage.

Small white *(Pieris rapae)*—W Similar distribution to above but smaller in size and less grey/black markings.

Green-veined white *(Pieris napi)*—W Very common. Veins on wings grey/green, found in wet meadows.

Orange tip *(Anthocharis cardamines)*—W Very common in May, male with distinctive orange wing-tip.

Brimstone *(Gonepteryx rhamni)*—W Large yellow butterfly abundant in Shannon region where its larval foodplant is buckthorn.

Dingy skipper *(Erynnis tages)*—O Small, mothlike, found in limestone grassland.

Painted lady (Cynthia cardui)—R Large migrant, pink beige with brown and white markings.

Red admiral *(Vanessa atalanta)*—R Large migrant, black with red and white markings.

Clouded yellow *(Colias croceus)*—R Large yellow migrant rarely visiting Ireland except in exceptionally hot summers.

Five other species of butterfly have been recorded in Ireland (**purple hairstreak**, **brown hairstreak**, **pearl bordered fritillary**, **grayling** and **gatekeeper**) but these are not likely to be found throughout the Shannon system.

MISCELLANEOUS AQUATIC ANIMALS

Leeches *(Hirundinea)*—O Wormlike or with broad flat body, head with up to eight eyes, posterior sucker, up to 100 mm long. Many parasitic on fish, snails or birds, moving by looping action or swimming. Look for them under stones or other objects.

Mussels and Snails *(Molluscs)*

Swan mussel (Anodonta cygnaea)—W Shell up to 100 mm long in two halves; larvae attach themselves to fish skin and furs. Adults live almost buried in mud in lakes and sheltered waters throughout the system.

Pond snails *(Lymnaea)*—W Shells coiled clockwise to a point. Many different species ranging from 10–50 mm and differing shapes, found in mud, lakeshores and on vegetation, rising to the water surface for oxygen.

Crustaceans

Freshwater crayfish *(Astacus pallipes)*—C Up to 12 cm, resembling a small lobster, seen at night crawling or darting backwards when disturbed. Probably widespread throughout Shannon systems in muddy banks or behind stones. Edible.

Freshwater shrimps, **water lice** and **water fleas** belong to this group too. Translucent, many jointed animals, they live on dead plant and animal material and on other aquatic animals.

AQUATIC INSECTS

True dragonflies *(Anisoptera)*—W Fore and hindwing differing in shape, wings held horizontally when resting, eyes almost meet across head. Usually over 50 mm long. A striking species is the common hawker, a large browny-green dragonfly which flies up and down its favourite beat devouring midges and mosquitoes.

Damselflies *(Zygoptera)*—W Wings similar in shape, folded back vertically when resting, slender body, eyes wide apart, usually under 50 mm long. There are a number of dainty blue damselfly species which skim the water surface distinguished by the pattern of blue and black on head, body and wings. Another common damselfly is the banded agrion, the males with a dark band on their wings, the females distinctly metallic green.

Caddisflies *(Trichoptera)*—W Mothlike, with long antennae, resting wings meet at an angle over body. Some caddis larvae live and move about under water in cases made from sand, shells, rushes or twigs. A very large and varied group, easily observed in the adult or larva stage.

Mayflies *(e.g. Ephemera danica)*—W Large four-winged fly, green wings on hatching, aging to grey and black. Body grey with three long 'tails'. Abundant in Loughs Ree and Derg, larvae hatching in unpolluted water or shallow bays in May particularly. Major component of the diet of brown trout in early summer.

Pond skaters *(Gerridae)*—W Carnivorous insects with pointed mouthparts which suck the juices of other animals that fall in or come to the surface for air. They support themselves on the tips of their legs, moving across the surface of the water by rowing or jumping movements.

Water boatmen *(Corixidae)*—W Live on or below water surface where they live on algae and detritus on the mud or can be carnivorous. They row themselves through the water. Widespread through the Shannon system.

Whirligig beetles *(Gyrinidae)*—C Often found in groups whirling around the water surface until disturbed when they disappear beneath the surface.

Diving beetles *(Dytiscidae)*—W Speedy and strong swimmers found in still, weedy waters voracious, carnivores even killing small fish. Can be seen resting on the water surface in an oblique position renewing their store of air.

Maybug *(Melolontha melolontha)*—C Large night-flying, non-aquatic beetle which is attracted by lighted portholes into which they crash noisily. Quite harmless!

Appendix - Birds of the River

The list which follows indicates the status and distribution of birds likely to be seen. Armed with a pair of binoculars and a good identification guidebook (see bibliography), the visitor who goes to a range of habitats should be able to see many of the birds listed. This list has been compiled with the assistance of Ian Herbert, Irish Wildbird Conservancy.

The key to the abbreviations used is as follows: R = resident bird SR = summer resident bird WR = winter resident bird PM = passage migrant bird V = vagrant bird

Great crested grebe *(Podiceps cristatus)*—R Widespread .

Little grebe *(Tachybaptus ruficollis)*—R Present in all sheltered waters, except where mink predominate.

Manx shearwater *(Puffinus puffinus)*—V Occurs almost every year on the two larger lakes.

Gannet *(Sula bassana)*—V Single bird seen upper Lough Derg in May.

Cormorant *(Phalacrocorax carbo)*—R Breeds in various areas, particularly Corrikeen Islands and Church Island, Lough Derg.

Grey heron *(Ardea cinerea)*—R Breeds in colonies throughout the system.

Mute swan *(Cygnus olor)*—R Widespread.

Bewick's swan *(Cygnus columbianus)*–WR Commonest in the Shannon Harbour area in large flocks, and Little Brosna near Cloghan Castle.

Whooper swan *(Cygnus cygnus)*—WR Widespread throughout the Shannon in medium-sized flocks. Single birds of this, and the preceding species, often remain all summer.

Greylag goose *(Anser anser)*—V Occasional in Mountshannon area.

Greenland white-fronted goose *(Anser albifrons flavirostris)*–WR Flocks of 30 to 100, scattered over the entire length of the river.

Wigeon *(Anas penelope)*—WR Throughout the river, often in large flocks.

Teal *(Anas crecca)*—R & WR Breeding population small and scattered. Numerous in winter.

Mallard *(Anas platyrhynchos)*—R & WR Widespread. Very common in reserves, esp. Inner Lakes, Lough Ree and forest park, Portumna.

Shoveller *(Anas clypeata)*—R & WR In small numbers, possibly no longer breeding. Most likely to be seen in the Clonmacnois area in spring–summer.

Pochard *(Aytha ferina)*—R & WR Large winter flocks in upper Shannon. Has possibly bred.

Tufted duck *(Aythya fuligula)*—R & WR Widespread.

Common scoter *(Melanitta nigra)*—SR Breeds centre area of Lough Ree.

Goldeneye *(Bucephala clangula)*—WR Small numbers, scattered throughout the river.

Red-breasted merganser *(Mergus serrator)*—R Breeds in small numbers on both the larger lakes. Few on river just below Athlone (4–5 pairs in 1987).

Osprey *(Pandion haliaetus)*–V Bred once Lough Derg.

Marsh harrier *(Circus aeruginosus)*–SR Possibly breeds in one area mid-Shannon.

Hen harrier *(Circus cyaneus)*—R Seen both ends of the system, breeding some distance from the river.

Peregrine *(Falco peregrinus)*—V Very occasionally seen.

Sparrowhawk *(Accipter nisus)*—R Scattered throughout the area.

Buzzard *(Buteo buteo)*—V Seen several years on north Lough Derg.

Kestrel *(Falco tinnunculus)*—R In fair numbers throughout the area.

Merlin *(Falco columbarius)*—V Occasional.

Grey partridge *(Perdix perdix)*—R Very scarce in the area.

Quail *(Coturnix coturnix)*—SR Has bred in Portumna area, Cappaleitrim, hay meadows, 2 calling birds 1987.

Pheasant *(Phasianus colchicus)*—R Widespread.

Water rail *(Rallus aquaticus)*—R Heard in most really swampy areas.

Corncrake *(Crex crex)*—SR While decreasing in numbers throughout Ireland can still be heard from Athlone to Portumna. Grants administered by Irish Wildbird Conservancy available to farmers who cut meadows after the breeding period and cut fields from the centre out.

Moorhen *(Gallinula chloropus)*—R Widespread in all reeded areas.

Coot *(Fulica atra)* as above species.

Oystercatcher *(Haematopus ostralegus)*—V Small flocks seen in Athlone area and north west side of Lough Derg.

Ringed plover *(Charadrius hiaticula)*—R Breeds in Lough Ree area and also Fin Lough, Clonmacnois.

Golden plover *(Pluvialis apricaria)*—WR Often large flocks in Athlone–Portumna area and Bullock Island, north of Banagher.

Lapwing *(Vanellus vanellus)*—R & WR Breeds throughout the area; large winter flocks.

Dunlin *(Calidris alpina)*—WR Shannon Harbour area.

Jack snipe *(Lymnocryptes minimus)*—WR Occasional.

Snipe *(Gallinago gallinago)*—R & WR Widespread.

Woodcock *(Scolopax rusticola)*—R & WR Found in most woodland areas.

Black-tailed godwit *(Limosa limosa)*—R Breeds in one area mid–Shannon.

Whimbrel *(Numenius phaeopus)*—PM Small flocks passing daily in spring and autumn.

Grey phalarope *(Phalaropus fulicarius)*—V Once seen Illaunmore area, Lough Derg, in October.

Curlew *(Numenius arquata)*—R & WR Widespread.

Redshank *(Tringa totanus)*—R & WR Widespread.

Greenshank *(Tringa nebularia)*—WR Mainly Shannon Harbour area.

Common sandpiper *(Actitis hypoleucos)*—SR Breeds on river banks and lake edges.

Long-tailed skua *(Stercorarius longicandatus)*—V Occasionally seen in spring passage.

Black-headed gull *(Larus ridibundus)*—R Breeds on many of the lakes and also Fin Lough, Clonmacnois.
Common gull *(Larus canus)*—R Occasionally seen in all areas, has bred on Lough Derg.
Herring gull *(Larus argentatus)*—R Breeds Lough Ree, seen in all areas.
Lesser black-backed gull *(Larus fuscus)*—R Breeds Lough Ree, seen in all areas.
Great black-backed gull *(Larus marinus)*—R Seen throughout the river.
Common tern *(Sterna hirundo)*–SR Breeds on larger lakes, especially Goat Island, Lough Derg.
Black tern *(Chlidonias niger)*—V Lough Derg.
Whiskered tern *(Chlidonias hydrida)*—V June–September, Lough Derg, 1987.
Stock dove *(Columba oenas)*—R Not common.
Woodpigeon *(Columba palumbus)*—R Widespread throughout the river.
Collared dove *(Streptopelia decaocto)*—R Present in most towns and villages.
Cuckoo *(Cuculus canorus)*—SR Widespread.
Barn owl *(Tyto alba)*—R Small numbers, widely spread over district.
Long–eared owl *(Asio otus)*—R Present in many woodland areas.
Short-eared owl *(Asio flammeus)*—WR Occasional mid-Shannon.
Nightjar *(Caprimulgus europaeus)*—V Possibly breeds in some areas.
Kingfisher *(Alcedo atthis)*—R Breeds on small tributaries. Widespread over river after autumn dispersal.
Belted kingfisher *(Ceryle alcyon)*—V Single bird spent some time in Killaloe.
Skylark *(Alauda arvensis)*—R & PM Breeds throughout. Large flocks, particularly in autumn on migration.
Swift *(Apus apus)*—SR Most common in towns and villages.
Sand martin *(Riparia riparia)*—SR Decreasing numbers breed in suitable areas.
Swallow *(Hirundo rustica)*—SR Breeds throughout; large numbers on passage in autumn.
House martin *(Delichon urbica)*—SR Declining numbers, breeding and on passage, large colony under Banagher Bridge.
Meadow pipit *(Anthus pratensis)*—R Widespread.
Grey wagtail *(Motacilla cinerea)*—R More common in Upper Shannon area, Jamestown–Roosky.
Pied wagtail *(Motacilla alba)*—R Breeds throughout area.
Wren *(Troglodytes troglodytes)*—R Widespread.
Dipper *(Cinclus cinclus)*—R Only found on derelict Ballinamore Canal, between locks 14 and 12.
Dunnock *(Prunella modularis)*—R Widespread.
Robin *(Erithacus rubecula)*—R Widespread.
Whinchat *(Saxicola rubetra)*—SR Breeds particularly in Portumna area, also Clonmacnois.
Stonechat *(Saxicola torquata)*—R Not very common, spread over whole area.
Wheatear *(Oenanthe oenanthe)*—SR As previous species.
Fieldfare *(Turdus pilaris)*—WR Large numbers in suitable field areas.
Ring ouzel *(Turdus torquatus)*—SR Breeds outside area in Cavan/Leitrim hills.
Blackbird *(Turdus merula)*—R Widespread.
Song thrush (Turdus philomelos)—R Widespread.
Redwing *(Turdus iliacus)*—WR Large numbers in suitable fields.
Mistle thrush *(Turdus viscivorus)*—R Fairly widespread throughout.
Grasshopper warbler *(Locustella naevia)*—SR Breeds in Drumsna area and Portland Island, near Portumna.
Sedge warbler *(Acrocephalus schoenobaenus)*—SR Widespread in all reeded areas.
Whitethroat *(Sylvia communis)*—SR Not very common, found in areas with gorse, especially Shannon Harbour.
Garden warbler *(Sylvia borin)*—SR Breeds particularly in Lough Ree area.
Blackcap *(Sylvia articapilla)*—SR Occasional, north end of Lough Ree. Small numbers breed throughout the system, especially Lough Derg.
Chiffchaff *(Phylloscopus collybita)*—SR Widespread.
Willow warbler *(Phylloscopus trochilus)*—SR Widespread .
Spotted flycatcher *(Muscicapa striata)*—SR Widespread in wooded areas.
Goldcrest *(Regulus regulus)*—R Widespread.
Long-tailed tit *(Aegithalos caudatus)*—R Throughout the river, particularly in Lough Ree area.
Coal tit *(Parus ater)*—R Widespread.
Blue tit (Parus caeruleus)—R Widespread.
Great tit *(Parus major)*—R Widespread.
Treecreeper *(Certhia familiaris)*—R In most wooded areas.
Jay *(Garrulus glandarius)*—R In all woodland areas.
Magpie *(Pica pica)*—R Widespread.
Jackdaw *(Corvus monedula)*—R widespread.
Rook *(Corvus frugilegus)*—R Widespread.
Hooded crow *(Corvus corone)*—R Widespread.
Raven *(Corvus corax)*—R Jamestown area and upper Lough Derg.
Starling *(Sturnus vulgaris)*—R & WR Widespread.
Very large flocks in winter.
House sparrow *(Passer domesticus)*—R Widespread.
Chaffinch *(Fringilla coelebs)*—R & WR Widespread.
Large numbers in winter.
Brambling *(Fringilla montifringilla)*—WR Occasional in chaffinch flocks.
Bulfinch *(Pyrrhula pyrrhula)*—R Common throughout river.
Greenfinch *(Carduelis chloris)*—R Widespread.
Goldfinch *(Carduelis carduelis)*—R Widespread.
Siskin *(Carduelis spinus)*—R Occasional throughout area.
Linnet *(Carduelis cannabina)*—R Local.
Redpoll *(Carduelis flammea)*—R Not very common.
Yellowhammer *(Emberiza citrinella)*—R Decreasing numbers in roadside hedges.
Reed bunting *(Emberiza schoeniclus)*—R Widespread in almost all reed beds and marshy area.

Appendix - General Information

The River Shannon

The River Shannon

from the source to Loop Head	344km
Catchment area	15,540 sq km

Shannon Navigation (including 18 lakes, the Boyle Water and Carnadoe Waters) approx.280 km.

Height above sea level (at normal summer levels):

Shannon Pot	152m	Lough Ree	38m
Lough Allen	50m	Lough Derg	33m

Administration:

Waterways Ireland

Number of locks:

Killaloe to Lough Allen	8	to Richmond Harbour	2
on the Boyle Water	1	Killaloe to Limerick	1 (double)
Lough Allen Canal	3		

Minimum size of Locks, Shannon Navigation:

Limerick to Killaloe 30m x 5.5m x 1.5m on cill

Killaloe to Lough Key 31.1m x 9.1m 1.5m on cill

River Camlin route and Lough Allen Canal 19.6.mx 4.1m x 1.2m on cill

Bridges:

There are two opening bridges and one swing bridge; the lowest fixed bridge on the main navigation is Lough Tap railway bridge with 4m but Carnadoe Bridge has only 3.5m at the centre of the arch and on the River Camlin route 3.6m. Charge per lock or movable bridge £1.20.

Local Phone Numbers :

Inspector of Navigation's Office, Athlone, Tel : 0902-94232

Portumna Bridge	0509-41011	Roosky	078-38018
Meelick	0509-51359	Albert Lock	078-37715
Athlone	0902-92026	Clarendon Lock	079-67011
Tarmonbarry	043-26117	Battlebridge	078-41552

Locks and Moveable Bridges:

PERIOD	WEEKDAYS	SUNDAYS
March 14 - April 3	09.00 - 18.30	10.30 - 16.00
April 4 - September 25	09.00 - 20.30	09.00 - 18.00
September 26 - November 1	09.00 - 19.30	10.00 - 16.00
November 2 - March 13	09.00 - 12.30	10.00 - 12.30
	Lunch Break 13.00 - 14.00	

Portumna Bridge only opens at the following times:

PERIOD	WEEKDAYS	SUNDAYS
March 14 - April 3	09.45 11.00 12.30	11.00 12.30
	14.30 16.30 17.30	14.30 16.00
April 4 - September 25	09.45 11.00 12.30	11.00 12.30
	15.00 17.30 19.30	15.00 17.30
September 26 - November 1	09.45 11.00 12.30	11.00 12.30
	15.00 17.00 18.30	14.30 16.00
November 2 - March 13	09.45 11.00 12.00	11.00 12.00

Overhead Cables:

Great care should be observed by masted craft. Minimum clearance at normal summer level is about 10.6m but is less on the upper reaches above Carrick bridge

Access by water:

Via the Shannon Estuary and Limerick - Maximum size of craft 30m x 5.5m with combined headroom and draft less than 5.2m

Via Dublin or Waterford Estuary and the Grand Canal - Maximum size of craft 18.4 x 3.9 x 1.2m with headroom under 2.7m (2.4 m in time of flood on Barrow Navigation).

Via Shannon-Erne Waterway - Maximum size of craft 24m x 4.5m x 1.2m.

Access by road:

Large craft launching facilities at Killaloe, Portumna, Banagher, Athlone, Inner Lakes, Carnadoe Marina, Carrick and Knockvicar.

Small craft slips at Dromineer, Mountshannon, Garrykennedy, Kilgarvan, Rossmore, Hodson Bay, Portrunny, Barley Harbour, Lanesborough, Kilglass, Roosky, Dromod, Cootehall and Rockingham.

Charts and Maps:

ECBA / Irish Boat Rental Association and ERA Maptec Ltd., Dublin, Cruising Ireland Captain's Handbook & Charts.

Lough Derg and Lough Ree: Admiralty charts nos. 5080 and 5078

Shannon Estuary: Admiralty charts nos. 1819, 1540, 1547, 1548, 1549 and 2254 (small scale)

Discovery Series, 1:50 000: Nos. 24,25,32,33,39,40,46,49,52,53,58, 59,65,66.

Shannon Boat Hire Companies:		Telephone
Athlone Cruisers Ltd.		++353(0)902-72892
Carrick Craft,	Base, Banagher	++353(0)509-51187
	Base, Carrick-on-Shannon	++353(0)78-20236
	Base, Knockninny	++44(0)28-677-48868
Shannon Erne Waterway Holidays	- Coothall	++353(0)79-76028
	- Erincurrach	++44(0)28-6864-1737
Crown Blue Line, Carrick		++353(0)78-21196
Ireland Line Cruisers, Killaloe		++353(0)61-375011
Emerald Star,	Base, Carrick-on-Shannon	++353(0)78-20234
	Base, Portumna	++353(0)509-41120
	Base, Belturbet	++353(0)49-9522933
Shannon Castle Line		++353(0)61-927042
Silver Line, Banagher		++353(0)509-51112
Tara Cruisers, Lough Key		++353(0)79-67777
Waveline Cruisers, Killinure, L.Ree		++353(0)902-85711

Grand Canal & Barrow Line

Celtic Canal Cruisers, Tullamore	0506-21861

Barrow Navigation

Barrowline Cruisers	0503-32545
Ceatharlach Moorings	0503-30411
Southstar Cruisers	0503-21406
Valley Boats	0503-24945

Barrow Line

Vicarstown Leisure Barges	0502-25189
Canalways Ireland, Rathangan	045-524646

Royal Canal

Leisureways Holidays	(01) 822-5034
Royal Canal Cruisers	(01) 820-5263

Prefex: Republic of Ireland to Northern Ireland (00 44 28)
Northern Ireland to Republic of Ireland (00353)

The Shannon-Erne Waterway and Erne Navigation

Shannon-Erne Waterway

Administration: Waterways Ireland

Leitrim to Upper Lough Erne	61km
Number of locks	16
Maximum size of craft,	24m x 4.5m x 1.2m.

Shannon-Erne Waterway Promotions, Ballinamore, Tel: 078-44855

Explore Erne, Belleek, Tel: 013656-58866

Headroom:

3.2m over 3m width.

Slipways:

Leitrim, Keshcarrigan, Ballinamore, Haughtons Shore, Ballyconnell and Aghalane.

Erne Navigation :

Administration: Waterways Ireland

Belturbet to Belleek	64km
Maximum size of craft	33.5m x 6m x 1.2m.
Headroom	6m

(except on alternative channel 4.5m)

Assistance On Shannon-Erne Waterway

Lock 16 Leitrim	088-2608569
Kilclare	088-2603663
Ballinamore	088-2602478
Ballyconnell	088-2603662
Lock I, Corraquill	04866-48976
Waterways Ireland, Ballyconnell	049-9526603 (Mon-Fri)
Rivers Agency Office (N.I)	04866-388529 (Mon-Fri)

Slipways:

For large craft: Belleek, Belturbet, Bellanaleck, Enniskillen, Castle Archdale, Muckross (Kesh).

For smaller craft: Blaney Bay, Corrindillar, Carrybridge, Derryad, Geaglum, Kilmore, Manor House and Rosseigh.

Overhead cables:

8.5m (except Kesh River 6m.)

Charts and Guides:

Dick Warners Guide to the Shannon-Erne Waterway, SEW Promotions Ltd.,

Navigational Guide to the Shannon-Erne Waterway, ERA Maptec Ltd., Dublin and ESB International 1: 20,000.

Upper and Lower Lough Erne Navigational Charts, Dept. of Agriculture Northern Ireland and ERA Maptec Ltd., Dublin, 1:25,000.

Irish Ordnance Survey half inch to the mile nos. 3, 7 & 8.

Rogers, Mary *Prospect of Erne* Fermanagh Field Club, 1967.

Boat Hire:	**Telphone**
Aghinver Boat Co., Lower Lough Erne	++44(0)28-686-31400
Belleek Charter Cruising, Lower Lough Erne	++44(0)28-686-58027
Carrybridge Boat Co., River Erne	++44(0)28-663-87034
Carrick Craft, - Carrick-on-Shannon	++353(0)78-20236
- Knockninny	++44(0)28-677-48868
- Banagher	++353(0)509-51187
Emerald Star, - Carrick-on-Shannon	++353(0)78-20234
- Portumna	++353(0)509-41120
- Belturbet	++353(0)49-9522933
Erincurrach Cruising, Lower Lough Erne	++44(0)28-686-41737
Erne Marine, Bellanaleck, River Erne	++44(0)28-663-48267
Lochside Cruisers, Enniskillen	++44(0)28-663-24368
Leitrim Quay, Leitrim Village	++353(0)78-22989
Locaboat Marina	++353(0)78-45300
Manor House Marine, Lower Lough Erne	++44(0)28-686-28100
Riversdale Barge Holidays, Ballinamore	++353(0)7844122
Shanon-Erne Waterway Holidays - Cootehall	++353(0)79-67028
- Erincurrach	++44(0)28-6864-1737

Appendix - Bibliography

Guides

Athlone, A Tourist Trail, Athlone 1987.
A useful guide for exploring the town.
Lough Key Forest Park, Dublin: Forest & Wildlife service.
A comprehensive guide to the history, flora and fauna of the park, including a guide to the nature trails.
McKnight, H., ***The Shell Book of Inland Waterways***, Newton Abbot: David & Charles 1975.
A guide to all the waterways of England, Scotland, Wales and Ireland.
Tipper, Bernadette, ***The River Shannon A Boater's Guide***, Dublin: Town House 1987. A guide to the towns, villages and places of interest along the river with useful details about restaurants, shops, etc.
Trodd, Valentine, ***Banagher on the Shannon***, Banagher 1985.
An indispensable guide when visiting Banagher.

General

Craig, Maurice, ***Portumna Castle***, Dublin: Gatherum 7 1976.
Detailed and informative booklet by Ireland's foremost architectural historian.
Delany Ruth, ***By Shannon Shores***, Dublin: Gill and Macmillan 1987.
An exploration of the river, its landscape, history, legends and personalities.
Delany Ruth, ***Ireland's Inland Waterways***, Belfast: Appletree 1986.
The history of the waterways with sections on the Shannon Navigation.
Feehan, John M., ***The Magic of the Shannon***, Cork: Mercier 1980.
A journey on the river meeting many interesting Shannon characters.
Gardner, R., ***Land of Time Enough***, London: Hodder & Stoughton 1977.
A trip on the Shannon, Grand Canal and Barrow by a visitor from England.
Hayward, R., ***Where the River Shannon Flows***, Dundalk: Dundalgan Press 1940.
A journey by road along the Shannon with carefully researched history and legends of the places visited.
Harbison, Peter, ***Guide to the Ancient Monuments of Ireland***, Dublin: Gill and Macmillan 1975.
Useful information about the ancient monuments.
Journals of the Old Athlone Society, Athlone 1970–1985. Contain a number of interesting papers on subjects relating to the Shannon by Harman Murtagh and other local historians.
Kerrigan, Paul, 'The Defences of Ireland 1793–1815', essays in ***An Cosantoir*** vols 34-7, 1974-7.
MacMahon, Michael, ***Portumna Castle and its Lords***, Nenagh 1983.
An interesting booklet with details about the Clanricards by a local historian.
Malet, H., ***Voyage in a Bowler Hat***, reprinted London: M & M Baldwin 1985.
A journey along the Shannon, Grand Canal and Barrow in the late 1950s.
Malet, H., ***In the Wake of the Gods***, London: Chatto & Windus 1970.
A sequel to his earlier book concentrating on the history and legends.
Murtagh, Harman (ed.), ***Irish Midland Studies***, Essays in commemoration of N.W.English, Athlone: Old Athlone Society 1980.
Contains a number of interesting essays on subjects relating to the Shannon.
O'Farrell, Padraic, ***Shannon Through her Literature***, Cork: Mercier Press 1983.
An anthology of some of the references to the river in prose and verse.
Praeger, R.L, ***The Way that I went,*** Dublin: Figgis 1969.
Contains an interesting chapter on the Shannon by this eminent botanist and scholar.
Rice, H .J, ***Thanks for the Memory***, Athlone Printing Works 1952 (re-printed 1975).
An exploration of the river, and in particular Lough Ree, by one of the founders of the Inland Waterways Association of Ireland.
Rolt, L.T C., ***Green & Silver***, London Allen & Unwin 1949.
One of the classics of the Irish waterways. Describes a journey on the Shannon and the canals in the late 1940s.

Landscape, flora and fauna

Areas of Scientific Interest in Ireland, Dublin An Foras Forbartha l981
Bellamy *D.*, ***Bellamy's Ireland: The Wild Boglands***, Dublin: Country House 1986.
An account of Ireland's bogs and their development and features.
d'Arcy, Gordon **The Birds of Ireland,** Belfast 1986. An illustrated guide to Ireland's birds.
de Buitléar, E. (ed.), ***Irish Rivers***, Dublin Amach Faoin Aer 1985.
A general account of the natural history of Irish rivers.
Fairley, J.S. ***An Irish Beast Book: A Natural History of Ireland's Furred Wildlife***, Belfast: Blackstaff 1975.
The natural history and folklore of Ireland's mammals
.Heery, S. **The Shannon Floodlands A Natural History of the Shannon Callows,** Kinvara, Co Galway, Tir Eolas 1993. An account of the natural history, landscape and farming of this special and irreplaceable part of the Shannon between Lough Derg with good bibliography.
Hutchinson, C., ***Ireland's Wetlands and their Birds***, Dublin: Irish Wildbird Conservancy 1977.
Includes information on birds of the Shannon system.
Martin, W K., ***The New Concise British Flora***,London: Ebury Press & Michael Joseph 1982.
A useful beginner's book for identifying plants—well illustrated.
Mitchell G. F., ***The Shell Guide to reading the Irish Landscape***, Dublin Country House 1986.
The story of the development of Ireland's landscape.
Ní Lamhna, E. (ed.), ***Provisional Distribution Atlas of Amphibians, Reptiles and Mammals in Ireland,*** Dublin: An Foras Forbartha 1979.
Praeger, K L., ***Natural History of Ireland*** Yorkshire: EP Publishing 1972.
A classic work on Ireland's natural history.
Praeger, K L., ***The Botanist in Ireland***, Yorkshire: EPPublishing 1974.
Sharrock, J.T.R., ***The Atlas of Breeding Birds in Britain and Ireland***, Dublin BTO/IWC 1976.
A most comprehensive account of Ireland's birds their distribution, habitat, description and sources of information.
Thomas, J. A. ***Butterflies of the British Isles***, London: Country Life Books 1986.
Tubridy, M & Jeffrey, D. W., ***The Heritage of Clonmacnois***, Environmental Sciences Unit, Trinity College Dublin & Co Offaly VEC, 1987.
A readable account of the natural history and historical geography of the Clonmacnois area, making a case for establishing a Heritage Zone.
Webb, D.W., ***An Irish Flora***, Dundalk: Dundalgan Press l977
Identification keys and brief descriptions of all Irish species.

Acknowledgments

This guide is published by ERA-Maptec Limited with the support of Irish Shell Limited and Waterways Ireland. Thanks are due to Gill & Macmillan for making available the revised text. Much of the original design by Jan de Fouw has been retained but the slightly smaller format and the change to full colour did necessitate some alterations which have been carried out by Gary Bowes and Paul Grimes. Thanks are due to the Inland Waterways Association of Ireland for permitting the incorporation of material from their earlier Guide to the River Shannon, to the family of John Weaving for making available the work which he had completed before his death and to the other contributors of the articles on various aspects of the river: Peter Harbison, Harman Murtagh, Hugh Gough, Gerrit van Gelderen and, in particular, Daphne Levinge who not only supplied the text for much of the flora and fauna section together with her husband Jonathan Shackleton, but also the unique hand-painted drawings. Other people who assisted with the text were Ian Herbert of the Wildbird Conservancy; Jeremy Addis who read the draft and made helpful suggestions, Hardress Waller and James Scully who provided local history details, Sandra and John Lefroy and many individual IWAI members who assisted with information and photographs. Ray Dunne, Waterways Ireland, Shannon Navigation engineer, has been very helpful in updating the Navigation Notes relating to the Limerick to Killaloe Navigation. The illustrations and line drawings come from many sources and are individually acknowledged. A special word of thanks must be made to Walter Borner, who first came to the Shannon as a visitor from Switzerland but who fell in love with the river, bought his own boat and now spends much time here. He not only provided some useful corrections to the German text but made available his extensive collection of photographs. For the past two editions he has become joint managing editor providing many new photographs and translating the new material into German.

I would like to add a personal word of thanks to Paul Kidney and Sharon O' Reilly of ERA-Maptec Limited for their commitment to this new edition. ERA-Maptec Limited are also responsible for the charts of the River Shannon, Erne Navigation and the Shannon-Erne Waterway and, as such, form a useful link between these navigation charts and this guidebook.

May 2000
RUTH DELANY

Index